navigating

the course to

college

Navigating the Course to College

A Compilation of College Admissions Statistics & Research Data
2011 - 2012

Ellen Richards

Truro Press
Los Angeles, California

Truro Press
Published by Truro Press
Los Angeles, California
www.TruroPress.com

ISBN-13: 978-0-6154-8925-4
ISBN-10: 0-6154-8925-7

First Printing: July 2011

Printed in the United States of America

10 9 8 7 6 5 4 3 2 1

Things may come to those who wait,
but only the things left by those who hustle.

- Abraham Lincoln

CONTENTS

13

COLLEGE LANDSCAPE
13 strengths college seek
14 factors in admissions
15 high school courses
16 GPA
17 ACT Score
18 competition

21

COMMON APPLICATION
21 the common application
26 common application schools
32 schools with no supplement

37

DECISION PLANS
37 types of decision plans
39 early versus overall acceptance
43 early decision acceptance rates
46 colleges with early decision 1
49 colleges with early decision 2

53

STANDARDIZED TESTS
53 act versus sat
55 score choice
60 average scores per school
67 college test policies
74 no tests required schools
89 sat subject tests
94 test schedule

97

APPLICATION ESSAYS
97 sample supplement topics
106 sample essays

119

RESUMES & PORTFOLIOS
119 sample resume
122 performing/visual arts
126 music majors & college
127 sample music resume
129 sample film resume
131 sample portfolio listing

133

INTERVIEWS & RECS
135 the interview
136 college interview policies
139 letters of recommendation

143

CALIFORNIA COLLEGES
143 overview
144 community college
146 california state colleges
151 university of california
169 private colleges

173

ADMISSIONS DATA
173 yields
177 liberal arts colleges near cities
178 america's best universities
181 america's best liberal arts colleges
183 second tier liberal arts colleges
184 lowest faculty to student ratios
185 schools that offer BA/MD
186 strong dance programs
187 strong drama programs
187 strong journalism programs
188 strong business programs
189 strong art/music programs
193 top schools for Jewish students
195 foreign language requirements
197 top 50 most stressful colleges
199 waitlist statistics 2010
203 college acceptance rates 2011

209

GEOGRAPHIC LOCATIONS
209 maps of colleges locations

225

FINANCIAL AID
225 college costs
227 need blind schools
229 $50,000 or more colleges
233 federal & institutional methods
239 financial aid forms
235 financial aid & early decision
236 independent students

college

landscape

Top Ten Strengths and Experiences Colleges
Look for in a High-School Student

1. A high school curriculum that challenges the student. Academically successful students should include several Honors and Advanced Placement classes.

2. Grades that represent strong effort and an upward trend. Grades should show an upward trend over the years. However, slightly lower grades in a rigorous program are preferred to all A's in less challenging course work.

3. Solid scores on standardized tests (SAT, ACT). These should be consistent with high school performance.

4. Passionate involvement in a few activities, demonstrating leadership and initiative. Depth, not breadth, of experience is most important.

5. Community service showing evidence of being a "contributor." Activities should demonstrate concern for other people and a global view.

6. Work or out-of-school experiences (including summer activities) that illustrate responsibility, dedication and development of areas of interest. Work or other meaningful use of free time can demonstrate maturity.

7. A well-written essay that provides insight into the student's unique personality, values and goals. The application essay should be thoughtful and highly personal. It should demonstrate careful and well-constructed writing.

8. Letters of recommendation from teachers and guidance counselor that give evidence of integrity, special skill, and positive character traits. Students should request recommendations from teachers who respect their work in an academic discipline.

9. Supplementary recommendations by adults who have had significant direct contact with the student. Letters from coaches or supervisors in long-term work or volunteer activities are valuable; however, recommendations from casual acquaintances or family friends, even if they are well known, are rarely given much weight.

10. Anything special that makes the student stand out from the rest of the applicants! Include honors, awards, evidence of unusual talent or experience, or anything else that makes the student unique. Overall, colleges are seeking students who will be active contributing members of the student body.

Source: Independent Educational Consultants Association

FACTORS IN THE ADMISSIONS PROCESS

Table 16. Percentage of colleges attributing different levels of importance to factors in the admission decision: 2009

Factor	Considerable importance	Moderate importance	Limited importance	No importance
Grades in college prep courses	86.5%	11.5%	1.6%	0.3%
Strength of curriculum	70.7	22.0	5.9	1.3
Admission test scores (SAT, ACT)	57.8	32.0	9.2	1.0
Grades in all courses	45.6	43.9	9.8	0.7
Essay or writing sample	26.4	37.5	19.9	16.3
Teacher recommendation	17.4	47.7	23.7	11.2
Student's demonstrated interest	20.7	27.0	27.6	24.7
Counselor recommendation	17.1	50.0	22.0	10.9
Class rank	16.3	42.2	31.7	9.8
Interview	6.6	26.3	31.9	35.2
Subject test scores (AP, IB)	7.0	27.2	33.6	32.2
Extracurricular activities	8.9	43.9	34.3	12.9
SAT II scores	5.0	11.0	28.0	56.0
Portfolio	8.4	11.0	35.8	44.8
State graduation exam scores	3.0	15.9	27.2	53.8
Work	1.7	20.2	43.7	34.4

SOURCE: NACAC Admission Trends Survey, 2009.

HOW COURSES AFFECT CHANCE OF ADMISSION

If you are wondering what increases a student's chance of gaining admission to college, more rigourous courses have the strongest impact. If an average 2004 applicant completed precalculus instead of stopping math coursework at trigonometry, his or her chances of gaining admission would have increased to 90%.

Second, higher college entrance exam scores affect admission.

A student's GPA counts the least among these three factors.

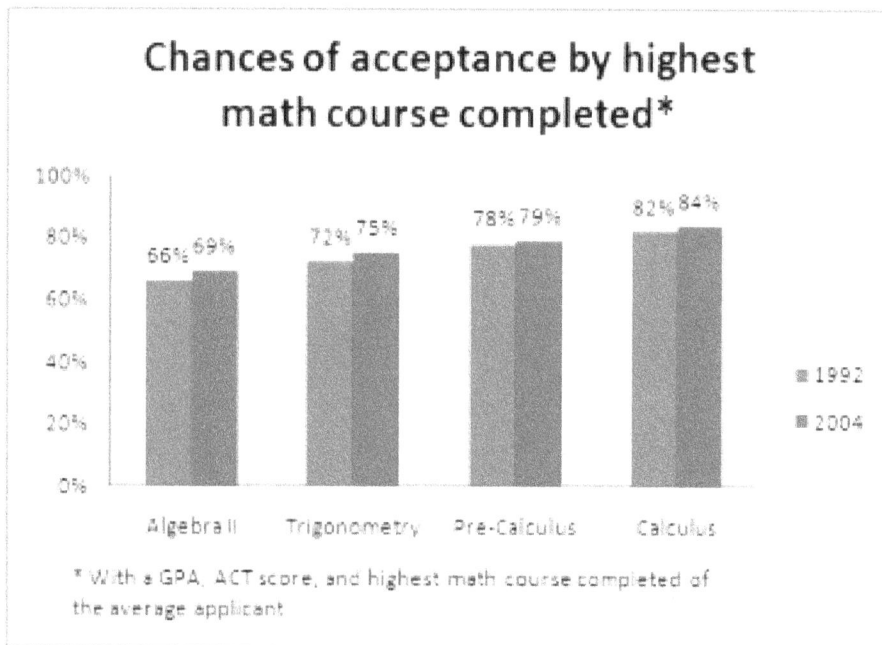

Chances of acceptance by highest math course completed*

Highest math course	1992	2004
Algebra II	66%	69%
Trigonometry	72%	75%
Pre-Calculus	78%	79%
Calculus	82%	84%

* With a GPA, ACT score, and highest math course completed of the average applicant

Source: Center for Public Education

EFFECT OF GPA ON ADMISSION TO COLLEGE

It would take a student raising his or her GPA drastically from a 3.1 to a 3.6 -- a B to an A- -- to increase the chance of getting into college as much as simply completing pre-calculus

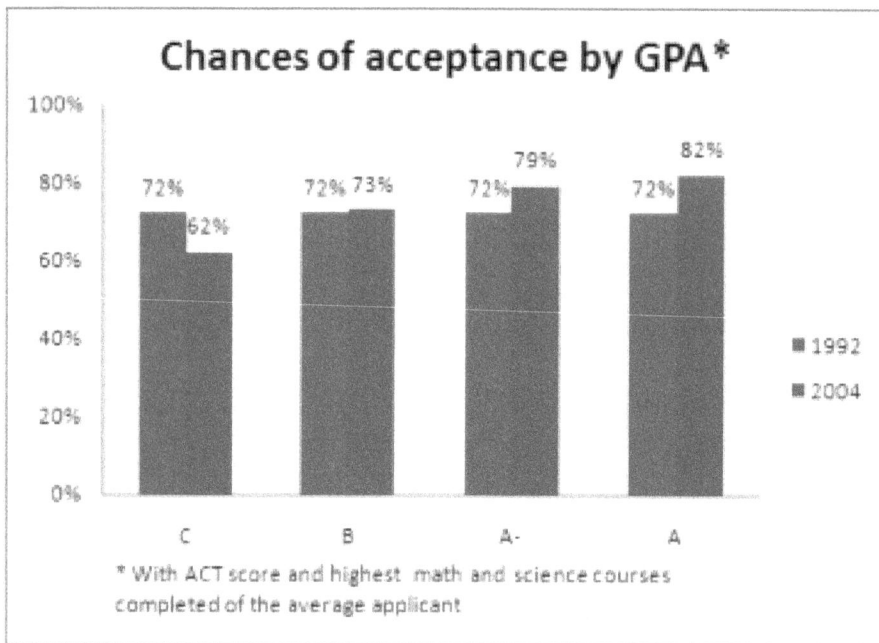

Chances of acceptance by GPA*

	1992	2004
C	72%	62%
B	72%	73%
A-	72%	79%
A	72%	82%

* With ACT score and highest math and science courses completed of the average applicant

Source: Center for Public Education

How ACT Scores Affect Chance of College Acceptance

If the average 2004 applicant scored a 22 on the ACT - the same as the average applicant in 1992 - his or her chance of getting into college would have risen from 75 percent to 78 percent.

This illustrates that a small increase in ACT scores OR taking more rigorous courses can increase a student's chance of getting into college MORE THAN raising a GPA can.

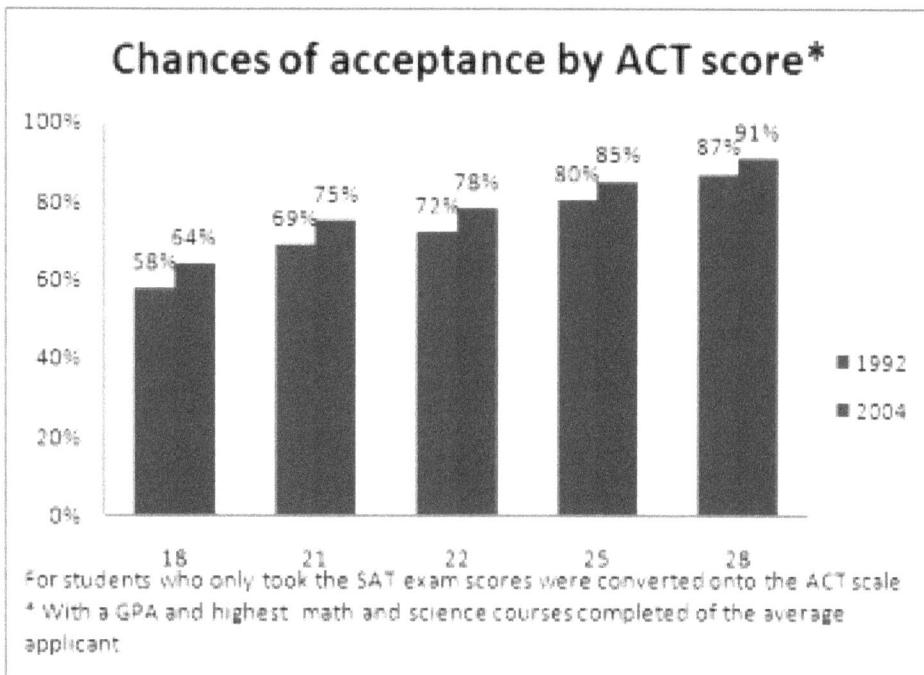

Chances of acceptance by ACT score*

For students who only took the SAT exam scores were converted onto the ACT scale
* With a GPA and highest math and science courses completed of the average applicant

Source: Center for Public Education

HOW COMPETITIVE IS ADMISSION TO COLLEGE?

The bottom line

- It is no more difficult for most students to get into college today than it was a decade ago. The shrinking acceptance rates cited in so many news reports likely come from a higher number of applications per student. However, the average applicant today has about the same chance of getting into a competitive college as an average applicant a decade ago.
- Taking more rigorous courses, especially in math and science, gives an applicant a better chance of getting into a competitive college than does raising his or her GPA. For instance, lower-achieving students could increase their chances by over 10 percent if they simply took trigonometry instead of stopping math at algebra II. Higher college admissions scores also increase a student's chances.
- Well-prepared minority applicants have just as good of a chance of getting into a competitive college as well-prepared white students. However, a much smaller percentage of minority applicants earn the necessary credentials.
- Well-prepared low-income applicants are less likely to get into a competitive college as well-prepared high-income applicants: 67 percent vs. 80 percent. Moreover, few low-income applicants earn the necessary credentials.

Source: Center for Public Education

common
application

2011 - 2012 COMMON APPLICATION

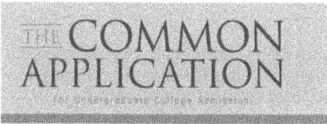

THE COMMON APPLICATION
for Undergraduate College Admission

2011-12 FIRST-YEAR APPLICATION
For Spring 2012 or Fall 2012 Enrollment

APPLICANT

Legal Name _____
Last/Family/Sur (Enter name *exactly* as it appears on official documents.)   First/Given   Middle (complete)   Jr., etc.

Preferred name, if not first name (only one) _____   Former last name(s) _____

Birth Date _____ ○ Female ○ Male   US Social Security Number, if any _____
mm/dd/yyyy   Required for US Citizens and Permanent Residents applying for financial aid via FAFSA

Preferred Telephone ○ Home ○ Cell   Home (_____) _____   Cell (_____) _____
Area/Country/City Code   Area/Country/City Code

E-mail Address _____   IM Address _____

Permanent home address _____
Number & Street   Apartment #

_____
City/Town   County or Parish   State/Province   Country   ZIP/Postal Code

If different from above, please give your current mailing address for all admission correspondence.   (from _____ to _____)
mm/dd/yyyy   mm/dd/yyyy

Current mailing address _____
Number & Street   Apartment #

_____
City/Town   County or Parish   State/Province   Country   ZIP/Postal Code

If your current mailing address is a boarding school, include name of school here: _____

FUTURE PLANS

Your answers to these questions will vary for different colleges. If the online system did not ask you to answer some of the questions you see in this section, this college chose not to ask that question of its applicants.

College _____   Deadline _____
mm/dd/yyyy

Entry Term: ○ Fall (Jul-Dec)   ○ Spring (Jan-Jun)   Do you intend to apply for need-based financial aid? ○ Yes ○ No

Decision Plan_____   Do you intend to apply for merit-based scholarships? ○ Yes ○ No

Academic Interests _____   Do you intend to be a full-time student? ○ Yes ○ No

_____   Do you intend to enroll in a degree program your first year? ○ Yes ○ No

_____   Do you intend to live in college housing? _____

Career Interest_____   What is the highest degree you intend to earn? _____

DEMOGRAPHICS

Citizenship Status _____

Non-US Citizenship _____

_____

_____

Birthplace _____
City/Town   State/Province   Country

Years lived in the US? _____ Years lived outside the US? _____

Language Proficiency (Check all that apply.)
S(Speak) R(Read) W(Write) F(First Language) H(Spoken at Home)

	S	R	W	F	H
_____	○	○	○	○	○
_____	○	○	○	○	○
_____	○	○	○	○	○

Optional The items with a gray background are optional. No information you provide will be used in a discriminatory manner.

Religious Preference _____

US Armed Services veteran status _____

1. Are you Hispanic/Latino?

○ Yes, Hispanic or Latino (including Spain) ○ No If yes, please describe your background.

_____

2. Regardless of your answer to the prior question, please indicate how you identify yourself. (Check one or more and describe your background.)

○ American Indian or Alaska Native (including all Original Peoples of the Americas)

Are you Enrolled? ○ Yes ○ No If yes, please enter Tribal Enrollment Number_____

○ Asian (including Indian subcontinent and Philippines)

_____

○ Black or African American (including Africa and Caribbean)

_____

○ Native Hawaiian or Other Pacific Islander (Original Peoples)

_____

○ White (including Middle Eastern)

_____

2011 - 2012 COMMON APPLICATION

FAMILY

Please list both parents below, even if one or more is deceased or no longer has legal responsibilities toward you. Many colleges collect this information for demographic purposes even if you are an adult or an emancipated minor. If you are a minor with a legal guardian (an individual or government entity), then please list that information below as well. If you wish, you may list step-parents and/or other adults with whom you reside, or who otherwise care for you, in the Additional Information section.

Household

Parents' marital status (relative to each other): ○ Never Married ○ Married ○ Civil Union/Domestic Partners ○ Widowed ○ Separated ○ Divorced (date _____)
mm/yyyy

With whom do you make your permanent home? ○ Parent 1 ○ Parent 2 ○ Both ○ Legal Guardian ○ Ward of the Court/State ○ Other

Parent 1: ○ Mother ○ Father ○ Unknown

Is Parent 1 living? ○ Yes ○ No (Date Deceased _____)
mm/yyyy

_____
Last/Family/Sur   First/Given   Middle   Title (Mr./Mrs./Ms./Dr.)

Country of birth _____

Home address **if different** from yours

_____

_____

Preferred Telephone: ○ Home ○ Cell ○ Work (_____) _____
Area/Country/City Code

E-mail _____

Occupation _____

Employer _____

College (if any) _____ CEEB _____

Degree _____ Year _____

Graduate School (if any) _____ CEEB _____

Degree _____ Year _____

Parent 2: ○ Mother ○ Father ○ Unknown

Is Parent 2 living? ○ Yes ○ No (Date Deceased _____)
mm/yyyy

_____
Last/Family/Sur   First/Given   Middle   Title (Mr./Mrs./Ms./Dr.)

Country of birth _____

Home address **if different** from yours

_____

_____

Preferred Telephone: ○ Home ○ Cell ○ Work (_____) _____
Area/Country/City Code

E-mail _____

Occupation _____

Employer _____

College (if any) _____ CEEB _____

Degree _____ Year _____

Graduate School (if any) _____ CEEB _____

Degree _____ Year _____

Legal Guardian *(if other than a parent)*

Relationship to you _____

_____
Last/Family/Sur   First/Given   Middle   Title (Mr./Mrs./Ms./Dr.)

Country of birth _____

Home address **if different** from yours

_____

_____

Preferred Telephone: ○ Home ○ Cell ○ Work (_____) _____
Area/Country/City Code

E-mail _____

Occupation _____

Employer _____

College (if any) _____ CEEB _____

Degree _____ Year _____

Graduate School (if any) _____ CEEB _____

Degree _____ Year _____

Marital Status _____

Spouse's Name _____

Siblings

Please give names and ages of your brothers or sisters. If they are enrolled in grades K-12 (or international equivalent), list their grade levels. If they have attended or are currently attending college, give the names of the undergraduate institution, degree earned, and approximate dates of attendance. If more than three siblings, please list them in the Additional Information section.

_____
Name   Age & Grade   Relationship

College Attended _____ CEEB _____

Degree earned _____ Dates _____
or expected   *mm/yyyy – mm/yyyy*

_____
Name   Age & Grade   Relationship

College Attended _____ CEEB _____

Degree earned _____ Dates _____
or expected   *mm/yyyy – mm/yyyy*

_____
Name   Age & Grade   Relationship

College Attended _____ CEEB _____

Degree earned _____ Dates _____
or expected   *mm/yyyy – mm/yyyy*

College Attended _____ CEEB _____

Degree Earned/Expected _____ Dates _____
                                             mm/yyyy – mm/yyyy

If you have children, how many? _____

2011 - 2012 COMMON APPLICATION

EDUCATION

Secondary Schools

Most recent secondary school attended _____

Entry Date _____ Graduation Date _____   School Type: ○ Public ○ Charter ○ Independent ○ Religious ○ Home School
mm/yyyy   *mm/dd/yyyy*

Address _____ CEEB/ACT Code _____
Number & Street

City/Town   *State/Province*   *Country*   *ZIP/Postal Code*

Counselor's Name _____ Counselor's Title _____

E-mail _____ Telephone (_____) _____ Fax (_____) _____
Area/Country/City Code   Number   Ext.   Area/Country/City Code   Number

List all other secondary schools you have attended since 9th grade, including summer schools or enrichment programs hosted on a secondary school campus:

School Name & CEEB/ACT Code   Location (City, State/Province, ZIP/Postal Code, Country)   Dates Attended (mm/yyyy)

_____   _____   _____

_____   _____   _____

Please list any community program/organization that has provided free assistance with your application process:_____

If your education was or will be interrupted, please indicate so here and provide details in the Additional Information section: _____

_____ Report all college attendance (including online) since 9th grade and indicate as College Course (CO) or Enrichment Program (EP) hosted on a college campus.

Were you issued a transcript for any work listed above? ○ Yes ○ No   If yes, please have an official transcript sent as soon as possible.

ACADEMICS

The self-reported information in this section is not intended to take the place of your official records. Please note the requirements of each institution to which you are applying and arrange for official transcripts and score reports to be sent from your secondary school and the appropriate testing agencies. Where "Best Scores" are requested, please report the highest individual scores you have earned so far, even if those scores are from different test dates.

Grades   Class Rank _____   Class Size _____   Weighted? ○ Yes ○ No   GPA _____   Scale _____   Weighted? ○ Yes ○ No
(if available)   *(if available)*

ACT	Exam Dates: _____ *(past & future)* *mm/yyyy*	_____ *mm/yyyy*	_____ *mm/yyyy*		Best Scores: _____ *(so far)*	COMP *mm/yyyy*	English *mm/yyyy*	Math *mm/yyyy*		
						Reading *mm/yyyy*	Science *mm/yyyy*	Writing *mm/yyyy*		
SAT	Exam Dates: _____ *(past & future)* *mm/yyyy*	_____ *mm/yyyy*	_____ *mm/yyyy*		Best Scores: _____ *(so far)*	Critical Reading *mm/yyyy*	Math *mm/yyyy*	Writing *mm/yyyy*		
TOEFL/ IELTS	Exam Dates: _____ *(past & future)* *mm/yyyy*	_____ *mm/yyyy*	_____ *mm/yyyy*		Best Score: _____ *(so far)*	Test	Score *mm/yyyy*			

AP/IB/SAT Subjects   Best Scores: _____
(per subject, so far)

mm/yyyy	Type & Subject	Score	*mm/yyyy*	Type & Subject	Score	
mm/yyyy	Type & Subject	Score	*mm/yyyy*	Type & Subject	Score	
mm/yyyy	Type & Subject	Score	*mm/yyyy*	Type & Subject	Score	
mm/yyyy	Type & Subject	Score	*mm/yyyy*	Type & Subject	Score	

Current Courses Please indicate title, level (AP, IB, advanced honors, etc.) and credit value of all courses you are taking this year. Indicate quarter classes taken in the same semester on the appropriate semester line.

Full Year/First Semester/First Trimester   Second Semester/Trimester   Third Trimester
or additional first/second term courses if more space is needed

_____   _____   _____

_____   _____   _____

_____   _____   _____

_____   _____   _____

_____   _____   _____

_____   _____   _____

_____   _____   _____

2011 - 2012 COMMON APPLICATION

Honors Briefly list any academic distinctions or honors you have received since the 9th grade or international equivalent (e.g., National Merit, Cum Laude Society).

S(School) S/R(State or Regional N(National) I(International)

Grade level or post-graduate (PG) 9 10 11 12 PG	Honor	
○ ○ ○ ○ ○	_____	○ ○ ○ ○
○ ○ ○ ○ ○	_____	○ ○ ○ ○
○ ○ ○ ○ ○	_____	○ ○ ○ ○
○ ○ ○ ○ ○	_____	○ ○ ○ ○
○ ○ ○ ○ ○	_____	○ ○ ○ ○

EXTRACURRICULAR ACTIVITIES & WORK EXPERIENCE

Please list your **principal** extracurricular, volunteer, and work activities **in their order of importance to you**. Feel free to group your activities and paid work experience separately if you prefer. Use the space available to provide details of your activities and accomplishments (specific events, varsity letter, musical instrument, employer, etc.). **To allow us to focus on the highlights of your activities, please complete this section even if you plan to attach a résumé.**

Grade level or post-graduate (PG) 9 10 11 12 PG	Approximate time spent — Hours per week / Weeks per year	When did you participate in the activity? School year / Summer/ School Break	Positions held, honors won, letters earned, or employer	If applicable, do you plan to participate in college?
○ ○ ○ ○ ○	____ ____	○ ○	_____	○
Activity _____				
○ ○ ○ ○ ○	____ ____	○ ○	_____	○
Activity _____				
○ ○ ○ ○ ○	____ ____	○ ○	_____	○
Activity _____				
○ ○ ○ ○ ○	____ ____	○ ○	_____	○
Activity _____				
○ ○ ○ ○ ○	____ ____	○ ○	_____	○
Activity _____				
○ ○ ○ ○ ○	____ ____	○ ○	_____	○
Activity _____				
○ ○ ○ ○ ○	____ ____	○ ○	_____	○
Activity _____				
○ ○ ○ ○ ○	____ ____	○ ○	_____	○
Activity _____				
○ ○ ○ ○ ○	____ ____	○ ○	_____	○
Activity _____				
○ ○ ○ ○ ○	____ ____	○ ○	_____	○
Activity _____				

2011 - 2012 COMMON APPLICATION

WRITING

Please briefly elaborate on one of your extracurricular activities or work experiences in the space below.

_____
_____
_____
_____
_____

Please write an essay of **250 – 500 words** on a topic of your choice or on one of the options listed below, and attach it to your application before submission. **Please indicate your topic by checking the appropriate box.** This personal essay helps us become acquainted with you as a person and student, apart from courses, grades, test scores, and other objective data. It will also demonstrate your ability to organize your thoughts and express yourself. _NOTE: Your Common Application essay should be the same for all colleges. Do not customize it in any way for individual colleges. Colleges that want customized essay responses will ask for them on a supplement form._

○ ❶ Evaluate a significant experience, achievement, risk you have taken, or ethical dilemma you have faced and its impact on you.

○ ❷ Discuss some issue of personal, local, national, or international concern and its importance to you.

○ ❸ Indicate a person who has had a significant influence on you, and describe that influence.

○ ❹ Describe a character in fiction, a historical figure, or a creative work (as in art, music, science, etc.) that has had an influence on you, and explain that influence.

○ ❺ A range of academic interests, personal perspectives, and life experiences adds much to the educational mix. Given your personal background, describe an experience that illustrates what you would bring to the diversity in a college community or an encounter that demonstrated the importance of diversity to you.

○ ❻ Topic of your choice.

_____ Please attach a separate sheet if you wish to provide details of circumstances or qualifications not reflected in the application.

Disciplinary History

① Have you ever been found responsible for a disciplinary violation at any educational institution you have attended from the 9th grade (or the international equivalent) forward, whether related to academic misconduct or behavioral misconduct, that resulted in a disciplinary action? These actions could include, but are not limited to: probation, suspension, removal, dismissal, or expulsion from the institution. ○ Yes ○ No

② Have you ever been adjudicated guilty or convicted of a misdemeanor, felony, or other crime? ○ Yes ○ No
[Note that you are not required to answer "yes" to this question, or provide an explanation, if the criminal adjudication or conviction has been expunged, sealed, annulled, pardoned, destroyed, erased, impounded, or otherwise ordered by a court to be kept confidential.]

If you answered "yes" to either or both questions, please attach a separate sheet of paper that gives the approximate date of each incident, explains the circumstances, and reflects on what you learned from the experience.

**Note: Applicants are expected to immediately notify the institutions to which they are applying should there be any changes to the information requested in this application, including disciplinary history.**

SIGNATURE

Application Fee Payment If this college requires an application fee, how will you be paying it?

○ Online Payment   ○ Will Mail Payment   ○ Online Fee Waiver Request   ○ Will Mail Fee Waiver Request

Required Signature

☐ _I certify that all information submitted in the admission process—including the application, the personal essay, any supplements, and any other supporting materials—is my own work, factually true, and honestly presented, and that these documents will become the property of the institutions to which I am applying and will not be returned to me. I understand that I may be subject to a range of possible disciplinary actions, including admission revocation, expulsion, or revocation of course credit, grades, and degree, should the information I have certified be false._

☐ _I acknowledge that I have reviewed the application instructions for each college receiving this application. I understand that all offers of admission are conditional, pending receipt of final transcripts showing work comparable in quality to that upon which the offer was based, as well as honorable dismissal from the school._

☐ _I affirm that I will send an enrollment deposit (or equivalent) to only one institution; sending multiple deposits (or equivalent) may result in the withdrawal of my admission offers from all institutions. [Note: students may send an enrollment deposit (or equivalent) to a second institution where they have been admitted from the waitlist, provided that they inform the first institution that they will no longer be enrolling.]_

Signature ✎ _____   Date _____
                                                                        mm/dd/yyyy

Common Application member institution admission offices do not discriminate on the basis of race, color, ethnicity, national origin, religion, creed, sex, age, marital status, parental status, physical disability, learning disability, political affiliation, veteran status, or sexual orientation.

Source: commonapp.org

COLLEGES THAT ACCEPT THE COMMON APPLICATION

Adelphi University
Agnes Scott College
Albion College
Albright College
Alfred University
Allegheny College
American University
Amherst College
Arcadia University
Assumption College
Augsburg College
Augustana College - Illinois
Augustana College - South Dakota
Austin College
Babson College
Baldwin-Wallace College
Bard College
Barnard College
Bates College
Belmont University
Beloit College
Bennington College
Bentley University
Berry College
Birmingham-Southern College
Boston College
Boston University
Bowdoin College
Bradley University
Brandeis University
Brown University
Bryant University
Bryn Mawr College
Bucknell University
Burlington College
Butler University
Cabrini College
Caldwell College (NJ)
California Institute of Technology (Caltech)
California Lutheran University

Canisius College
Carleton College
Carnegie Mellon University
Carroll College (Montana)
Carroll University (WI)
Case Western Reserve University
Castleton State College*
Cazenovia College
Cedar Crest College
Centenary College
Centenary College of Louisiana
Centre College
Champlain College
Chapman University
Chatham College
Christian Brothers University
Christopher Newport University*
Claremont McKenna College
Clark University
Clarkson University
Coe College
Cogswell Polytechnical College
Colby College
Colby-Sawyer College
Colgate University
College of Mount Saint Vincent
College of St. Benedict (St. John's University)
College of the Atlantic
College of the Holy Cross
College of William & Mary*
College of Wooster
Colorado College
Colorado State University*
Cornell College
Cornell University
Creighton University
Curry College
Daemen College
Dartmouth College
Davidson College

COLLEGES THAT ACCEPT THE COMMON APPLICATION

Denison University
DePauw University
DeSales University
Dickinson College
Dominican University of California
Dowling College
Drake University
Drew University
Drexel University
Drury University
Duke University
Earlham College
Eastern Connecticut State University*
Eckerd College
Elizabethtown College
Elmira College
Emerson College
Emmanuel College
Emory University
Erskine College
Fairfield University
Fisk University
Flagler College
Florida Southern College
Fordham University
Franklin & Marshall College
Franklin College Switzerland
Franklin Pierce University
Franklin W. Olin College of Engineering
Furman University
George Fox University
Gettysburg College
Gonzaga University
Goshen College
Goucher College
Green Mountain College
Grinnell College
Guilford College
Gustavus Adolphus College
Hamilton College

Hamline University
Hampden-Sydney College
Hampshire College
Hanover College
Hartwick College
Harvard College
Harvey Mudd College
Haverford College
Hendrix College
Hillsdale College
Hiram College
Hobart & William Smith Colleges
Hofstra University
Hollins University
Hood College
Hope College
Howard University
Illinois College
Illinois Institute of Technology
Illinois Wesleyan University
Immaculata University
Iona College
Ithaca College
John Cabot University
John Carroll University
John F. Kennedy University
Johns Hopkins University
Juniata College
Kalamazoo College
Keene State College*
Kenyon College
Keystone College
King's College
Knox College
La Salle University
Lafayette College
Lake Erie College
Lake Forest College
Lasell College
Lawrence Technological University

COLLEGES THAT ACCEPT THE COMMON APPLICATION

Lawrence University
Lees-McRae College
Lehigh University
LeMoyne College
Lesley College
Lewis & Clark College
Linfield College
Lipscomb University
List College, The Jewish Theological Seminary
Long Island University - C.W. Post Campus
Long Island University Brooklyn Campus
Loyola Marymount University
Loyola University Maryland
Loyola University New Orleans
Luther College
Lycoming College
Lyndon State College*
Lynn University
Macalester College
Manhattan College
Manhattanville College
Marietta College
Marist College
Marlboro College
Marquette University
Marymount Manhattan College
Maryville University of St. Louis
Mass. College of Pharmacy & Health Sciences
McDaniel College
Menlo College
Mercyhurst College
Meredith College
Merrimack College
Miami University (Ohio)*
Middlebury College
Mills College
Millsaps College
Moravian College
Morehouse College
Mount Holyoke College

Mount St. Mary's College
Muhlenberg College
Naropa University
Nazareth College
New College of Florida*
New England College
New School University - Eugene Lang College
New York Institute of Technology
New York University
Newbury College
Niagara University
Nichols College
Northeastern University
Northland College
Northwestern University
Notre Dame de Namur University
Oberlin College
Occidental College
Oglethorpe University
Ohio Northern University
Ohio Wesleyan University
Oklahoma City University
Pace University
Pacific Lutheran University
Pacific University
Pepperdine University
Philadelphia University
Pitzer College
Plymouth State University*
Polytechnic Institute of New York University
Pomona College
Presbyterian College
Prescott College
Princeton University
Providence College
Quinnipiac University
Ramapo College of New Jersey*
Randolph College
Randolph-Macon College
Reed College

COLLEGES THAT ACCEPT THE COMMON APPLICATION

Regis College
Regis University
Rensselaer Polytechnic Institute
Rhode Island College*
Rhodes College
Rice University
Richard Stockton College of New Jersey*
Rider University
Ringling College of Art & Design
Ripon College
Rochester Institute of Technology
Rockhurst University
Roger Williams University
Rollins College
Rosemont College
Russell Sage College
Sacred Heart University
Sage College of Albany
Saint Anselm College
Saint Francis University
Saint Joseph's College
Saint Joseph's University
Saint Leo University
Saint Leo University
Saint Louis University
Saint Martin's University
Saint Mary's College of California
Saint Mary's College of Indiana
Saint Mary's University of Minnesota
Saint Michael's College
Saint Peter's College
Saint Vincent College
Salem College
Salisbury University*
Salve Regina University
Samford University
Santa Clara University
Sarah Lawrence College
Scripps College
Seattle Pacific University

Seattle University
Seton Hall University
Sewanee: The University of the South
Siena College
Sierra Nevada College
Simmons College
Skidmore College
Smith College
Southern Methodist University
Southern New Hampshire University
Southwestern University
Spelman College
Spring Hill College
St. Bonaventure University
St. Catherine University
St. Edward's University
St. John Fisher College
St. John's University (College of St. Benedict)
St. Joseph's College - Brooklyn Campus
St. Joseph's College - Long Island Campus
St. Lawrence University
St. Mary's College of Maryland*
St. Norbert College
St. Olaf College
St. Thomas Aquinas College
Stanford University
Stetson University
Stevens Institute of Technology
Stevenson University
Stonehill College
Suffolk University
SUNY Binghamton University*
SUNY Buffalo State College*
SUNY College at Brockport*
SUNY College at Geneseo*
SUNY College at Old Westbury*
SUNY College at Oneonta*
SUNY College of Environmental Science
SUNY Cortland*
SUNY Fredonia*

COLLEGES THAT ACCEPT THE COMMON APPLICATION

SUNY Institute of Technology*
SUNY New Paltz*
SUNY Oswego*
SUNY Plattsburgh*
SUNY Purchase College*
SUNY Stony Brook University*
SUNY University at Albany*
SUNY University at Buffalo*
Susquehanna University
Swarthmore College
Sweet Briar College
Syracuse University
Texas Christian University
The American University of Paris
Catholic University of America
The College of Idaho
The College of New Jersey
College of New Rochelle*
The College of Saint Rose
George Washington University
Thiel College
Thomas College
Towson University*
Transylvania University
Trinity College
Trinity University
Tufts University
Union College
University of Chicago
University of Dallas   University of Dayton
University of Delaware*
University of Denver
University of Evansville
University of Findlay
University of Great Falls
University of Hartford
University of Kentucky*
University of LaVerne
University of Maine at Farmington*
University of Maine at Machias*

University of Maine*
University of Mary Washington*
University of Massachusetts Amherst*
University of Massachusetts Boston*
University of Massachusetts Dartmouth*
University of Massachusetts Lowell*
University of Miami
University of Michigan - Flint*
University of New England
University of New Hampshire*
University of New Haven
University of New Orleans*
University of North Carolina at Chapel Hill*
University of North Carolina at Wilmington*
University of Notre Dame
University of Pennsylvania
University of Portland
University of Puget Sound
University of Redlands
University of Rhode Island*
University of Richmond
University of Rochester
University of San Diego
University of San Francisco
University of Scranton
University of Southern California
University of Southern Maine*
University of St Andrews*
University of Tampa
University of the Pacific
University of the Sciences in Philadelphia
University of Tulsa
University of Vermont*
University of Virginia*
Ursinus College
Utica College
Valparaiso University
Vanderbilt University
Vassar College
Villanova University

Colleges That Accept the Common Application

Virginia Wesleyan College
Wabash College
Wagner College
Wake Forest University
Wartburg College
Washington & Jefferson College
Washington and Lee University
Washington College
Washington University in St. Louis
Webster University
Wellesley College
Wells College
Wentworth Institute of Technology
Wesleyan University
Westminster College - Missouri
Westminster College - Pennsylvania
Westminster College - Utah
Wheaton College
Wheeling Jesuit University
Wheelock College
Whitman College
Whittier College
Willamette University
William Jewell College
Williams College
Wilson College
Wittenberg University
Wofford College
Worcester Polytechnic Institute
Xavier University
Yale University

* Public institution

Source: commonapp.org

COMMON APPLICATION SCHOOLS - NO SUPPLEMENT

Albright College

Alfred University

American University

Augustana College

Berry College

Birmingham-Southern College

Bradley University

Butler University

California Lutheran University

Canisius College

Carroll College (Montana)

Cazenovia College

Cedar Crest College

Centenary College of Louisiana

Chatham University

Coe College

Colby-Sawyer College

College of Mount Saint Vincent

College of Notre Dame of Maryland

College of the Holy Cross

Concordia University

Converse College

Daemen College

Dominican University of California

Eckerd College

Elmira College

Emmanuel College

Erskine College

Fisk University

Florida Institute of Technology

Florida Southern College

Fontbonne University

Franklin Pierce University

Furman University

Green Mountain College

Hamline University

Hampden-Sydney College

Hanover College

Hollins University

Hood College

Husson University

King's College

La Salle University

Lake Erie College

Le Moyne College

Loyola University New Orleans

Lycoming College

Manhattanville College

Marietta College

McDaniel College

Menlo College

Meredith College

Mills College

Millsaps College

Morrisville State College

New England College

Common Application Schools - No Supplement

Newbury College	The Catholic University of America
Nichols College	The College at Brockport
Northland College	Trinity College (Connecticut)
Notre Dame de Namur University	Trinity University (San Antonio)
Oglethorpe University	University at Albany, State Univ. of New York
Ohio Wesleyan University	University of Dayton
Randolph College	University of Denver
Randolph-Macon College	University of Findlay
Regis University (Colorado)	University of Great Falls
Rhodes College	University of La Verne
Ripon College	University of Maine at Machias
Rosemont College	University of Portland
Saint Mary's University of Minnesota	University of Southern Maine
Saint Peter's College	University of Tampa
Saint Vincent College	University of Tulsa
Salem College (North Carolina)	Utica College
Southwestern University	Virginia Wesleyan College
Spelman College	Wabash College
Spring Hill College	Washington & Jefferson College
St. Catherine University	Washington College (Maryland)
St. Norbert College	Wells College
Stephens College	Westminster College (Utah)
Stetson University	Wheelock College
Stevens Institute of Technology	William Jewell College
SUNY Cortland	Wilson College
SUNY New Paltz	Xavier University of Louisiana
SUNY Oswego	
Texas Christian University	
The American University of Rome	

decision
plans

Types of Decision Plans

Early Action

Students who apply under a college's Early Action plan receive a decision before the standard response date but are not required to accept an offer of admission or to make a deposit prior to May 1. Most Early Action deadlines are in November, December, or January, with notification some weeks later. Approximately 200 colleges have Early Action plans. Students should be sure to read the college policy carefully. Some colleges have Single Choice Early Action plans. In these plans, colleges place some restrictions on the applicant's right to make applications to other Early Decision or Early Action plans. Some schools offering Early Action plans include: Boston College, Georgetown and MIT.

Early Decision

A binding plan that states that a student agrees to matriculate if offered admission. Students can only apply Early Decision to one school. Some schools offer an Early Decision II plan which is still binding but has an application deadline later than November 1. Typically Early Decision candidates, if accepted, are required to make a deposit at the university to secure their place in the class. Students who apply under Early Decision commit to enroll at the college if they are admitted and offered a satisfactory financial aid package. Application deadlines are usually in mid-November, with a mid- to late-December notification date. Approximately 230 colleges have an Early Decision plan. Some colleges have both an Early Decision and an Early Action plan.

Open Admissions

Under this policy, a college admits students without regard to conventional academic qualifications, such as taking appropriate high school subjects and receiving suitable high school grades and admission test scores. Virtually all applicants with high school diplomas or the equivalent are accepted. Most community colleges practice open admissions, although many have requirements for certain programs—for example, nursing.

Early Evaluation and Early Notification

With Early Evaluation and Early Notification plans, universities send a preliminary letter indicating the likelihood of acceptance in late February with the official decision being mailed in early April.

TYPES OF DECISION PLANS

Rolling Admissions

In this frequently used procedure, a college considers each student's application a soon as all the required credentials, such as school record and test scores, have been received. The college usually notifies an applicant of its decision without delay. At many colleges, rolling admissions allow for early notification and work much like nonbinding Early Action programs. Many state universities render decision as applications become complete. Therefore, students should apply to state universities with rolling admission plans (for example, University of Michigan or University of Wisconsin) by late September.

Candidates Reply Date Agreement

With the exception of candidates who apply under the Early Decision plan, applicants offered admission as first-year students must notify the college of their decision to attend (or to accept an offer of financial aid) before May 1 of the year the applicant intends to enroll. The purpose of the agreement is to give students time to hear from all the colleges to which they have applied before having to make a commitment to any of them.

Take the Early Application Challenge
Determine if applying early is right for you.

1. Is there a college you really like? Yes or No.

    If your answer is yes, continue. If you answer is no, STOP.
    You are definitely not applying early anywhere.

2. Is there a single college that you like more than any other college? Yes or No.

    If yes, continue. If no, STOP. You are not applying early.

3. Have you visited the college that you like more than any other college? Yes or No.

    If yes, continue. If no, STOP. You are not applying early.

If you have answered yes to each of the above questions, then you should consider the options more closely and research more about the EA/ED process before making a final decision.

If you answered no to any of the above, you are not applying early!

EARLY ACCEPTANCE VS OVERALL ACCEPTANCE - 2010-2011

	Program Offered	Early Acceptance	Overall Acceptance
American University	ED	71.53%	41.44%
Amherst College	ED	36.56%	12.76%
Babson College	ED/EA		33.19%
Barnard College	ED		25.00%
Bates College	ED	50.99%	26.87%
Boston College	REA	43.55%	27.88%
Boston University	ED	42.11%	47.69%
Bowdoin College	ED	33.69%	15.59%
Brandeis University	EA	21%	38.63%
Brown University	ED		8.70%
Bucknell University	ED	60.74%	27.23%
Caltech University	EA		12.00%
Carleton College	ED		29.60%
Carnegie Mellon University	ED		30.40%
Case Western University	ED		48.20%
Claremont McKenna College	ED		13.81%
Clark University	EA		67.20%
Colby College	ED	55.31%	29.08%
Colgate University	EA	60.00%	29.00%
Colorado College	ED/EA		28.97%
Columbia University	ED	19.57%	6.93%
Connecticut College	ED		33.16%
Cooper Union	ED		7.22%
Cornell University	ED	35.16%	17.95%
Dartmouth College	ED	24.87%	9.73%
Davidson College	ED	47.26%	25.06%
Denison University	ED	60.00%	
DePauw University	ED	77.65%	
Dickinson College	ED/EA	69.00%	41.76%
Duke University	ED	28.26%	12.59%
Elon University	ED	84.68%	56.90%
Emerson College	EA		48.4%

EARLY ACCEPTANCE VS OVERALL ACCEPTANCE - 2010-2011

	Program Offered	Early Acceptance	Overall Acceptance
Emory University	ED		25.90%
Fordham University	EA		40.10%
Franklin & Marshall College	ED	80.73%	
Furman University	ED		
George Washington	ED	35.90%	32.05%
Georgetown University	EA	16.86%	17.00%
Georgia Tech	EA		47.90%
Gettysburg University	ED		
Hamilton College	ED	43.09%	26.75%
Harvard College	EA	6.20%	6.17%
Harvey Mudd College	ED	28.97%	19.53%
Haverford College	ED	49.06%	24.88%
College of Holy Cross	ED		33.27%
Johns Hopkins University	ED	38.84%	18.31%
Julliard School of Music	RD		5.50%
Kenyon College	ED	60.24%	33.15%
Lafayette College	ED	49.27%	40.25%
Lehigh University	ED		32.93%
Macalester College	ED		31.69%
Marist College	ED/EA		
Miami University	ED/EA	71.69%	
Middlebury College	ED	38.71%	17.74%
Muhlenberg College	ED		42.40%
New York University	ED		25.64%
Northeastern University	EA		34.31%
Northwestern University	EA	33.62%	18.00%
Notre Dame University	ED		24.15%
Oberlin College	ED		29.70%
Pennsylvania State	RD		46.66%
Occidental College	ED		38.01%
University of Pennsylvania	ED	26.14%	12.26%
Pitzer College	ED	45.42%	

EARLY ACCEPTANCE VS OVERALL ACCEPTANCE - 2010-2011

	Program Offered	Early Acceptance	Overall Acceptance
Pomona College	ED	30.93%	13.58%
Princeton University	RD		8.39%
Purdue University	ED		66.11%
Rensselaer Polytechnic (RPI)	ED		38.48%
Reed College	ED		
Rhodes College	ED/EA		
Rice University	ED	28.76%	18.60%
University of Richmond	ED	43.18%	31.73%
University of Rochester	ED	36.87%	33.66%
Sarah Lawrence College	ED	66.67%	60.52%
Scripps College	ED		36.14%
Skidmore College	ED		41.79%
Smith College	ED	58.93%	45.47%
Southern Methodist University	EA		42.90%
St. Olaf College	ED		
Stanford University	REA	12.72%	7.07%
SUNY, Binghamton			40.19%
Stevens Institute of Technology	ED	68.26%	
Swarthmore College	ED		14.92%
Trinity College	ED		26.70%
Tufts University	ED		21.80%
Tulane University	EA		24.80%
University of California, Los Angeles	RD		25.00%
University of Chicago	EA		15.80%
University of Colorado, Boulder	EA		84.30%
University of Connecticut	EA		40.00%
University of Florida	EA		39.00%
University of Maryland, College Park	EA		44.80%
University of North Carolina, Chapel Hill	EA		29.40%
University of Southern California	RD		22.80%
University of Texas, Austin	RD		45.60%
University of Virginia	RD		32.30%

EARLY ACCEPTANCE VS OVERALL ACCEPTANCE - 2010-2011

	Program Offered	Early Acceptance	Overall Acceptance
University of Wisconsin, Madison	EA		49.80%
Vanderbilt University	ED	29.71%	15.45%
Vassar College	ED		22.28%
Villanova University	EA	39.77%	42.60%
Virginia Tech	ED	53.56%	64.47%
Wake Forest University	ED/EA		
Washington and Lee	ED	47.31%	17.37%
Wellesley College	ED		
Wesleyan College	ED		23.60%
Wheaton College	ED		59.00%
College of William and Mary	ED	50.23%	34.58%
Williams College	ED	40.21%	17.06%
Yale University	REA	13.88%	7.35%

EARLY DECISION ACCEPTANCE RATES 2011 VERSUS 2010

	Early Apps 2011	% change over 2010	Early acceptances 2011	% of early applicants accepted 2011	% of early applicants accepted 2010	Overall Acceptance Rate 2010	Freshman Class Size	% of freshman class filled
American	576	7.06%	412	71.53%	77.51%	44%	1500	27.47%
Amherst	413	-5.06%	151	36.56%	33.79%	15%	465	32.47%
Babson	212	17.78%			61.44%	40%	471	
Barnard	550	38.53%			51.83%	31%	577	
Bates	353	7.95%	180	50.99%	54.43%	31%	500	36.00%
Boston College	6200	7.36%	2700	43.55%	44.68%	31	2500	
Boston U	893	-0.45%	376	42.11%	44.04%	58%	4000	9.40%
Bowdoin	561	9.78%	189	33.69%	36.20%	20%	485	38.97%
Brandeis	278	12.55%			57.49%	40%	781	
Brown	2,765	-3.00%			22.34%	9.3%	1500	
Bucknell	540	30.43%	328	60.74%	71.98%	31%	940	34.89%
Claremont McKenna	250	32.28%				17%	282	
Colby	273	9.20%	151	55.31%	60.80%	34%	490	30.81%
Colorado College	263	39.15%			51.74%	34%	536	
Columbia	3,229	8.25%	632	19.57%	21.25%	9.16%	1419	45.00%
Connecticut College	256	2.81%			70.75%	32%	502	
Cooper Union	725	6.62%			13.08%	8%	198	
Cornell	3,456	-3.84%	1215	35.16%	32.69%	18.4%	3182	38.18%
Dartmouth	1,785	11.98%	444	24.87%	28.92%	11.53%	1100	40.36%
Davidson	402	39.58%	190	47.26%	55.90%	30%	490	38.78%
Denison	150	15.38%	90	60%	81.37%	50%	605	14.88%
DePauw	85	-10.53%	66	77.65%	64.21%	57%	640	10.31%
Dickinson	300	15.38%	207	69%	77.69%	48%	600	34.50%
Duke	2,282	13.7%	645	28.26%	29.90%	15%	1705	37.83%
Elon	346	-15.19%	293	84.68%	86.03%	48%	1291	20.93%

EARLY DECISION ACCEPTANCE RATES 2011 VERSUS 2010

	Early Apps 2011	% change over 2010	Early acceptances 2011	% of early applicants accepted 2011	% of early applicants accepted 2010	Overall Acceptance Rate 2010	Freshman Class Size	% of freshman class filled
Emory	749	1.22%			31.05%	29%		
Franklin & Marshall	275	-7.09%	222	80.73%	71.46%	48%	600	37%
Furman	805	58.77%			71.34%	68%	655	
George Washington	1,725	18.56%			47.44%	31%	2592	
Gettysburg	265				71.78%	40%	739	
Hamilton	376	24.10%	162	43.09%	49.50%	29%	480	33.75%
Harvey Mudd	145	22.88%	42	28.97%	39.83%	25%	198	21.21%
Haverford	265	14.22%	130	49.06%	54.31%	26%	325	40%
Holy Cross	450	6.00%			73.13%	35%	727	
Johns Hopkins	1,330	15.15%	518	38.95%	42.68%	21%	1235	41.94%
Kenyon	249	19.14%	150	60.24%	58.85%	39%	460	32.61%
Lafayette	343	27.04%	169	49.27%	41.85%	42%	620	27.26%
Lehigh	614	14.34%			64.50%	33%	1193	
Macalester	150	2.74%			53.11%	46%	565	
Marist	268	54.02%			84.62%	36%	1000	
Miami	498	-6.92%	357	71.69%	78.13%	79%	3550	10.06%
Middlebury	682	4.28%	264	38.71%	41.59%	17%	690	38.26%
N.Y.U.	3,154	**			43.30%	38%	5000	
Northwestern	2,127	25.86%	715	33.62%	36.51%	23%	2025	35.31%
Oberlin	261	12.99%			65.48%	34%	806	
Occidental	128	-17.95%			45.13%	44%	576	
U. of Pennsylvania	4,571	18.70%	1195	26.14%	31.19%	14.2%	2420	49.38%
Pitzer	139	-2.11%	63	45.32%	48.00%	20%	250	25.20%
Pomona	236	0.85%	73	30.93%	31.62%	18%	390	18.72%
Reed	149	43.27%			52.51%	43%	373	
Rhodes	41	28.12%			23.93%	45%	502	
Rice	1,036	18.81%	298	28.76%	33.72%	21%	950	31.37%

EARLY DECISION ACCEPTANCE RATES 2011 VERSUS 2010

	Early Apps 2011	% change over 2010	Early acceptances 2011	% of early applicants accepted 2011	% of early applicants accepted 2010	Overall Acceptance Rate 2010	Freshman Class Size	% of freshman class filled
Richmond	579	37.86%	250	43.18%	69.13%	39%	770	32.47%
U. of Rochester	594	2.06%	219	36.87%	33.16%	39%	1150	19.04%
Sarah Lawrence	84	15.07%	56	66.67%	62.91%	58%	360	15.56%
Scripps	75	-15.73%			53.97%	33%	203	
Skidmore	271	-3.56%				42%	664	
Smith	224	13.71%	132	58.93%	55.89%	47%	640	20.63%
St. Olaf	198	3.13%			88.46%	57%	778	
Stanford	5929	6.54%	754	12.72%	13.53%	7.2	1725	
Stevens Institute of Technology	293	26.29%	200	68.26%	66.80%	51%	565	35.40%
Swarthmore	307	5.13%			33.40%	16%	394	
Trinity	80	60%			91.25%	59%	642	
Tufts						27%	1312	
Vanderbilt	1,666	30.77%	495	29.71%	42.07%	16.3%	1585	31.23%
Vassar	395	4.22%			43.41%	24%	659	
Virginia Tech	2,022	-2.74%	1083	53.56%	55.41%	67%	5137	21.08%
Wake Forest	401	-11.09%			41.86%	38%	1197	
Washington and Lee	372	0.54%	176	47.31%	44.86%	19%	472	37.29%
Wellesley					58.82%	35%	589	
Wesleyan	515	3%			41.10%	21%	745	
William and Mary	1,079	-0.19%	542	50.23%	53.42%	34%	1400	38.71%
Williams	572	6.31%	230	40.21%	40.01%	20%	550	41.82%
Yale	5257	-0.08%	761	14.48%	13.88%	7.5	1350	

COLLEGES THAT OFFER EARLY DECISION

	Date		Date
Albany College of Pharmacy & Health Sciences	11/1	Cornell University	11/1
Alfred University	12/1	Dartmouth College	11/1
Allegheny College	11/15	Davidson College	11/15
American University	11/15	Denison University	11/15
Amherst College	11/15	DePauw University	11/1
Babson College	11/1	Dickinson College	11/15
Barnard College	11/15	Drew University	11/1
Bates College	11/15	Duke University	11/1
Bennington College	11/15	Earlham College	12/1
Bentley University	11/1	Elmira College	11/15
Boston University	11/1	Emmanuel College	11/1
Bowdoin College	11/15	Emory University	11/1
Brandeis University	11/15	Eugene Lang New School	11/1
Brown University	11/1	Florida Southern College	11/1
Bryant University	11/15	Franklin and Marshall College	11/15
Bryn Mawr College	11/15	Furman University	11/15
Bucknell University	11/15	Geneseo, State Univ. of New York	11/15
Carleton College	11/15	George Washington University	11/10
Carnegie Mellon University	11/1	Gettysburg College	11/15
Champlain College	11/15	Goucher College	11/15
Claremont McKenna College	11/15	Grinnell College	11/15
Clarkson University	12/1	Hamilton College	11/15
Colby College	11/15	Hampden-Sydney College	11/15
Colgate University	11/15	Hampshire College	11/15
College of the Atlantic	12/1	Hartwick College	11/15
College of the Holy Cross	12/15	Harvey Mudd College	11/15
College of William & Mary	11/1	Haverford College	11/15
College of Wooster	11/15	Hillsdale College	11/15
Colorado College	11/15	Hobart and William Smith Colleges	11/15
Columbia University	11/1	Hollins University	12/1
Connecticut College	11/15	Hood College	11/1
Cornell College (Iowa)	11/1	Illinois Institute of Technology	11/1

COLLEGES THAT OFFER EARLY DECISION

	Date		Date
Ithaca College	11/1	Reed College	11/15
Johns Hopkins University	11/1	Rensselaer Polytechnic Institute	11/1
Juniata College	12/1	Rhodes College	11/1
Kalamazoo College		Rice University	11/1
Kenyon College	11/15	Rochester Institute of Technology	12/1
Lafayette College	11/15	Rollins College	11/15
Lake Forest College	12/1	Sacred Heart University	12/1
Lawrence University	11/15	Saint Mary's College (Indiana)	11/15
Lehigh University	11/15	Sarah Lawrence College	11/1
List College, Jewish Theological Seminary	11/15	Scripps College	11/1
		Sewanee University of the South	11/15
Macalester College	11/15	Siena College	12/1
Manhattan College	11/15	Skidmore College	11/15
Manhattanville College	12/1	Smith College	11/15
Marist College	11/16	Southwestern University	11/1
Marlboro College	12/1	Spelman College	11/1
Meredith College	10/30	St. John Fisher College	12/1
Miami University (Ohio)	11/1	St. Lawrence University	11/15
Middlebury College	11/15	St. Olaf College	11/15
Millsaps College	11/15	Stephens College	11/15
Moravian College	2/1	Stetson University	11/1
Mount Holyoke College	11/15	Stevens Institute of Technology	11/15
Muhlenberg College	2/15	Stonehill College	11/1
Nazareth College	11/15	SUNY Buffalo State College	11/1
New York University	11/1	SUNY Fredonia	11/1
Northwestern University	11/1	SUNY Oswego	11/15
Oberlin College	11/15	SUNY Plattsburgh	11/1
Occidental College	11/15	Susquehanna University	11/15
Pitzer College	11/15	Swarthmore College	11/15
Polytechnic Institute of NYU	11/6	Syracuse University	11/15
Pomona College	11/1	The College of New Jersey	11/15
Presbyterian College	11/1	Trinity College (Connecticut)	11/15
Prescott College	12/1	Trinity College (San Antonio)	11/1

COLLEGES THAT OFFER EARLY DECISION

	Date
Tufts University	11/1
Union College (New York)	11/15
University at Buffalo (SUNY)	11/1
University of Great Falls	11/15
University of Miami	11/1
University of New England	12/1
University of Pennsylvania	11/1
University of Puget Sound	11/15
University of Richmond	11/15
University of Rochester	11/1
Ursinus College	1/15
Vanderbilt University	11/1
Vassar College	11/15
Wabash College	11/15
Wagner College	12/15
Wake Forest University	1/1
Washington & Jefferson College	12/1
Washington and Lee University	11/15
Washington College (Maryland)	11/15
Washington University in St. Louis	11/15
Wellesley College	11/1
Wells College	12/15
Wesleyan University	11/15
Wheaton College (Mass.)	11/15
Whitman College	11/15
Williams College	11/10
Wittenberg University	11/15
Wofford College	11/15

COLLEGES THAT OFFER EARLY DECISION 2

	ED 1	ED 2		ED 1	ED 2
Bates College	11/15	1/1	Lehigh University	11/15	1/1
Bennington College	11/15	1/3	List College	11/15	1/15
Bowdoin College	11/15	1/1	Macalester College	11/15	1/3
Brandeis University	11/15	1/1	Middlebury College	11/15	12/31
Bryant University	11/15	1/14	Mount Holyoke College	11/15	1/1
Bryn Mawr College	11/15	1/1	New York University	11/1	1/1
Bucknell University	11/15	1/15	Oberlin College	11/15	1/2
Carleton College	11/15	1/15	Occidental College	11/15	1/3
Carnegie Mellon University	11/1	12/1	Pomona College	11/1	12/28
Champlain College	11/15	1/1	Reed College	11/15	12/20
Claremont McKenna College	11/15	1/2	Rensselaer Polytechnic Institute	11/1	12/15
Colby College	11/15	1/1			
Colgate University	11/15	1/15	Rollins College	11/15	1/15
College of the Atlantic	12/1	1/10	Sarah Lawrence College	11/1	1/1
Colorado College	11/15	1/1	Scripps College	11/1	1/1
Connecticut College	11/15	1/1	Sewanee	11/15	1/2
Cornell College (Iowa)	11/1	2/1	Skidmore College	11/15	1/15
Davidson College	11/15	1/2	Smith College	11/15	1/1
Denison University	11/15	1/15	St. Lawrence University	11/15	1/15
Dickinson College	11/15	1/15	St. Olaf College	11/15	1/15
Drew University	11/1	1/15	Stevens Institute of Technology	11/15	1/15
Elmira College	11/15	1/15			
Emory University	11/1	1/1	Swarthmore College	11/15	1/3
Franklin and Marshall College	11/15	1/15	Trinity College (Connecticut)	11/15	1/1
George Washington University	11/10	1/10	Tufts University	11/1	1/3
Gettysburg College	11/15	1/15	Union College (New York)	11/15	1/15
Goucher College	11/15	1/15	University of Puget Sound	11/15	1/2
Grinnell College	11/15	1/2	University of Richmond	11/15	1/15
Hamilton College	11/15	1/1	Vanderbilt University	11/1	1/3
Harvey Mudd College	11/15	1/2	Vassar College	11/15	1/1
Hobart & William Smith Colleges	11/15	1/1	Washington and Lee University	11/15	1/3
Kenyon College	11/15	1/15	Wesleyan University	11/15	1/1
Lafayette College	11/15	2/1	Wheaton College	11/15	1/15
			Whitman College	11/15	1/1

standardized tests

ACT VERSUS THE SAT

	ACT	SAT
Length	3 hours, 25 minutes (Including the 30 minute optional Writing Test)	3 hours, 45 minutes
Sections	4 sections (5 with the Writing Test)	10 sections (One of which is not scored)
Areas Tested	English, Math, Reading, Science	Critical Reading, Math, Writing (includes the essay), Experimental (not scored)
Reading (ACT)/ Critical Reading (SAT)	4 Reading Comprehension passages 10 questions per passage	Mix of Reading Comprehension and Sentence Completion questions (requires vocabulary expertise)
Science	Science reasoning (Requires ability to use logic & think critically; does not test knowledge of science)	Science not included
Math	1/4 of overall score Topics: Algebra, Geometry, Trigonometry (4 questions)	1/3 of overall score Topics: Algebra, Geometry and Algebra II
Essay	Last section (optional) 30 minutes	First section (required) 25 minutes
Scoring	Composite score of 1-36 (Based on the average of the 4 tests)	Scored out of possible 2400 points
Wrong Answer Penalty	No wrong answer penalty	Point deduction: 1/4 point per wrong answer (Excluding the math grid-in section)
Sending Score Options	Student decides scores to send	Score choice available (Some schools do not honor it)

ACT versus the SAT

The SAT may be a better test for you if:

- You performed really well on the PSAT.

- You possess a better than average vocabulary.

- You can ace grammar. In addition to the essay section, the Writing section of the SAT includes several sub-sections that test a student's knowledge of grammar rules.

- You find it easier to write essays that use illustrative examples rather than persuasive arguments. On the SAT, the essay prompt requires a student to use anything from the Civil Rights Movement to The Scarlet Letter as evidence, while the ACT essay prompt more likely expects examples from personal experience.

- You consider yourself quick-thinking. At some level, the math section of the SAT is based on reasoning. The reading section is about seeing things the same way as the test-makers.

- You are high-energy or impulsive. Comprised of nine sections and an essay, the SAT is 20 minutes longer than the ACT. However, there are more starts and stops on the SAT — which for some test takers makes it feel as though it's moving along faster than the ACT.

The ACT may be a better test for you if:

- You scored well on the PLAN (the equivalent of the "PSAT" for the ACT) or had a PSAT or SAT score inconsistent with your academic performance in school.

- Your vocabulary is not as strong as your reading ability. You read well and relatively quickly. Arguably, the ACT is a test that is three parts verbal — English, Reading and Science (the latter section requires no knowledge outside of what the test presents).

- You are accustomed to editing papers. The English portion of the ACT is more a test of punctuation and sentence and paragraph structure. Many students find the English to be common sense, much like proof-reading a paper.

- You prefer to write essays about everyday issues in your life or school.

- You want guaranteed score choice. If, when you register, you do not indicate schools you want to receive your scores, you can wait until you have taken the ACT several times and then select the best scores to send. On the SAT, students are offered "score choice," but many colleges still require all SAT scores from all test dates.

- You are more academic than "test savvy." The ACT is more curriculum-based than the SAT and thus more straightforward.

SCORE CHOICE

Score Choice Overview

The College Board offers "Score Choice," which gives students the option to hand select the SAT scores they send to colleges. They may choose SAT scores by test date and SAT Subject Test scores by each individual test. If students choose not to utilize Score Choice, the College Board automatically sends all scores.

Students will be encouraged to follow the score-reporting requirements of each college to which they apply, but their scores will not be released for admission purposes without their specific consent. Colleges and universities will only receive the scores that students send them.

Schools that require students to submit all SAT scores regardless of Score Choice

ABINGTON MEM HOSP DIXON SCH OF NURSING
ACADEMY COLLEGE
AIMS COMMUNITY COLLEGE
ALDERSON-BROADDUS COLLEGE
AMBASSADOR BAPTIST COLLEGE
AMERICAN CAREER COLLEGE
AMERICAN COLLEGE OF HIGHER EDUCATION
AMERICAN INTERCONTINENTAL UNIVERSITY
AMERICAN UNIVERSITY BULGARIA
AMERICAN UNIVERSITY COLLEGE OF SCIENCE & TECHNOLOGY
ANDREWS UNIVERSITY
ARGOSY UNIVERSITY
ARNOT-OGDEN MEDICAL CENTER
ART ACADEMY OF CINCINNATI
ART INSTITUTE OF NEW YORK CITY
ASHWORTH COLLEGE
ATLANTIC COLLEGE UNIVERSIDADES
AUGUSTA STATE UNIVERSITY
AULTMAN COLLEGE OF NURS & HLTH SCI
AUSTIN COMMUNITY COLLEGE TEXAS
AVERETT UNIVERSITY
BAKER COLLEGE CENTER FOR GRAD STUDIES ONLINE
BARNARD COLLEGE
BARRY UNIVERSITY
BAUDER COLLEGE
BELLIN COLLEGE NURSING
BLINN COLLEGE
BLUE MOUNTAIN COLLEGE

BLUE RIDGE COMMUNITY AND TECHNICAL COLLEGE
BRIGHAM YOUNG UNIVERSITY HAWAII CAMPUS
BROCKTON HOSPITAL SCHOOL OF NURSING
CALUMET COLLEGE SAINT JOSEPH
CALVARY BIBLE COLLEGE
CAMERON UNIVERSITY
CARIBBEAN UNIVERSITY COLLEGE
CARL ALBERT STATE COLLEGE
CARNEGIE MELLON UNIVERSITY
CARNEGIE MELLON UNIVERSITY-QATAR
CAROLINAS COLLEGE OF HEALTH SCIENCES
CASTLETON STATE COLLEGE
CAZENOVIA COLLEGE
CENTRAL ARIZONA COLLEGE
CENTRAL FLORIDA COMMUNITY COLLEGE
CENTRAL METHODIST UNIVERSITY
CHAMINADE UNIVERSITY OF HONOLULU
CHINESE UNIVERSITY OF HONG KONG
CHOWAN COLLEGE
CHRIST COLLEGE OF NURSING AND HEALTH SCIENCES
CHRIST HOSPITAL SCHOOL OF NURSING JERSEY CITY
CINCINNATI CHRISTIAN UNIVERSITY
CLINTON COMMUNITY COLLEGE
COASTAL CAROLINA COMMUNITY COLLEGE
COLGATE UNIVERSITY
COLUMBIA COLLEGE SOUTH CAROLINA
COLUMBIA INTERNATIONAL UNIVERSITY
COLUMBIA UNIVERSITY UNDERGRAD ADMISSIONS
COLUMBUS TECHNICAL COLLEGE

Score Choice

Schools that require students to submit all SAT scores regardless of Score Choice

COMMUNITY COLLEGE OF DENVER
COMPASS FILM ACADEMY
CONSERVATORY MUSIC PUERTO RICO
COOPER UNION
CORBAN COLLEGE
CORNELL UNIVERSITY
CORNERSTONE UNIVERSITY
COSSATOT COMMUNITY COLLEGE
CUNY BARUCH COLLEGE
CUNY BOROUGH OF MANHATTAN COMM COLLEGE
CUNY BRONX COMMUNITY COLLEGE
CUNY BROOKLYN COLLEGE
CUNY COLLEGE OF STATEN ISLAND
CUNY HOSTOS COMMUNITY COLLEGE
CUNY HUNTER COLLEGE
CUNY JOHN JAY COLLEGE OF CRIMINAL JUSTICE
CUNY KINGSBOROUGH COMMUNITY COLLEGE
CUNY LAGUARDIA COMMUNITY COLLEGE
CUNY LEHMAN COLLEGE
CUNY MEDGAR EVERS COLLEGE
CUNY NEW YORK CITY COLLEGE OF TECHNOLOGY
CUNY QUEENS COLLEGE
CUNY QUEENSBOROUGH COMMUNITY COLLEGE
CUNY THE CITY COLLEGE OF NEW YORK
CUNY UAPC
CUNY YORK COLLEGE
CURTIS INSTITUTE OF MUSIC
DALLAS CHRISTIAN COLLEGE
DELAWARE STATE UNIVERSITY
DEVRY INSTITUTE OF TECHNOLOGY MIRAMAR FLORIDA
DIGIPEN INSTITUTE OF TECHNOLOGY SINGAPORE
DORDT COLLEGE
DUQUESNE UNIVERSITY
EAST CENTRAL UNIVERSITY
EMORY UNIVERSITY MEDICAL IMAGING PROGRAM
FAIRMONT STATE UNIVERSITY
FLORIDA AGRICULTURAL MECHANICAL UNIVERSITY
FLORIDA CHRISTIAN COLLEGE
FORT RANGE COMMUNITY COLLEGE LARIMER CAMPUS

FORT VALLEY STATE UNIVERSITY
FRONT RANGE COMMUNITY COLLEGE
GEORGETOWN UNIVERSITY
GERMANNA COMMUNITY COLLEGE
GOUCHER COLLEGE POST-BACCALAUREATE PRE-MEDICAL PRG
GRACE COLLEGE
GRACE UNIVERSITY
GRAMBLING STATE UNIVERSITY
HALLMARK INSTITUTE OF TECHNOLOGY
HARRINGTON INSTITUTE INTERIOR DESIGN
HARVEY MUDD COLLEGE
HOBE SOUND BIBLE COLLEGE
HOLY APOSTLES COLLEGE AND SEMINARY
HOPE COLLEGE
HOWARD COLLEGE
HOWARD PAYNE UNIVERSITY
INDIANA UNIVERSITY OF PENNSYLVANIA
INDIANA UNIVERSITY PURDUE UNIVERSITY COLUMBUS
INDIANA WESLEYAN UNIVERSITY
INTER-AMERICAN UNIVERSITY OF PUERTO RICO
PONCE INTERNATIONAL AMERICAN UNIVERSITY
INTERNATIONAL UNIVERSITY OF BUSINESS AND AGRICULTURE
IOWA WESTERN COMMUNITY COLLEGE COUNCIL BLUFFS
IVY TECH COMMUNITY COLLEGE
IVY TECH COMMUNITY COLLEGE BLOOMINGTON
IVY TECH COMMUNITY COLLEGE MUNCIE
JAMES A RHODES STATE COLLEGE
JAMESTOWN COLLEGE
JEFFERSON STATE COMMUNITY COLLEGE
JOHN WESLEY COLLEGE
JOHNS HOPKINS UNIVERSITY BACCALAUREATE PROGRAM
JUDSON COLLEGE ALABAMA
JUDSON COLLEGE ILLINOIS
KANSAS WESLEYAN UNIVERSITY
KENT STATE UNIVERSITY STARK CAMPUS
KENTUCKY CHRISTIAN UNIVERSITY

SCORE CHOICE

Schools that require students to submit all SAT scores regardless of Score Choice

KEY COLLEGE
LAKE SUMTER COMMUNITY COLLEGE
LETOURNEAU UNIVERSITY
LITTLE PRIEST TRIBAL COLLEGE
LONG ISLAND UNIVERSITY BROOKLYN
LOUISIANA STATE UNIVERSITY ALEXANDRIA
LOUISIANA STATE UNIVERSITY SHREVEPORT
LOUISIANA TECHNICAL COLLEGE
LUMS SCHOOL OF SCIENCE & ENGINEERING
MACALESTER COLLEGE
MACCORMAC COLLEGE
MACMURRAY COLLEGE
MADISONVILLE COMMUNITY AND TECHNICAL COLLEGE
MARION MILITARY INSTITUTE
MARTIN COMMUNITY COLLEGE
MAYVILLE STATE UNIVERSITY
MCGILL UNIVERSITY
METRO BUSINESS COLLEGE JEFFERSON CITY
MIAMI INTERNATIONAL UNIVERSITY OF ART AND DESIGN
MICHLALAH COLLEGE
MIDWESTERN STATE UNIVERSITY
MILLS COLLEGE
MISR INTERNATIONAL UNIVERSITY
MONTGOMERY COMMUNITY COLLEGE
MOTLOW STATE COMMUNITY COLLEGE
MOUNT MERCY COLLEGE
MOUNT SAINT MARYS UNIVERSITY
MUHLENBURG REGIONAL MEDICAL CENTER
NEUMONT UNIVERSITY
NEW COLLEGE OF FLORIDA
NEW ENGLAND BIBLE COLLEGE
NEW ENGLAND COLLEGE OF FINANCE
NEW MEXICO JUNIOR COLLEGE
NEW YORK SCHOOL OF INTERIOR DESIGN
NEWCASTLE UNIVERSITY
NICHOLLS STATE UNIVERSITY
NIPISSING UNIVERSITY
NORMANDALE COMMUNITY COLLEGE
NORTH CENTRAL TEXAS COLLEGE

NORTH DAKOTA STATE COLLEGE OF SCIENCE
NORTHEAST ALABAMA STATE COMMUNITY COLLEGE
NORTHEAST COMMUNITY COLLEGE
NORTHERN CARIBBEAN UNIVERSITY
NORTHLAND BAPTIST BIBLE COLLEGE
NOSSI COLLEGE OF ART
OAK HILLS CHRISTIAN COLLEGE
OAKLAND CITY UNIVERSITY
OLIVET NAZARENE UNIVERSITY
OLYMPIC COLLEGE
ORANGEBURG-CALHOUN TECHNICAL COLLEGE
OWENS COMMUNITY COLLEGE
OWENS COMMUNITY COLLEGE FINDLAY
PANOLA COLLEGE
PATRICIA STEVENS COLLEGE
PEACE COLLEGE
PIKES PEAK COMMUNITY COLLEGE
POINT LOMA NAZARENE UNIVERSITY
POMONA COLLEGE
PRAIRIE VIEW AGRICULTURAL MECHANICAL UNIV
PUEBLO COMMUNITY COLLEGE
PUERTO RICO TECHNICAL JUNIOR COLLEGE
QATAR UNIVERSITY
QUINNIPIAC UNIVERSITY
RASMUSSEN COLLEGE
REINHARDT COLLEGE
RICE UNIVERSITY
RICHARD STOCKTON COLLEGE OF NEW JERSEY
ROBERT MORRIS COLLEGE ILLINOIS
ROCHESTER COMMUNITY AND TECH COLLEGE
ROCKFORD COLLEGE
ROGERS STATE UNIVERSITY
ROSEDALE TECHNICAL INSTITUTE
SABANCI UNIVERSITY
SACRED HEART MAJOR SEMINARY
SACRED HEART UNIVERSITY
SAINT ELIZABETH COLLEGE OF NURSING
SAINT GREGORY THE GREAT SEMINARY
SAINT JOSEPH SEMINARY COLLEGE

SCORE CHOICE

Schools that require students to submit all SAT scores regardless of Score Choice

SAINT LOUIS CHRISTIAN COLLEGE
SAINT LOUIS UNIVERSITY MISSOURI
SAINT LUKES COLLEGE
SAINT MARYS COLLEGE CALIFORNIA
SAINT MARYS COLLEGE SAINT MARY KANSAS
SAINT XAVIER UNIVERSITY
SALEM COMMUNITY COLLEGE
SAN JACINTO COLLEGE SOUTH
SANDERSVILLE TECHNICAL COLLEGE
SCRIPPS COLLEGE
SENTARA SCHOOL OF HEALTH PROFESSIONS
SHIPPENSBURG UNIVERSITY OF PENNSYLVANIA
SOKA UNIVERSITY OF AMERICA
SOUTH HILLS BUSINESS SCHOOL
SOUTH LOUISIANA COMMUNITY COLLEGE
SOUTH PLAINS COLLEGE
SOUTH UNIVERSITY ALABAMA
SOUTH UNIVERSITY COLUMBIA CAMPUS
SOUTHEAST COMMUNITY COLLEGE
SOUTHEAST MISSOURI HOSPITAL COLL NUR & HEALTH SCI
SOUTHEASTERN UNIVERSITY
SOUTHERN ARKANSAS UNIVERSITY MAGNOLIA
SOUTHWEST GEORGIA TECH COLLEGE
SOUTHWESTERN COLLEGE ARIZONA
SOUTHWESTERN COMMUNITY COLLEGE
SOUTHWESTERN OKLAHOMA STATE UNIVERSITY
SPENCERIAN COLLEGE LEXINGTON
SPOON RIVER COLLEGE
ST EDWARDS UNIVERSITY
STANFORD UNIVERSITY
STATE UNIVERSITY OF NEW YORK
STETSON UNIVERSITY
SUSQUEHANNA UNIVERSITY
SWINBURNE UNIVERSITY TECHNOLOGY
SYRACUSE UNIVERSITY
TARLETON STATE UNIVERSITY
TECHNICAL COLLEGE OF THE LOW COUNTRY

TEMPLE COLLEGE
TEMPLE UNIVERSITY
TENNESSEE TECHNOLOGICAL UNIVERSITY
TENNESSEE TEMPLE UNIVERSITY
TEXAS A&M UNIVERSITY COLLEGE STATION
TEXAS A&M UNIVERSITY KINGSVILLE
TEXAS WESLEYAN UNIVERSITY, THE CITADEL
THREE RIVERS COMMUNITY COLLEGE
TIDEWATER COMMUNITY COLLEGE CHESAPEAKE
TOURO COLLEGE LOS ANGELES
TOURO COLLEGE/LANDER
TRIDENT TECHNICAL COLLEGE NORTH
TRINIDAD STATE JUNIOR COLLEGE
TRINITY CHRISTIAN COLLEGE
TRINITY VALLEY COMMUNITY COLLEGE
TRUCKEE MEADOWS COMMUNITY COLLEGE
TUFTS UNIVERSITY
UNION COLLEGE NEBRASKA
UNITED STATES AIR FORCE HEALTH CARE SCIENCE
UNITED STATES MERCHANT MARINE ACADEMY
UNIVERSITY ALASKA SOUTHEAST SITKA CAMPUS
UNIVERSITY COLORADO DENVER
UNIVERSITY NORTH ALABAMA
UNIVERSITY NORTH CAROLINA CHARLOTTE
UNIVERSITY OF ARKANSAS LITTLE ROCK
UNIVERSITY OF CALIFORNIA BERKELEY
UNIVERSITY OF CALIFORNIA DAVIS
UNIVERSITY OF CALIFORNIA IRVINE
UNIVERSITY OF CALIFORNIA LOS ANGELES
UNIVERSITY OF CALIFORNIA MERCED
UNIVERSITY OF CALIFORNIA RIVERSIDE
UNIVERSITY OF CALIFORNIA SAN DIEGO
UNIVERSITY OF CALIFORNIA SANTA BARBARA
UNIVERSITY OF CALIFORNIA SANTA CRUZ
UNIVERSITY OF DUBLIN TRINITY COLLEGE
UNIVERSITY OF GLASGOW
UNIVERSITY OF KENTUCKY LEXINGTON
UNIVERSITY OF LIMERICK

SCORE CHOICE

Schools that require students to submit all SAT scores regardless of Score Choice

UNIVERSITY OF LOUISIANA AT MONROE
UNIVERSITY OF MARYLAND COLLEGE PARK
UNIVERSITY OF MASSACHUSETTS LOWELL
UNIVERSITY OF MEDICINE & DENTISTRY OF NJ PA PRG
UNIV OF PENN COLL LIBERAL/ PROFESSIONAL STUD
UNIVERSITY OF PENNSYLVANIA
UNIVERSITY OF PUERTO RICO CAYEY
UNIVERSITY OF PUERTO RICO HUMACAO
UNIVERSITY OF PUERTO RICO PONCE
UNIVERSITY OF REGINA
UNIVERSITY OF SAINT MARY LEAVENWORTH
UNIVERSITY OF SOUTH CAROLINA COLUMBIA
UNIVERSITY OF SOUTH CAROLINA LANCASTER
UNIVERSITY OF SOUTH CAROLINA SUMTER
UNIVERSITY OF TEXAS BROWNSVILLE
UNIVERSITY OF TEXAS
UNIVERSITY OF TORONTO
UNIVERSITY OF WARWICK THE
UNIVERSITY OF WASHINGTON
UNIVERSITY OF WISCONSIN PLATTEVILLE
UNIVERSITY OF WISCONSIN WAUSAU
UNIVERSITY ST FRANCIS INDIANA
UTAH STATE UNIVERSITY
VALENCIA COMMUNITY COLLEGE
VICTORIAN TERTIARY ADMISSIONS CENTRE
VILLA MARIA ACADEMY

Source: The College Board

Average SAT and ACT Scores

	Math SAT	Verbal SAT	ACT
Agnes Scott College	590	560	25
Albertson College of Idaho	571	563	24
Albion College	580	600	25
Allegheny College	607	601	26
American University	640	620	28
Amherst College	760	770	34
Arizona State University	530	540	23
Auburn University	570	600	26
Austin College	614	613	25
Barnard College	660	670	29
Baylor University	660	650	
Bellarmine University	545	550	25
Beloit College	640	610	27
Birmingham-Southern College	570	570	26
Boston College	720	710	
Boston University			
Bradley University	540	520	25
Brandeis University	730	730	
Brigham Young University	N/A	N/A	
Brown University	770	760	34
Bryn Mawr College	660	630	31
Bucknell University	640	670	29
California College of the Arts	530	540	22
California Polytechnic State University	594	639	28
Calvin College	600	600	26
Carleton College	740	750	33
Carnegie Mellon University	780	720	33
Catawba College	488	494	20
Chapman University	604	623	27
Claremont McKenna College	750	750	
Clark University	600	590	26
Clemson University	600	630	27
Colby College	710	720	31
Colgate University	730	730	32
College of Charleston	606	605	25
College of the Atlantic	642	565	25

Average SAT and ACT Scores

	Math SAT	Verbal SAT	ACT
College of William and Mary	720	730	32
Colorado College	660	660	27
Colorado School of Mines	610	610	26
Columbia University	780	770	34
Connecticut College	660	650	27
Cooper Union	660	720	33
Cornell College	610	610	
Cornell University	770	730	33
Creighton University	580	600	26
CUNY - Hunter	557	575	34
Dartmouth College	780	770	
Davidson College	630	630	32
Denison University	630	620	30
DePaul University	556	551	23
DePauw University	680	690	27
Dickinson College	690	700	31
Drexel University	580	620	
Duke University	790	750	35
Duquesne University	539	568	25
Earlham College	640	590	27
Elon College	611	614	27
Emerson College	623	592	26
Emory University	740	730	33
Eugene Lang College			
Fairfield University	570	570	25
Fisk University	492	484	19
Flagler College	550	540	23
Fordham University	660	670	
George Mason University	560	570	25
George Washington University	690	690	
Georgetown University	730	730	32
Georgia Institute of Technology	730	690	31
Gettysburg College	690	690	30
Gonzaga University	580	600	26
Goucher College	620	570	26
Grinnell College	720	740	32

AVERAGE SAT AND ACT SCORES

	Math SAT	Verbal SAT	ACT
Grove City College	630	629	28
Guilford College	570	550	25
Hamilton College	730	720	31
Hampden-Sydney College	561	562	22
Hampton University	526	516	20
Hanover College	550	560	25
Harvard University	790	780	34
Haverford College	740	750	
Hendrix College	635	617	29
Hiram College	526	521	23
Hofstra University	580	600	26
Hollins College	595	550	24
Hope College	585	597	26
Illinois Wesleyan University	630	660	28
Indiana University-Bloomington	570	600	27
Ithaca College	580	580	
Johns Hopkins University	760	730	33
Kalamazoo College	630	630	28
Kenyon College	730	700	32
Knox College	660	620	29
Lafayette College	700	670	30
Lake Forest College			
Lehigh University	710	640	
Lewis & Clark College			
Loyola Marymount University	580	600	26
Loyola University	600	590	27
Loyola University Chicago	600	590	27
Macalester College	710	740	32
Manhattanville College	530	540	24
Marist College	506	565	24
Marquette University			
Mary Washington College	613	595	27
Mass College of Pharmaceutical & Health Sciences	525	570	24
Massachusetts Institute of Technology	715	770	33
Miami University of Ohio	580	610	26
Middlebury College	740	740	32

Average SAT and ACT Scores

	Math SAT	Verbal SAT	ACT
Mills College	600	550	25
Millsaps College	580	580	26
Monmouth University	530	550	23
Montana Tech of the Univ. of Montana	530	539	22
Morehouse College	530	550	23
Mount Holyoke College	660	660	29
Muhlenberg College	610	610	20
New College of Florida	693	637	27
New York University	720	710	29
Northeastern University	680	660	
Northwestern University	770	750	34
Notre Dame	760	740	34
Oberlin College	710	740	32
Occidental College	650	650	30
Oglethorpe University	600	570	25
Ohio State University, Columbus	600	640	27
Ohio University	540	550	23
Ohio Wesleyan University	602	608	27
Pace University	539	547	
Pepperdine University	680	670	29
Pitzer College			
Pomona College	760	770	34
Princeton University	790	790	35
Purdue University	555	606	26
Quinnipiac University	560	580	25
Randolph-Macon College	560	560	24
Reed College	710	760	32
Rensselaer Polytechnic Institute	650	700	27
Rhodes College	630	640	28
Rice University	780	750	34
Ripon College	599	602	24
Rollins College	610	611	
Rose-Hulman Institute of Technology	610	670	29
Rutgers University - Camden	510	560	580
Rutgers University - New Brunswick	580	620	
Rutgers University - Newark	510	560	

Average SAT and ACT Scores

	Math SAT	Verbal SAT	ACT
Saint Anselm College	551	556	23
Salve Regina University	540	550	23
Samford University	580	570	25
San Diego State University	590	570	22
Santa Clara University			
Sarah Lawrence College			
Scripps College	690	660	
Seattle University			
Seton Hall University	539	548	25
Siena College	559	583	24
Simmons College	551	541	24
Simon's Rock College of Bard	662	587	27
Skidmore College	630	620	27
Smith College	660	640	29
Southern Methodist University	610	630	28
St. Bonaventure University	523	531	22
St. John Fisher College	700	620	27
St. Lawrence University	603	610	
St. Olaf College	660	640	29
Stanford University	780	760	34
Stetson University	558	550	24
Stonehill College	590	610	26
SUNY - Albany	560	590	25
SUNY - Binghamton	690	650	29
SUNY- Stony Brook	660	620	26
Swarthmore College	760	780	33
Sweet Briar College			
Temple University	579	561	22
Texas A&M University, College Station			
Trinity College			
Tufts University	740	750	
Tulane University	680	690	31
Union College (NY)	630	660	28
University of California, Berkeley	760	700	32
University of California, Davis	580	630	26
University of California, Irvine	670	620	

Average SAT and ACT Scores

	Math SAT	Verbal SAT	ACT
University of California, Los Angeles	720	680	31
University of California, Merced	600	570	
University of California, Riverside	620	570	
University of California, San Diego	710	660	30
University of California, Santa Barbara	593	612	27
University of Chicago	760	770	33
University of Cincinnati	550	570	24
University of Colorado, Boulder	520	600	24
University of Connecticut	600	630	27
University of Dayton	560	580	25
University of Denver	600	600	22
University of Florida	690	670	
University of Maryland, College Park	700	680	
University of Massachusetts, Amherst	575	594	25
University of Miami	690	680	29
University of Michigan, Ann Arbor	740	690	31
University of New Hampshire	553	570	
University of North Carolina, Chapel Hill	700	690	31
University of Notre Dame	760	750	
University of Pennsylvania	780	800	34
University of Pittsburgh	620	640	27
University of Puget Sound	640	616	
University of Rochester	720	700	30
University of San Diego	540	620	27
University of South Carolina, Columbia	588	604	26
University of Southern California	740	720	
University of Texas, Austin			
University of the Pacific	575	610	27
University of Virginia	730	710	32
University of Wisconsin, Madison	730	670	30
Vanderbilt University	760	740	33
Vassar College	710	750	32
Wagner College	560	520	25
Wake Forest University	710	700	
Washington and Lee University	740	740	31
Washington University in St. Louis	780	760	34

Average SAT and ACT Scores

	Math SAT	Verbal SAT	ACT
Wellesley College	730	750	32
Wesleyan University	740	750	32
Wheaton College	630	620	29
Williams College	730	750	33
Yale University	780	800	34

INDIVIDUAL COLLEGE TEST POLICIES

	SUPER SCORE	SAT SCALE	SCORE CHOICE	SUBJECT TESTS
Albion College	Y			
American University	Y	1600	Y	not required
Amherst College	Y	2400	Y	2 w/ SAT
Arizona State University		1600	Y	not required
Auburn University			Y	not required
Babson College	Y			
Barnard College		2400	N	2 w/ SAT
Bates College		2400 if submitted	Y	not required
Baylor University		1600	Y	not required
Beloit College	Y	1600	N	not required
Birmingham Southern College	Y			
Boston College	Y	1600	Y	2 w/ SAT
Boston University		2400	Y	2 w/ SAT
Bowdoin College	Y	1600	Y	not required
Brandeis University	Y	1600	Y	not required
Brown University	Y	2400	Y	2 w/ SAT
Bryn Mawr College	Y	1600	Y	test-flexible policy
Butler University	Y			
California Institute of Technology	Y			
California State University System	Y			
Carnegie Mellon University	Y		N	
Case Western		2400	Y	not required
Catholic University of America		1600	Y	used for placement
Chapman University	Y			
Claremont McKenna College		1600	Y	not required
Clark University		1600	Y	not required
Clemson University		1600		not required
Colby College	Y	2400	Y	3 in lieu of SAT/ACT
Colgate University		1600	N	not required
College of Charleston		1600	Y	not required
College of the Holy Cross	Y	1600	Y	not required
College of William & Mary		2400	Y	not required
Colorado College		1600	Y	not required
Columbia University		2400	N	2 required
Connecticut College	Y	2400	Y	2 in lieu of SAT/ACT
Cooper Union				
Cornell University	Y	2400	N	2 required

INDIVIDUAL COLLEGE TEST POLICIES

	SUPER SCORE	SAT SCALE	SCORE CHOICE	SUBJECT TESTS
Dartmouth College		2400	Y	2 required
Davidson College		2400	Y	1 math & other recommended
Denison University		1600	Y	not required
DePauw University	Y			
Dickinson College		1600	Y	not required
Drexel University		2400	Y	not required
Duke University	Y	2400	Y	2 w/ SAT
Eckerd College	Y			
Elon University	Y	2400	Y	not required
Emory University		2400	N	recommended
Fairfield University		2400	Y	not required
Florida Atlantic University	Y			
Florida State University	Y	2400	Y	not required
Fordham University	Y	2400	Y	not required
Franklin W. Olin College of Engineering	Y			
George Mason University		2400	N	not required
George Washington University	Y	2400	N	not required
Georgetown University		1600	N	3 recommended
Georgia Institute of Technology	Y	2400	Y	not required
Gettysburg College		1600	Y	not required
Hamden-Sydney College	Y	1600	Y	not required
Hamilton College	Y	2400	Y	not required
Harvard University		2400	Y	2 required
Harvey Mudd College		2400	N	2 required
Haverford College	Y	2400		2 required
Hawaii Pacific University	Y			
Hendrix College	Y			
Hollins	Y	1600	N	not required
Indiana University		1600	Y	not required
Ithaca College			Y	not required
James Madison University		1600	N	not required
Johns Hopkins University		1600	N	up to 3 recommended
Kalamazoo College	Y			
Kenyon College	Y	1600 primarily but look at writing	Y	not required

INDIVIDUAL COLLEGE TEST POLICIES

	SUPER SCORE	SAT SCALE	SCORE CHOICE	SUBJECT TESTS
Lafayette College		near 2400; less focus on writing	Y	recommended
Lawrence University	Y			
Lehigh University		1600	Y	recommended
Loyola University in Maryland		1600	Y	not required
Macalester College				
Marquette University		1600 scale given most weight	N	not required
Marymount University		2400	Y	not required
Massachusetts Institute of Technology	Y	2400	Y	Math Level 1 or 2 & a science
McGill University		1600	N	2 w/ SAT
Miami University		1600	Y	not required
Middlebury College	Y	2400	Y	3 in lieu of SAT/ACT
Millsap College	Y			
Mills College				
Muhlenberg College		1600 scale given most weight	Y	not required
New York University	Y	1600 primarily but writing also used	Y	not required
North Carolina State University	Y	1600; high writing scores noted	Y	not required
Northeastern University	Y	2400	Y	not required
Northwestern University		1600 primarily but writing also used	Y	3 recommended
Oberlin College			Y	2 recommended
Occidental College		2400	Y	not required
Ohio State University		2400	Y	not required
Pennsylvania State University	Y	2400	Y	not required
Pepperdine University	Y			
Pitzer College	Y	1600	Y	not required
Pomona College	Y	2400	N	2 w/ SAT
Princeton University		2400	Y	2 required
Purdue University	Y	2400	Y	not required
Quinnipiac University				
Randolph-Macon College		near 2400; less focus on writing	Y	not required
Reed College		1600	Y	not required

INDIVIDUAL COLLEGE TEST POLICIES

	SUPER SCORE	SAT SCALE	SCORE CHOICE	SUBJECT TESTS
Regis University	Y			
Rice University		2400	Y	2 w/ SAT
Rollins College		1600	Y	not required
Rose-Hulman Institute of Technology	Y			
Rutgers University		2400	Y	not required
Santa Clara University		1600	N	not required
Sarah Lawrence College				not required
Scripps College		near 2400; less focus on writing	N	recommended
Shenandoah University		1600	Y	not required
Skidmore College			Y	2 recommended
Smith College		2400	Y	not required
Spring Hill College	Y			
St. John's University	Y			
St. Joseph University		1600	no policy	not required
St. Mary College of Maryland		1600	Y	not required
Stanford University	Y	2400	N	2 strongly recommended
SUNY Buffalo	Y			
Swarthmore College		2400	Y	2 w/ SAT
Syracuse University		2400	N	not required
Texas A&M University		2400 for students	N	not required
Towson University	Y	2400	Y	not required
Trinity College	Y			
Trinity University (TX)	Y			
Tufts University	Y	2400	Y	2 w/ SAT
Tulane University		2400	no preference	not required
Union College		1600	Y	not required
United States Air Force Academy	Y			
United States Coast Guard Academy	Y			
United States Merchant Marine Academy	Y			
United States Military Academy at West Point	Y			
United States Naval Academy	Y	1600	Y	not required
University of Arizona		1600	Y	not required

INDIVIDUAL COLLEGE TEST POLICIES

	SUPER SCORE	SAT SCALE	SCORE CHOICE	SUBJECT TESTS
University of Arkansas- Fayetteville	Y			
University of California, Berkeley		2400	N	not required
University of California, Davis		2400	N	not required
University of California, Irvine		2400	N	not required
University of California, Los Angeles		2400	N	not required
University of California, San Diego		2400	N	not required
University of California, Santa Barbara		2400	N	not required
University of California, Santa Cruz		2400	N	not required
University of Chicago		1600	Y	not required
University of Colorado, Boulder	Y	1600	Y	not required
University of Connecticut	Y	1600	Y	not required
University of Dayton	Y			
University of Delaware	Y	1600	Y	recommended
University of Denver	Y	1600	Y	not required
University of Florida		2400	Y	not required
University of Georgia	Y	near 2400; less focus on writing	request all scores	recommended
University of Illinois	Y		request all scores	not required
University of Illinois, Urbana-Champaign	Y	1600	request all scores	not required
University of Indiana, Bloomington	Y			
University of Louisiana, Lafayette	Y			
University of Mary Washington		1600; use writing score as needed	Y	not required
University of Maryland, Baltimore County		2400	Y	not required
University of Maryland, College Park		1600	N	not required
University of Massachusetts, Amherst		1600	Y	not required
University of Miami	Y	1600	Y	not required
University of Michigan, Ann Arbor		1600	Y	not required
University of New Hampshire		2400	Y	not required
University of North Carolina, Chapel Hill		2400	Y	used for placement only

INDIVIDUAL COLLEGE TEST POLICIES

	SUPER SCORE	SAT SCALE	SCORE CHOICE	SUBJECT TESTS
University of North Carolina, Greensboro		1600	Y	not required
University of North Carolina, Wilmington		1600	Y	not required
University of North Texas	Y			
University of Notre Dame		1600	Y	recommended
University of Pennsylvania		2400	N	2 w/ SAT
University of Pittsburgh		1600	Y	not required
University of Puget Sound	Y			
University of Rhode Island		1600 is main focus	Y	not required
University of Richmond		2400	Y	not required
University of Rochester		near 2400; less focus on writing	Y	not required
University of San Diego	Y			
University of San Francisco		1600	Y	not required
University of South Carolina, Columbia		1600	N	not required
University of Southern California		2400	Y	recommended
University of South Florida	Y			
University of Tampa	Y	1600	Y	not required
University of Tennessee, Knoxville	Y	1600	Y	not required
University of Texas, Austin	Y	2400	Y	not required
University of Vermont		near 2400; less focus on writing	Y	not required
University of Virginia		1600 primarily but writing also used	Y	2 recommended
University of Washington		2400	N	not required
University of Wisconsin, Madison		2400	N	not required
Vanderbilt University		1600	Y	not required
Vassar College		near 2400; less focus on writing	Y	2 w/ SAT
Villanova University		1600 mostly but writing also used	N	not required
Virginia Polytechnic University		1600; writing used for placement	N	not required
Wagner College				
Wake Forest University		1600 is focus (if submitted)	Y	not required

INDIVIDUAL COLLEGE TEST POLICIES

	SUPER SCORE	SAT SCALE	SCORE CHOICE	SUBJECT TESTS
Washington and Lee University	Y	2400	Y	2 required
Washington State University	Y			
Washington University- St. Louis	Y	2400	Y	recommended
Wellesley College		2400	Y	2 w/ SAT
Wesleyan University	Y	2400	Y	2 w/ SAT
West Virginia University		1600	Y	not required
Wheaton College	Y	1600	Y	not required
Williams College	Y	2400	Y	2 required
Yale University		2400	N	2 w/ SAT
Xavier University	Y			

SCHOOLS THAT DO NOT REQUIRE SAT OR ACT SCORES

The following colleges and univiersities include accredited, bachelor-degree granting colleges and universities that deemphasize the use of standardized tests by making admissions decisions factoring in SAT or ACT test scores. Please check with the school's admissions office to learn more about specific admissions requirements, particularly for international or non-traditional students.

Academy College, Minneapolis, MN

Academy of Art College, San Francisco, CA

Agnes Scott College, Decatur, GA

Alabama State University, Montgomery, AL

Albright College, Reading, PA

Alcorn State University, Alcorn, MS

Allen University, Columbia, SC

Alliant International University, San Diego, CA

American Academy of Art, Chicago, IL

Am. Baptist College of ABT Seminary, Nashville, TN

Am. College of Computer and Information Sciences, Birmingham, AL

Am. College of Pre-hospital Medicine, Navarre, FL

Am. Indian College of Assemblies of God, Phoenix

American Intercontinental University, Los Angeles

American Intercontinental Univ, Fort Lauderdale, FL

American Intercontinental University, Atlanta, GA

American Intercontinental Univ., Dunwoody, GA

American Military University, Charles Town, WV

American Public University, Charles Town, WV

American University of Puerto Rico, Bayamon, PR

Andrew Jackson University, Birmingham, AL

Angelo State University, Angelo, TX

Angley College, Deland, FL

Antioch Coll. of Antioch Univ, Yellow Springs, OH

Aquinas College, Nashville, TN

Arizona State University, Tempe, AZ

Arkansas Baptist College, Little Rock, AR

Arkansas State University, State University, AR

Arlington Baptist College, Arlington, TX

Armstrong University, Berkeley, CA

Art Center College of Design, Pasadena, CA

Art Center Design College, Tucson, AZ

Art Center Design College, Albuquerque, NM

Art Institute of Atlanta, Atlanta, GA

Art Inst. of Boston at Lesley University, Boston, MA

Art Inst. of California, Los Angeles, Los Angeles, CA

Art Inst. of California, Orange County, Santa Ana, CA

Art Institute of California, San Diego, San Diego, CA

Art Inst. of CA San Francisco, San Francisco, CA

Art Institute of Chicago, Chicago, IL

Art Institute of Colorado, Denver, CO

Art Institute of Dallas, Dallas, TX

Art Institute of Ft. Lauderdale, Ft. Lauderdale, FL

Art Institute of Houston, Houston, TX

Art Institute of Las Vegas, Las Vegas, NV

Art Institute of Philadelphia, Philadelphia, PA

Art Institute of Phoenix, Phoenix, AZ

Art Institute of Pittsburgh, Pittsburgh, PA

Art Institute of Portland, Portland, OR

SCHOOLS THAT DO NOT REQUIRE SAT OR ACT SCORES

Art Institute of Southern CA, Laguna Beach, CA

Art Institute of Washington, Arlington, VA

Ashford University, Clinton, IA

Assumption College, Worcester, MA

Atlantic College, Guaynabo, PR

Audrey Cohen College, New York, NY

Augustana College, Rock Island, IL

Austin Peay State University, Clarksville, TN

Bais Binyomin Academy, Stamford, CT

Baker College of Auburn Hills, Auburn Hills, MI

Baker College of Cadillac, Cadillac, MI

Baker College of Flint, Flint, MI

Baker College of Mt. Clemens, Clinton Township, MI

Baker College of Muskegon, Muskegon, MI

Baker College of Owosso, Owosso, MI

Baker College of Port Huron, Port Huron, MI

Baldwin-Wallace College, Berea, OH

Baltimore Hebrew University, Baltimore, MD

Baltimore International College, Baltimore, MD

Baptist Bible College, Springfield, MO

Barber-Scotia, Concord, NC

Bard College, Annandale-on-Hudson, NY

Bard College at Simon's Rock, Great Barrington, MA

Bartlesville Wesleyan College, Bartlesville, OK

Bates College, Lewiston, ME

Bayamon Central University, Bayamon, PR

Beacon College, Rockledge, FL

Beis Medrash Heichal Dovid, Far Rockaway, NY

Bellevue University, Omaha, NE

Belmont Abbey College, Belmont, NC

Bemidji State University, Bemidji, MN

Benedict College, Columbia, SC

Benedictine College, Atchison, KS

Benjamin Franklin Institute of Tech, Boston, MA

Bennett College for Women, Greensboro, NC

Bennington College, Bennington, VT

Berkeley College, West Patterson, NJ

Berkeley College, White Plains, NY

Berkeley College of New York City, New York, NY

Berklee College of Music, Boston, MA

Beth HaMedrahs Shaarei Yosher, Brooklyn, NY

Beth HaTalmud Rabbinical College, Brooklyn, NY

Beth Medrash Govoha, Lakewood, NJ

Bethany Coll of Assemblies of God, Scotts Valley, CA

Bethesda Christian University, Anaheim, CA

Beulah Heights Bible College, Atlanta, GA

Black Hills State University, Spearfish, SD

Bluefield State College, Bluefield, WV

Boricua College, New York, NY

Boston Architectural College, Boston, MA

Boston Conservatory, Boston, MA

Bowdoin College, Brunswick, ME

Briarcliffe College, Bethpage, NY

Brooks Institute of Photography, Santa Barbara, CA

Brown College, Mendota Heights, MN

Burlington College, Burlington, VT

Calif. College for Health Sciences, National City, CA

California College of the Arts, San Francisco, CA

SCHOOLS THAT DO NOT REQUIRE SAT OR ACT SCORES

CA Institute of Integral Studies, San Francisco, CA

California Institute of the Arts, Valencia, CA

California Maritime Academy, Vallejo, CA

Calif. Nat. Univ. for Advanced Studies, Northridge, CA

Calumet College of St. Joseph, Hammond, IN

Cambridge College, Cambridge, MA

Cameron University, Lawton, OK

Campbell University, Morrisville, NC

Campbell Univ., New River Jacksonville, NC

Campbell University, Fort Bragg, Fayetteville, NC

Campbell Univ., Pope Air Force Base, Fayetteville, NC

Capella University, Minneapolis, MN

Carlos Albizu University, Miami, FL

Cascade College, Portland, OR

Cazenovia College, Cazenovia, NY

Central Baptist College, Conway, AK

Central Bible College, Springfield, MO

Central Christian College, McPherson, KS

Central Washington University, Ellensburg, WA

Central Yeshiva Tomchei Tmimim-Lebavitch, Brooklyn

Chadron State College, Chadron, NE

Chaparral College, Tuscon, AZ

Charles R. Drew Univ.: College of Allied Health, LA

Charter College, Anchorage, AK

Charter Oak State College, Newington, CT

Chatham College, Pittsburgh, PA

Chester College of New England, Chester, NH

Christopher Newport University, Newport News, VA

Cincinnati College of Mortuary Science, Cincinnati

City College, Ft. Lauderdale, FL

City University, Bellevue, WA

City University of Seattle, Seattle, WA

Clear Creek Baptist Bible College, Pineville, KY

Cleary University, Ypsilanti, MI

Cogswell Polytechnical College, Sunnyvale, CA

Colby College, Waterville, ME

Colby-Sawyer College, New London, NH

Coleman College, La Mesa, CA

College America, Cheyenne, WY

College America, Colorado Springs, CO

College America, Denver, CO

College America, Flagstaff, AZ

College America, Fort Collins, CO

College America, Phoenix, AZ

College for Lifelong Learning, Durham, NC

College of Health Sciences, Roanoke, VA

College of New Rochelle: School, NY

College of the Atlantic, Bar Harbor, ME

College of the Holy Cross, Worcester, MA

College of the Humanities and Sciences, Tempe, AZ

College of the Southwest, Hobbs, NM

College of Visual Arts, St. Paul, MN

Collins College, Tempe, AZ

Colorado Technical University, Colorado Springs, CO

Columbia College, Chicago, IL

Columbia College, Caguas, PR

Columbia College: Hollywood, Tarzana, CA

Columbia Southern University, Orange Beach, AL

SCHOOLS THAT DO NOT REQUIRE SAT OR ACT SCORES

Concordia College, Selma, AL

Concordia University, Portland, OR

Connecticut College, New London, CT

Conservatory of Music of Puerto Rico, San Juan, PR

Cornish College of the Arts, Seattle, WA

Crown College, Tacoma, WA

CSU Bakersfield, Bakersfield, CA

CSU Chico, Chico, CA

CSU Dominguez Hills, Dominguez Hills, CA

CSU East Bay, Hayward, CA

CSU Fresno, Fresno, CA

CSU Fullerton, Fullerton, CA

CSU Long Beach, Long Beach, CA

CSU Los Angeles, Los Angeles, CA

CSU Monterey Bay, Seaside, CA

CSU Northridge, Northridge, CA

CSU Sacramento, Sacramento, CA

CSU San Bernardino, San Bernardino, CA

CSU San Marcos, San Marcos, CA

CSU Stanislaus, Stanislaus, CA

Culinary Institute of America, Hyde Park, NY

Curry College, Milton, MA

Curtis Institute of Music, Philadelphia, PA

Daemen College, Amherst, NY

Dakota State University, Madison, SD

Dalton State College, Dalton, GA

Darkei Noam Rabbinical College, Brooklyn, NY

Davenport University, Alma, MI

Davenport University, Bad Axe, MI

Davenport University, Battle Creek, MI

Davenport University, Bay City, MI

Davenport University, Caro, MI

Davenport University, Dearborn, MI

Davenport University, Flint, MI

Davenport University, Gaylord, MI

Davenport University, Grand Rapids, MI

Davenport University, Holland, MI

Davenport University, Kalamazoo, MI

Davenport University, Lansing, MI

Davenport University, Lapeer, MI

Davenport University, Main Campus, Grand Rapids

Davenport University, Merrillville, IN

Davenport University, Midland, MI

Davenport University, Romeo, MI

Davenport University, Saginaw, MI

Davenport Univ, South Bend/Mishawaka, Granger

Davenport University, Traverse City, MI

Davenport University, Warren, MI

Denison University, Granville, OH

Design Institute of San Diego, San Diego, CA

DeVry Institute of Technology, New York, NY

DeVry University, West Hills, CA

DeVry University, Addison, IL

DeVry University, Alpharetta, GA

DeVry University, Atlanta, GA

DeVry University, Chicago, IL

DeVry University, Colorado Springs, CO

DeVry University, Columbus, OH

SCHOOLS THAT DO NOT REQUIRE SAT OR ACT SCORES

DeVry University, Crystal City, VA

DeVry University, Denver, CO

DeVry University, Freemont, CA

DeVry University, Houston, TX

DeVry University, Irving, TX

DeVry University, Kansas City, MO

DeVry University, Long Beach, CA

DeVry University, Orlando, FL

DeVry University, Philadelphia, PA

DeVry University, Phoenix, AZ

DeVry University, Pomona, CA

DeVry University, Seattle, WA

DeVry University, South Florida, Miramar, FL

DeVry University, Tinley Park, IL

Dickinson College, Carlisle, PA

Dickinson State University, Dickinson, ND

DigiPen Institute of Technology, Redmond, WA

Divine Word College, Epworth, IA

Dixie State College, Saint George, UT

Dowling College, Oakdale, NY

Drew University, Madison, NJ

East Central University, Ada, OK

East Tennessee State University, Johnson City, TN

East-West University, Chicago, IL

Eastern Kentucky University, Richmond, KY

Eastern Oregon State College, LaGrande, OR

Eastern Washington University, Cheney, WA

Eastman School of Music, University of Rochester

Edward Waters College, Jacksonville, FL

Electronic Data Processing College, Hato Rey, PR

Elizabethtown College, Elizabethtown, PA

Emporia State University, Emporia, KS

Eugene Bible College, Eugene, OR

Everest University, Brandon, Tampa, FL

Everest University, Jacksonville, FL

Everest University, Lakeland, FL

Everest University, Melbourne, FL

Everest University, North Orlando, FL

Everest University, Orange Park, FL

Everest University, Clearwater, FL

Everest University, Pompano Beach, FL

Everest University, South Orlando, FL

Everest University, Tampa, FL

Everglades College, Fort Lauderdale, FL

Excelsior College, Albany, NY

Fairfield University, Fairfield, CT

Fairmont State College, Fairmont, WV

Faith Baptist Coll & Theological Seminary, Ankeny, IA

Fashion Institute of Technology, New York, NY

Ferris State University, Grand Rapids, MI

Finlandia University, Hancock, MI

Fisher College, Boston, MA

Five Towns College, Dix Hills, NY

Florida Christian College, Kissimmee, FL

Florida Memorial University, Miami, FL

Fort Hays State University, Hays, KS

Fort Lewis College, Durango, CO

Franklin and Marshall College, Lancaster, PA

SCHOOLS THAT DO NOT REQUIRE SAT OR ACT SCORES

Franklin University, Columbus, OH

Free Will Baptist Bible College, Nashville, TN

Friends World Program, Long Island Univ, Brooklyn

Furman University, Greenville, SC

Gainesville State College, Gainesville, GA

Gallaudet University, Washington, DC

George Mason University, Fairfax, VA

Georgian Court University, Lakewood, NJ

Gettysburg College, Gettysburg, PA

Glenville State College, Glenville, WV

Global University, Springfield, MS

God's Bible School and College, Cincinnati, OH

Goddard College, Plainfield, VT

Golden Gate University, San Francisco, CA

Goucher College, Baltimore, MD

Grace Bible College, Grand Rapids, MI

Grambling State University, Grambling, LA

Grand Canyon University, Phoenix, AZ

Granite State College, Concord, NH

Grantham College of Engineering, Sidell, LA

Gratz College, Melrose Park, PA

Great Basin College, Elko, NV

Green Mountain College, Poultney, VT

Guilford College, Greensboro, NC

Gustavus Adolphus College, St. Peter, MN

Hamilton College, Clinton, NY

Hamilton College, Cedar Falls, IA

Hamilton College, Cedar Rapids, IA

Hamilton College, Des Moines, IA

Hamilton College, Mason City, IA

Hampshire College, Amherst, MA

Harrington College of Design, Chicago, IL

Harrisburg Univ. of Science and Tech., Harrisburg

Hartwick College, Oneonta, NY

Haskell Indian Nations University, Lawrence, KS

Hawaii Pacific University, Honolulu, HI

Heritage Christian University, Florence, AL

Heritage University, Toppenish, WA

Herzing College, Homewood, AL

Herzing College, New Orleans, LA

Herzing College, Atlanta, GA

Hesser College, Manchester, NH

Hilbert College, Hamburg, NY

Hobart and William Smith Colleges, Geneva, NY

Hobe Sound Bible College, Hobe Sound, FL

Hodges University, Naples, FL

Holy Apostles Coll. and Seminary, Cromwell, CT

Holy Trinity Orthodox Seminary, Jordanville, NY

Humboldt State University (CSU), Arcata, CA

Humphreys College, Stockton, CA

Huron University, Huron, SD

Hussian School of Art, Philadelphia, PA

Illinois College, Jacksonville, IL

Illinois Institute of Art, Schaumburg, IL

Indiana State University, Terre Haute, IN

Indiana University East, Richmond, IN

Institute of Computer Technology, Los Angeles, CA

Inter-American University of Puerto Rico: Metropolitan Campus, San Juan, PR

SCHOOLS THAT DO NOT REQUIRE SAT OR ACT SCORES

Interior Designers Institute, Newport Beach, CA

Int. Acad. of Design and Tech., Chicago, IL

Int. Acad. of Design and Tech., Orlando, FL

Int. Acad. of Design and Tech., Tampa, FL

International Business College, Fort Wayne, IN

International Fine Arts College (Miami International University of Art and Design), Miami, FL

ITT Technical Institute, Albuquerque, NM

ITT Technical Institute, Anaheim, CA

ITT Technical Institute, Arnold, MI

ITT Technical Institute, Birmingham, AL

ITT Technical Institute, Boise, ID

ITT Technical Institute, Chicago, IL

ITT Technical Institute, Duluth, GA

ITT Technical Institute, Ft. Lauderdale, FL

ITT Technical Institute, Greenfield, WI

ITT Technical Institute, Indianapolis, IN

ITT Technical Institute, Jacksonville, FL

ITT Technical Institute, Knoxville, TN

ITT Technical Institute, Lathrop, CA

ITT Technical Institute, Los Angeles, CA

ITT Technical Institute, Louisville, KY

ITT Technical Institute, Maitland, FL

ITT Technical Institute, Miami, FL

ITT Technical Institute, Oxnard, CA

ITT Technical Institute, Phoenix, AZ

ITT Technical Institute, Rancho Cordova, CA

ITT Technical Institute, Saint Rose, LA

ITT Technical Institute Salt Lake City, Murray, UT

ITT Technical Institute, San Bernardino, CA

ITT Technical Institute, Seattle, WA

ITT Technical Institute, Spokane, WA

ITT Technical Institute St. Louis, Earth City, MI

ITT Technical Institute, Sylmar, CA

ITT Technical Institute, Tampa, FL

ITT Technical Institute, Thornton, CO

ITT Technical Institute, Torrance, CA

ITT Technical Institute, Tucson, AZ

ITT Technical Institute, West Covina, CA

Jamestown College, Jamestown, ND

Jarvis Christian College, Hawkins, TX

John F. Kennedy University, Pleasant Hill, CA

John F. Kennedy University, Orinda, NY

John Jay College (CUNY), New York, NY

John Wesley College, High Point, NC

Johnson & Wales University, Charlotte, NC

Johnson & Wales University, Denver, CO

Johnson & Wales University, North Miami, FL

Johnson & Wales University, Providence, RI

Jones College, Jacksonville, FL

Jones International University, Centennial, CO

Juilliard School, New York, NY

Juniata College, Huntington, PA

Kansas State University, Manhattan, KS

Kaplan University, Davenport, IA

Kehilath Yakov Rabbinical Seminary, Brooklyn, NY

Kendall College, Chicago, IL

Kent State University, Stark, OH

Kent State Univ., Tuscarawas, New Philadelphia, OH

Schools That Do Not Require SAT or ACT Scores

Keuka College, Keuka Park, NY

King's College, Wilkes-Barre, PA

Kings College, The, Van Nuys, CA

Knox College, Galesburg, IL

Knoxville College, Knoxville, TN

Kol Yaakov Torah Center, Monsey, NY

La Sierra University, Riverside, CA

Lake Erie College, Painesville, OH

Lake Forest College, Lake Forest, IL

Lamar University, Beaumont, TX

Lancaster Bible College, Lancaster, PA

Langston University, Langston, OK

Laura & Alvin Siegel Coll of Judaic Studies, Cleveland

Lawrence Technological University, Southfield, MI

Lawrence University, Appleton, WI

Lebanon Valley College, Annville, PA

Lester Cox Coll of Nursing & Health Science, Springfield, MO

Lewis and Clark College, Portland, OR

Life Pacific College, San Dimas, CA

Lincoln University, Jefferson City, MO

Lincoln University, Oakland, CA

Lindsey Wilson College, Columbia, KY

Loma Linda University, Loma Linda, CA

Long Island Univ.: Brooklyn Campus, Brooklyn, NY

Longy School of Music, Cambridge, MA

Louisiana State University, Shreveport, LA

Lourdes College, Sylvania, OH

Loyola University, Baltimore, MD

Lycoming College, Williamsport, PA

Lyndon State College, Lydonville, VT

Machzikei Hadath Rabbinical College, Brooklyn, NY

Macon State College, Macon, GA

Magnolia Bible College, Kosciusko, MS

Manhattan Christian College, Manhattan, KS

Manhattan School of Music, New York, NY

Marahishi Univ. of Management, Fairfield, IA

Marlboro College, Marlboro, VT

Martin Methodist College, Pulaski, TN

Martin University, Indianapolis, IN

Marylhurst University, Marylhurst, OR

Masters College, Santa Clarita, CA

Mayville State University, Mayville, ND

McDaniel Coll. (Western MD Coll.), Westminster, MD

McNeese State University, Lake Charles, LA

McPherson College, McPherson, KS

Medaille College, Buffalo, NY

Medgar Evers College (CUNY), Brooklyn, NY

Memphis College of Art, Memphis, TN

Mercy College, Dobbs Ferry, NY

Merrimack College, North Andover, MA

Mesivta of Eastern Pkwy Rabbinical Sem, Brooklyn, NY

Mesivta Tifereth Jerusalem of America, NY, NY

Mesivta Torah Vodaath Seminary, Brooklyn, NY

Messiah College, Grantham, PA

Metropolitan College, Oklahoma City, OK

Metropolitan College of New York, New York, NY

SCHOOLS THAT DO NOT REQUIRE SAT OR ACT SCORES

Metropolitan State College of Denver, Denver, CO

Metropolitan State University, St. Paul, MN

Michigan Jewish Institute, Oak Park, MI

Mid-America Bible College, Oklahoma City, OK

Mid-Continent Baptist Bible College, Mayfield, KY

Middle Tennessee State Univ, Murfreesboro, TN

Middlebury College, Middlebury, VT

Midland Lutheran College, Fremont, NE

Midwestern State University, Wichita Falls, TX

Miles College, Fairfield, AL

Milwaukee Institute of Art & Design, Milwaukee, WI

Minnesota Bible College, Rochester, MN

Minnesota State University, Mankato, MN

Minot State University, Minot, ND

Mirrer Yeshiva, Brooklyn, NY

Mississippi University for Women, Columbus, MS

Mississippi Valley State University, Itta Bena, MS

Missouri Southern State University, Joplin, MO

Missouri Technical School, St. Louis, MO

Missouri Western State College, St. Joseph, MO

Mitchell College, New London, CT

Montana State University: Billings, MT

Montana State University: Bozeman, MT

Montana State University: Northern, Havre, MT

Montana Tech of the Univ. of Montana, Butte, MT

Montserrat College of Art, Beverly, MA

Moorehead State University, Moorhead, MN

Morris College, Sumter, SC

Morrison University, Reno, NV

Mount Angel Seminary, St. Benedict, OR

Mount Holyoke College, South Hadley, MA

Mount Sierra College, Monrovia, CA

Mountain State University, Beckley, WV

Muhlenberg College, Allentown, PA

NAES College, Chicago, IL

Naropa University, Boulder, CO

National American University, Albuquerque, NM

National American University, Kansas City, MO

National American University, Rapid City, SD

National American University, St. Paul, MN

National Business College, Roanoke, VA

National Hispanic University, San Jose, CA

National Labor College, Silver Spring, MD

National University, La Jolla, CA

Nazarene Bible College, Colorado Springs, CO

Nazareth College, Rochester, NY

Nebraska Christian College, Norfolk, NE

Nebraska Wesleyan University, Lincoln, NE

Ner Israel Rabbinical College, Baltimore, MD

Nevada State College, Henderson, NV

New England College, Henniker, NH

New England Conservatory, Boston, MA

New England Inst. of Art & Comm, Brookline, MA

New England Institute of Technology, Warwick, RI

N.E. School of Communications, Bangor, ME

New Mexico Highlands University, Las Vegas, NM

New Orleans Theological Seminary, New Orleans

New School, New York, NY

Schools That Do Not Require SAT or ACT Scores

New School of Architecture, San Diego, CA

New York City College of Tech. (CUNY), Brooklyn, NY

New York University, New York, NY

Newbury College, Brookline, MA

Nicholls State University, Thibodaux, LA

Northcentral University, Prescott, AZ

Northeastern Illinois University, Chicago, IL

Northeastern State University, Tahlequah, OK

Northern Arizona University, Flagstaff, AZ

Northern Kentucky University, Highland Heights, KY

Northern State University, Aberdeen, OK

Northrop-Rice Aviation Inst. of Tech, Inglewood, CA

Northwest Missouri State University, Maryville, MO

Northwest Nazarene College, Nampa, ID

Northwestern College, Saint Paul, MN

Northwestern Oklahoma State University, Alva, OK

Northwestern State University, Natchitoches, LA

Nyack College, Nyack, NY

Oak Hills Christian College, Bemidji, MN

Oakland University, Rochester, MI

Oakwood University, Huntsville, AL

Oglala Lakota College, Kyle, SD

Ohio State University, ATI Wooster, OH

Ohio State University, Mansfield, OH

Ohio State University, Marion, OH

Ohio State University, Newark, OH

Ohio University: Eastern Campus, St. Clairsville, OH

Ohio University: Lima Campus, Lima, OH

Ohio Univ.: Southern Campus at Ironton, OH

Ohio University: Zaneville Campus, Zaneville, OH

Ohr HaMeir Theological Sem, Courtland Manor, NY

Ohr Somayach-Tanenbaum Ed. Center, Monsey, NY

Oklahoma Univ. of Science & Arts, Oklahoma City

Oklahoma City University, Oklahoma City, OK

Oklahoma Panhandle State University, Goodwell

Oklahoma State University, Stillwater, OK

Oklahoma Wesleyan University, Bartlesville, OK

Olivet College, Olivet, MI

Oregon College of Art & Craft, Portland, OR

Oregon Institute of Technology, Klamath Falls, OR

Oregon State Univ., Cascades Campus, Bend, OR

Ottawa University, Ottawa, KS

Pacific Northwest College of Art, Portland, OR

Pacific Union College, Angwin, CA

Paine College, Augusta, GA

Patten University, Oakland, CA

Paul Quinn College, Dallas, TX

Peirce College, Philadelphia, PA

Pennsylvania College of Tech., Williamsport, PA

Peru State College, Peru, NE

Philander Smith College, Little Rock, AR

Piedmont Baptist College, Winston-Salem, NC

Pikeville College, Pikeville, KY

Pittsburg State University, Pittsburg, KS

Pitzer College, Claremont, CA

Prairie View A&M University, Prairie View, TX

Prescott College, Prescott, AZ

Presentation College, Aberdeen, SD

Schools That Do Not Require SAT or ACT Scores

Providence College, Providence, RI

Rabbi Jacob Joseph School, Edison, NY

Rabbinical Acad Mesivta Rabbi Chaim Berlin, Brooklyn

Rabbinical College Beth Shraga, Monsey, NY

Rabbinical Coll Bobover Yeshiva Bnci Zion, Brooklyn

Rabbinical College Ch'san Sofer, Brooklyn, NY

Rabbinical College of America, Morristown, NJ

Rabbinical College of Long Island, Long Island, NY

Rabbinical Coll of Ohr Shimon Yisroel, Brooklyn, NY

Rabbinical College of Telshe, Wickliffe, OH

Rabbinical Seminary Adas Yereim, Brooklyn, NY

Rabbinical Seminary M'kor Chaim, Brooklyn, NY

Rabbinical Seminary of America, Forest Hills, NY

Remington College, Colorado Springs, CO

Remington College, Denver, CO

Remington College, Honolulu, HI

Remington College, Memphis, TN

Remington College, San Diego, CA

Remington College, Tampa, FL

Remington College, Tempe, AZ

Ringling College of Art and Design, Sarasota, FL

Roanoke College, Salem, VA

Robert Morris College, Chicago, IL

Rocky Mountain College, Billings, MT

Rollins College, Winter Park, FL

Russell Sage College, Troy, NY

Rust College, Holly Springs, MS

Sacred Heart Major Seminary, Detroit, MI

Sacred Heart University, Fairfield, CT

Saint Ambrose University, Davenport, IA

Saint Augustine College, Chicago, IL

Saint Augustine's College, Raleigh, NC

Saint Charles Borromeo Seminary, Overbrook, PA

Saint Cloud University, Saint Cloud, MN

Saint Gregory's University, Shawnee, OK

Saint John's College, Annapolis, MD

Saint John's College, Santa Fe, NM

Saint Lawrence University, Canton, NY

Saint Michael's College Colchester, VT

Saint Thomas University, Miami, FL

Salem International University, Salem, WV

Salisbury University, Salisbury, MD

Salish Kootenai College, Pablo, MT

Sam Houston State University, Huntsville, TX

San Francisco Art Institute, San Francisco, CA

San Francisco Conservatory of Music, S.F., CA

San Francisco State Univ. (CSU), San Francisco, CA

San Jose State University (CSU), San Jose, CA

Sarah Lawrence College, Bronxville, NY

Sewanee: The University of the South, Sewanee, TN

Schiller International University, Dunedin, FL

School of the Visual Arts, New York, NY

Selma University, Selma, AL

Seton Hill University, Greensburg, PA

Shaw University, Raleigh, NC

Shawnee State University, Portsmouth, OH

Sheldon Jackson College, Sitka, AK

Shimer College, Chicago, IL

SCHOOLS THAT DO NOT REQUIRE SAT OR ACT SCORES

Shor Yoshuv Rabbinical College, Far Rockaway, NY

Siegal College of Judaic Studies, Cleveland, OH

Silicon Valley College, Emeryville, Emeryville, CA

Silicon Valley College, Fremont, Fremont, CA

Silicon Valley College, San Jose, San Jose, CA

Silicon Valley Coll., Walnut Creek, Walnut Creek, CA

Simon's Rock College of Bard, Great Barrington, MA

Sinte Gleska University, Rosebud, SD

Smith College, Northampton, MA

Sojourner-Douglass College, Baltimore, MD

Sonoma State University (CSU), Rohnert Park, CA

South College, Montgomery, AL

South Dakota Sch. of Mines and Tech., Rapid City

South Dakota State University, Brookings, SD

South University West Palm Beach, FL

Southeastern Coll of Assemblies of God, Lakeland

Southeastern Louisiana University, Hammond, LA

Southeastern Oklahoma State Univ, Durant, OK

Southeastern University, Washington, DC

Southern California Inst. of Tech, Anaheim, CA

Southern CA International Coll., Santa Ana, CA

Southern Christian Academy, Decatur, GA

Southern Nazarene University, Bethany, OK

Southern Oregon University, Ashland, OR

Southern Univ. & A&M College, Baton Rouge, LA

Southwest State University, Marshall, MN

Southwestern Adventist University, Keene, TX

Southwestern Christian College, Terrell, TX

Southwestern Oklahoma State, Weatherford, OK

State University of New York - Potsdam, NY

State U of NY/Empire State Coll., Saratoga Springs

State University of New York, Delhi, NY

Stephen F. Austin State University, Nacogdoches, TX

Sterling College, Craftsbury Common, VT

Stevens-Henager College, Ogden, UT

Stillman College, Tuscaloosa, AL

Stonehill College, Easton, MA

Stratford University, Falls Church, VA

Stratford University, Woodbridge, AL

Strayer College, Washington, DC

Sul Ross State University, Alpine, TX

Susquehanna University, Selinsgrove, PA

Talladega College, Talladega, AL

Talmudic College of Florida, Miami Beach, FL

Talmudical Academy of New Jersey, Adelphia, NJ

Talmudical Inst. of Upstate New York, Rochester, NY

Talmudical Seminary Oholei Torah, Brooklyn, NY

Talmudical Yeshiva of Philadelphia, Philadelphia, PA

Tarleton State University, Stephenville, TX

Teikyo University, Waterbury, CT

Telshe Yeshiva, Chicago, IL

Texas A&M International University, Laredo, TX

Texas A&M Univ., College Station, TX

Texas A&M University, Commerce, TX

Texas A&M University, Corpus Christi, TX

Texas A&M University, Galveston, TX

Texas A&M University, Kingsville, TX

Texas College, Tyler, TX

SCHOOLS THAT DO NOT REQUIRE SAT OR ACT SCORES

Texas Southern University, Houston, TX	University of Arkansas, Fort Smith, AR
Texas State University, San Marcos, TX	University of Arkansas, Little Rock, AR
Texas Tech University, Lubbock, TX	University of Arkansas, Monticello, AR
Texas Women's University, Denton, TX	University of Arkansas, Pine Bluff, AR
Thomas Edison State College, Trenton, NJ	Univ of Arkansas, Medical Sciences, Little Rock, AR
Thomas Moore Coll. of Liberal Arts, Merrimack, NH	University of Central Oklahoma, Edmond, OK
Thomas University, Thomasville, GA	University of Findlay, Findlay, OH
Tiffin University, Tiffin, OH	University of Great Falls, Great Falls, MT
Torah Temimah Talmudical Seminary, Brooklyn, NY	University of Guam, Mangilao, GU
Tougaloo College, Tougaloo, MS	University of Houston, Houston, TX
Touro College, New York, NY	University of Houston-Downtown, Houston, TX
Trevecca Nazarene University, Nashville, TN	University of Idaho, Moscow, ID
Trinity Lutheran College, Issaquah, MA	University of Kansas, Lawrence, KS
Trinity University, Washington, DC	University of Louisiana at Monroe, Monroe, LA
Turabo University, Gurabo, PR	University of Maine at Augusta, Augusta, ME
Union College, Lincoln, NE	Univ. of Maine at Farmington, Farmington, ME
Union College, Schenectady, NY	University of Maine at Ft. Kent, Ft. Kent, ME
Union Institute & University, Cincinnati, OH	Univ. of Maine at Presque Isle, Presque Isle, ME
Union University, Jackson, TN	Univ of Management and Technology, Arlington, VA
United Talmudical Seminary, Brooklyn, NY	University of Mary Hardin-Baylor, Belton, TX
Unity College, Unity, ME	Univ. of Maryland University Coll., Adelphi, MD
Univ. Adventista de las Antillas, Mayaguez, PR	University of Memphis, Memphis, TN
Universidad del Este, Carolina, AL	University of Michigan, Flint, MI
University of Action Learning, Boulder, CO	Univ. of Minnesota, Crookston, MN
University of Advancing Technology, Tempe, AZ	University of Minnesota, Duluth, MN
University of Alaska, Anchorage, AK	University of Minnesota, Morris, MN
University of Alaska, Fairbanks, AK	University of Mississippi, Oxford, MS
University of Alaska, Southeast, Juneau, AK	University of Montana, Missoula, MT
University of Arizona, Tuscon, AZ	University of Montana, Western, Dillon, MT

Schools That Do Not REquire SAT or ACT Scores

University of Nebraska at Kearney, Kearney, NE

University of Nebraska at Lincoln, Lincoln, NE

University of Nevada, Las Vegas, NV

University of Nevada, Reno, NV

University of New Orleans, New Orleans, LA

University of North Alabama, Florence, AL

University of North Texas, Denton, TX

University of Northern Iowa, Cedar Falls, IA

University of Northwestern Ohio, Lima, OH

University of Oklahoma, Norman, OK

University of Oregon, Eugene, OR

University of Phoenix, Phoenix, AZ

University of Rio Grande, Rio Grande, OH

Univ of Science & Arts of Oklahoma, Chickasha, OK

University of Scranton, Scranton, PA

University of South Dakota, Vermillion, SD

University of Southern Indiana, Evansville, IN

University of Texas of the Permian Basin, Odessa, TX

University of Texas, Arlington, TX

University of Texas, Austin, TX

University of Texas, Brownsville, TX

University of Texas, Dallas, Richardson, TX

University of Texas, El Paso, TX

University of Texas, Pan American, Edinburg, TX

University of Texas, San Antonio, TX

University of Texas, Tyler, TX

Univ of the District of Columbia, Washington, DC

Univ of the State of NY/Excelsior College, Albany, NY

University of the Virgin Islands, St. Croix, VI

University of the Virgin Islands, St. Thomas, VI

University of Toledo, Toledo, OH

Univ of West LA, Inglewood, Woodland Hills, CA

University of Wisconsin, Parkside, Kenosha, WI

University of Wisconsin, Whitewater, WI

University of Wyoming, Laramie, WY

Ursinus College, Collegeville, PA

Utica College, Utica, NY

Valley City State University, Valley City, ND

Villa Maria College, Buffalo, NY

Virginia College, Birmingham, AL

Voorhees College, Denmark, SC

Wake Forest University, Winston-Salem, NC

Walsh College, Troy, MI

Washburn University of Topeka, Topeka, KS

Washington & Jefferson College, Washington, PA

Washington Adventist University, Takoma Park, MD

Washington College, Chestertown, MD

Washington State University, Pullman, WA

Wayne State College, Wayne, NE

Wayne State University, Detroit, MI

Weber State University, Ogden, UT

West Texas A&M University, Canyon, TX

WV University at Parkersburg, Parkersburg, WV

West Virginia Univ. Inst. of Tech., Montgomery, WV

Western Governors University, Salt Lake City, UT

Western International University, Phoenix, AZ

Western Kentucky University, Bowling Green, KY

Western New Mexico University, Silver City, NM

SCHOOLS THAT DO NOT REQUIRE SAT OR ACT SCORES

Western Oregon University, Monmouth, OR

Westwood Coll of Technology South, Woodridge, IL

Westwood College of Technology, Anaheim, CA

Westwood College of Technology, Denver, CO

Westwood College of Tech., Los Angeles, CA

Wheaton College, Norton, MA

White Pines College, Chester, NH

Whitworth College, Spokane, WA

Wichita State University, Wichita, KS

Wilberforce University, Wilberforce, OH

Wiley College, Marshall, TX

Wilmington University, New Castle, DE

Wilson College, Chambersburg, PA

Wittenberg University, Springfield, OH

Woodbury College, Montpelier, VT

Worcester Polytechnic Institute, Worcester, MA

Yeshiva and Kolel Harbotzas Torah, Brooklyn, NY

Yeshiva Beth Moshe, Scranton, PA

Yeshiva Beth Yehuda-Yeshiva, Oak Park, MI

Yeshiva D'Monsey Rabbinical College, Monsey, NY

Yeshiva Derech Chaim, Brooklyn, NY

Yeshiva Gedolah Imrei Yosef D'Spinka, Brooklyn, NY

Yeshiva Gedolah Rabbinical College, Miami Beach

Yeshiva Karlin Stolin, Brooklyn, NY

Yeshiva Mikdash Melech, Brooklyn, NY

Yeshiva of Nitra, Mt. Kisco, NY

Yeshiva of the Telshe Alumni, Riverdale, NY

Yeshiva Ohr Elchonon Chabad/West Coast Talmudical Seminary, Los Angeles, CA

Yeshiva Shaar HaTorah Talmudic, Kew Gardens, NY

Yeshiva Shaarei Torah of Rockland, Suffern, NY

Yeshiva Toras Chaim Talmudical Sem, Denver, CO

Yeshiva Viznitz, Monsey, NY

Yeshivas Novominsk, Brooklyn, NY

Yeshivath Zichron Moshe, South Fallsburg, NY

York College, York, NE

Youngstown State University, Youngstown, OH

Zion Bible Institute, Barrington, RI

Source: fairtest.org

SAT Subject Tests

Some colleges require students to take SAT Subject Tests. The SAT Subject Tests are one hour in length.

Students may take up to three SAT Subject Tests on the same day, but they may not take the SAT Reasoning Test and Subject Tests on the same day. It is important to check the dates on which each Subject Test is given because they are not administered on all seven annual testing dates.

How are the SAT Subject Tests Scored?

SAT Subject Tests are graded on a scale of 200-800. Just like on the SAT Reasoning Test, students receive 1 point for correct answers, and ¼ point is subtracted for every incorrect answer. No points are added or deducted for questions left blank.

English

Literature

History and Social Studies

United States History

World History

Mathematics

Mathematics Level 1 (formerly Mathematics IC)

Mathematics Level 2 (formerly Mathematics IIC)

Science

Biology E/M

Chemistry

Physics

Languages

Chinese with Listening

French

French with Listening

German

German with Listening

Spanish

Spanish with Listening

Modern Hebrew

Italian

Latin

Japanese with Listening

Korean with Listening

SAT Subject Tests

How colleges use the Subject Tests

Some colleges require the results of one or more Subject Tests. Colleges should explain to students whether the results are used for admissions and/or for placement purposes once a student enrolls. If a college requires a particular Subject Test for placement purposes only, students may delay taking that test until the spring of their senior year, especially if it is not in their area of academic strength. Because there is so much variation in which exams colleges require, students must be responsible for checking college websites, catalogs, and similar sources to be sure they have the most up-to-date information.

When should students take the Subject Tests?

Students should take Subject Tests as near as possible to the completion of their studies in a given discipline at the high school level. Thus, a ninth- or tenth-grade student who is taking biology and does not expect to take a more advanced biology course in high school may want to take the SAT Subject Test in Biology in May or June of that year. Likewise, a student taking Spanish III in eleventh grade who does not plan to take Spanish IV as a senior can take the SAT Subject Test in Spanish in May or June of the junior year.

The colleges that require SAT Subject Tests tend to be selective and competitive. For that reason, taking a few Subject Tests in grades 9 to 11 is a good strategy.

SAT Subject Test Percentiles

Score	Literature	History and Social Studies		Mathematics		Science				Score
		U.S. History	World History	Math Level I	Math Level II	Ecological Biology	Molecular Biology	Chemistry	Physics	
800	99	98	95	99	88	99	98	93	90	800
790	99	97	94	99	86	98	97	89	87	790
780	98	96	92	98	83	97	94	86	85	780
770	97	94	90	98	81	96	91	83	82	770
760	96	92	88	96	78	94	89	80	78	760
750	94	89	85	94	75	92	85	76	75	750
740	92	87	82	92	72	90	81	73	72	740
730	90	85	81	89	70	87	78	70	69	730
720	88	82	78	86	68	84	73	67	65	720
710	85	79	76	83	65	82	70	63	62	710
700	82	76	73	79	62	78	66	61	59	700
690	80	72	71	75	60	76	61	57	55	690
680	77	69	67	72	57	72	58	54	53	680
670	74	67	65	68	54	69	54	51	49	670
660	71	63	62	65	51	65	50	49	45	660
650	67	60	60	61	48	61	47	45	42	650
640	65	57	56	58	45	58	43	43	39	640
630	62	53	55	55	42	55	39	40	36	630
620	58	51	52	49	39	51	36	37	33	620
610	55	48	50	45	35	48	33	35	30	610
600	53	45	47	41	33	44	30	33	27	600
590	50	42	43	38	30	41	27	30	25	590
580	46	40	41	35	26	38	25	28	22	580
570	44	37	39	32	24	35	22	26	20	570
560	41	35	36	29	21	32	20	24	18	560
550	38	32	33	26	19	29	18	22	16	550
540	35	30	30	24	16	27	16	20	14	540
530	32	28	29	22	14	24	15	18	13	530
520	30	25	26	20	12	22	13	16	11	520
510	28	23	24	17	11	19	12	15	9	510

SAT SUBJECT TEST PERCENTILES

Score	Literature	History and Social Studies		Mathematics		Science				Score
		U.S. History	World History	Math Level I	Math Level II	Ecological Biology	Molecular Biology	Chemistry	Physics	
500	25	21	22	15	9	17	10	13	8	500
490	22	19	19	14	7	16	9	12	7	490
480	20	17	17	12	6	14	8	10	6	480
470	18	15	15	10	5	12	7	9	5	470
460	16	13	13	9	4	11	7	7	4	460
450	14	11	10	8	3	10	6	6	3	450
440	12	10	9	7	2	8	5	5	2	440
430	10	8	7	6	2	7	5	4	2	430
420	8	7	6	5	1	6	4	3	1	420
410	6	5	5	4	1	5	3	2	1	410
400	5	4	4	3	1	4	3	2	1-	400
390	4	3	3	3	1-	4	2	1	1-	390
380	3	2	2	2	1-	3	2	1-	1-	380
370	2	2	2	1	1-	2	1	1-	1-	370
360	1	1	1	1	1-	2	1	1-	1-	360
350	1	1	1	1	1-	1	1	1-	1-	350
340	1	1-	1-	1-	1-	1	1-	1-	–	340
330	1-	1-	1-	1-	1-	1	1-	1-	–	330
320	1-	1-	1-	1-	1-	1-	1-	–	–	320
310	1-	1-	1-	1-	1-	1-	1-	–	–	310
300	1-	1-	1-	1-	1-	1-	1-	–	–	300
290	1-	1-	1-	1-	–	1-	1-	–	–	290
280	1-	1-	1-	1-	–	1-	1-	–	–	280
270	1-	1-	1-	–	–	1-	1-	–	–	270
260	1-	–	1-	–	–	–	1-	–	–	260
250	1-	–	1-	–	–	–	–	–	–	250
240	1-	–	–	–	–	–	–	–	–	240
230	1-	–	–	–	–	–	–	–	–	230
220	–	–	–	–	–	–	–	–	–	220
210	–	–	–	–	–	–	–	–	–	210
200	–	–	–	–	–	–	–	–	–	200
N.	123,408	123,229	16,818	85,109	163,713	38,502	41,739	67,891	42,407	N.
Mean	580	601	605	605	649	601	638	644	658	Mean
S.D.	111	115	120	101	107	108	104	114	103	S.D.
SEM	30	30	30	30	30	30	20	20	30	SEM
SED	50	40	40	40	40	40	30	30	40	SED

SAT SUBJECT TEST PERCENTILES

Score	Languages — Listening						Languages — Reading						Score
	Chinese	French	German	Japanese	Korean	Spanish	French	German	Modern Hebrew	Italian	Latin	Spanish	
800	57	87	89	86	63	95	89	91	84	89	96	92	800
790	44	85	88	73	45	91	88	88	81	81	95	91	790
780	37	83	85	65	36	88	86	86	80	78	92	88	780
770	31	81	83	61	28	84	84	84	76	74	90	85	770
760	27	81	79	54	24	76	81	82	73	69	89	81	760
750	23	77	78	51	21	71	80	80	72	66	86	77	750
740	20	75	75	47	18	66	77	76	69	63	83	75	740
730	18	74	73	45	16	63	75	74	69	59	80	69	730
720	15	70	71	42	13	59	73	72	68	57	78	67	720
710	14	68	69	39	12	56	70	71	67	54	76	63	710
700	12	65	67	37	11	54	68	69	64	51	71	61	700
690	11	63	65	35	10	52	65	67	62	48	69	57	690
680	9	59	63	34	9	47	63	64	61	45	66	54	680
670	8	57	61	32	8	45	60	62	61	42	63	51	670
660	8	53	60	30	6	43	58	59	59	39	59	48	660
650	7	49	57	29	6	42	55	57	56	36	56	45	650
640	6	47	55	28	5	38	52	54	53	33	54	42	640
630	6	44	55	27	4	37	50	52	52	30	51	39	630
620	5	41	53	25	4	34	48	50	49	29	48	36	620
610	5	38	51	24	3	32	45	48	47	27	44	34	610
600	4	34	49	23	3	30	42	46	45	25	42	31	600
590	3	32	48	22	2	28	40	44	44	23	39	29	590
580	3	29	44	20	2	27	37	41	40	20	36	27	580
570	3	27	42	19	2	25	35	39	39	19	33	25	570
560	2	25	40	17	1	23	33	37	37	18	31	23	560
550	2	22	37	16	1	22	31	35	36	18	29	21	550
540	2	21	36	15	1	19	28	32	34	17	25	19	540
530	2	19	33	13	1	17	26	30	32	16	23	17	530
520	1	16	30	12	1	15	24	27	30	15	19	16	520
510	1	14	28	11	1-	14	21	25	28	14	17	14	510
500	1	12	25	10	1-	12	19	23	26	14	15	12	500
490	1	11	23	10	1-	11	17	22	22	12	13	11	490
480	1	10	22	9	1-	10	15	19	20	11	10	10	480
470	1-	8	20	8	1-	8	13	15	17	11	8	8	470
460	1-	7	17	7	1-	7	12	13	15	10	6	7	460

Source: The College Board

STANDARDIZED TEST SCHEDULE
2011-2012

Date	Test	Registration Deadline	Late Registration Deadline
September 10	ACT	August 12	August 26
October 1	SAT/SAT II	September 9	Septemeber 21
October 12/15	PSAT offered		
October 22	ACT	September 16	September 30
November 5	SAT/SAT II	October 7	October 21
December 3	SAT/SAT II	November 8	November 20
December 11	ACT	November 4	November 18
January 28	SAT/SAT II	December 30	January 13
February 11	ACT	January 13	January 20
March 10	SAT Only	February 10	Februrary 24
April 14	ACT	March 9	March 23
May 2-13	AP exams	March 15	
May 5	SAT/SAT II	April 6	April 20
June 2	SAT/SAT II	May 8	May 22
June 9	ACT	May 4	May 18

college essay

College Application Essay Overview

Like the application form, the essay (or essays, in some cases) provides you with an opportunity to convey something about yourself that goes beyond the objective data. Above all, the essay should be well written and carefully edited, and you should strive to keep it within the prescribed length. (If no length is prescribed, aim for no more than two single-spaced, typed pages.) Again, you should consider your audience. Admissions officers want to read essays that are short, lively, and graceful that will tell them about you as a person. Write about something that is important to you. The presentation of yourself through the essay is a key component in shaping an admission officer's impression of you as a candidate.

Unless the college specifically asks for it, avoid the general autobiographical essay. If the application essay question is specific, make sure you answer the question. Make sure that the essay you write suits the application and the college for which you are writing.

Most importantly, be true to yourself. Don't think too much about what it is you think the admission officers want to hear. Focus on what you want to convey and how to say it. Let your voice come through. Where people commonly falter is approaching this as an academic exercise. The college application essay is usually the first time that you asked to think about your own life experiences and write an essay for total strangers to read.

Don't use the essay to apologize for some perceived failing on your part. Explain unusual circumstances in your life without making excuses.

Try to avoid much-used topics (unless they are addressed in a unique way). Don't go overboard in your attempts to be original or memorable or profound. Avoid anything that smacks of weirdness, cuteness, or elitism.

Think of the essay as an opportunity to add a new dimension to your folder. Avoid repeating facts, figures, or activities mentioned previously in the application, unless they have a particular bearing on the development of your character.

Get some feedback on your finished product. Have others read and critique your essay for its form and content. It should sound like it was written by you and only you. Listen to the advice of others, but make the decisions that are right for you.

Spell check is not always your friend. It will not pick up homonyms or keep you from accidentally sending your Oberlin essay to USC.

SAMPLE COLLEGE SUPPLEMENT ESSAY QUESTIONS

The Common Application

Essay Question (250-500 words). Select one topic.

- Evaluate a significant experience, achievement, risk you have taken, or ethical dilemma you have faced and its impact on you.

- Discuss some issue of personal, local, national, or international concern and its importance.

- Indicate a person who has had a significant influence on you, and describe that influence.

- Describe a character in fiction, an historical figure, or a creative work (as in art, music, science, etc.) that has had an influence on you, and explain that influence.

- A range of academic interests, personal perspectives, and life experiences adds much to the educational mix. Given your personal background, describe an experience that illustrates what you would bring to the diversity in a college community, or an encounter that demonstrated the importance of diversity to you.

- Topic of your choice

Bard College

One hundred years ago, in 1912, the Austrian writer and social critic Karl Kraus, famous for his provocative aphorisms, wrote "Civilization ends, since barbarians erupt from it." Write a short commentary on what you think this might mean from your perspective 100 years later, and whether it makes any sense.

Bennington College

Design an experiment that attempts to determine whether toads can hear. Provide the rationale for your design--explain your reasons for setting up the experiment as you did. Strive for simplicity and clarity.

Berea College

Please answer all questions using 500 words or less per question.

- What motivates you to seek a college education?

- Why is Berea College a good choice for you?

- What would you like the Admissions Decision Team to know about you prior to making their decision (that they are unlikely to learn otherwise)?

Brandeis University

If you could choose to be raised by robots, dinosaurs, or aliens, who would you pick? Why?

Sample College Supplement Essay Questions

Brown University

Please respond to one of the following essay topics: A, B, or C.

- Tell us about an intellectual experience, project, class, or book that has influenced or inspired you.

- What is the best piece of advice you've ever been given, and why?

- French novelist Anatole France wrote: "An education isn't how much you have committed to memory, or even how much you know It's being able to differentiate between what you do know and what you don't." What don't you know?

California Institute of Technology

CalTech students have long been known for their quirky sense of humor and creative pranks and for finding unusual ways to have fun. What is something that you find fun or humorous?

Catholic University

Please write an essay on one of the following topics:

- If you could add or remove one item/aspect of contemporary society, what would it be and why?

- Describe how a work of art, music, dance, theater or literature has inspired you.

- In his essay, Self Reliance, Ralph Waldo Emerson wrote: "Who so would be a man must be a nonconformist." React to this quotation and relate your own experience.

Claremont McKenna College

Write an analytical essay responding to the following prompt. There is no minimum or maximum length requirement, but the Admission Committee expects a thoughtful and analytical response to the following:

- Leadership is a constant theme and emphasis at CMC. In fact, one of the ways we describe CMC students is "Leaders in the Making." Choose someone, fictional or nonfictional, historical or contemporary, whom you consider to be a leader.

- Suppose you are this person's primary advisor. How would you advise this person and why?

Duke University

Choose one of the following questions and indicate which question you've chosen. We ask that you limit your essay more than 2–3 pages and use double spacing if the essay is typed or computer printed.

- Have you witnessed a person who is close to you doing something you considered seriously wrong? Describe the circumstances, your thoughts, and how you chose to respond. If you discussed it with the person, was his/her justification valid? In retrospect, what if anything would you have done differently and why?

- What has been your most profound or surprising intellectual experience?

Sample College Supplement Essay Questions

Eugene Lang The New School

Along with one of the Common Application essay questions, please answer both the short answer and the essay question below.

- Short Answer Question: Tell us about a time you were in the minority. (approximately 250 words)

- Essay Question: Eugene Lang College was originally known as The Seminar College, marked by discussion-based classes held around a table where students and professors gathered to share ideas. At Lang, students are expected to take an active role in their education. This is your chance to design your ideal class. Give us a brief description of what the course will entail. What lasting impact will this class have on you and the learning community at Lang? (approximately 500 words)

Florida State University

How has your family history, culture, or environment influenced who you are?

Fordham University

Discuss a political, social, or cultural issue that has had an impact on society and discuss why it is important to you.

Howard University

Howard University is interested in you as a person, as well as how you express your thoughts. Please submit a 500-word essay describing how you would contribute to the Howard University legacy.

Johns Hopkins University

If you had only $10 to plan a day's adventure, where would you go, what would you and whom would you take with you?

Kenyon College

Along the edge of ancient maps it used to say, "Here there be monsters." What does it say at the edge of your map, and why does it say that?

New York University

Select a creative work—a novel, a film, a musical piece, a painting, or other work of art—that has influenced the way you view the world, or the way you view yourself. Discuss the impact the work has had on you. (We are more interested in how the work has affected you rather than reading a detailed plot summary or a description of the work.)

SAMPLE COLLEGE SUPPLEMENT ESSAY QUESTIONS

Northwestern University

An old expression says, "What is right is not always popular, and what is popular is always right." Give an example of a time when you made a choice that was not popular but you felt was right. Why did you make this choice? What happened as a result?

Pitzer College

Pitzer College's educational foundation is built upon four core values: social responsibility, intercultural understanding, interdisciplinary learning, and student autonomy. Our students utilize these values to create solutions to our world's current and future challenges, both big and small. Keeping our core values in mind, please answer one of the following prompts.

- Incorporating one or more of our values, propose a solution to a local or global issue you deem important.

- Tell us about an accomplishment of yours. How did you use one or more of our core values to reach your goal?

Pomona College

Choose one of the following options. Lease limit your response to one or two pages.

- At Pomona, we see the ability to question and to think critically as essential to the learning experience. Tell us about something you once thought you knew with certainty but have since reevaluated.

- Pomona College's approach to education includes, among other things, a strong emphasis on collaboration. How has collaboration played a role in your learning experience thus far, and how do you see it affecting your college experience.

- Pick a topic of your own choosing that will give you the opportunity to express to us a sense of how you think, what issues and ideas are most important to you, and a sense of your personal philosophy, traits, goals, etc.

- Reinvent your high school. What is essential? What would you change?

Princeton University

In addition to the essay you have written for the Common Application, please select one of the following themes and write an essay of about 500 words in response.

- Tell us about a person who has influenced you in a significant way.

- Using the statement below as a starting point, tell us about an event or experience that helped you define one of your values or changed how you approach the world.

SAMPLE COLLEGE SUPPLEMENT ESSAY QUESTIONS

- "Princeton in the Nation's Service" was the title of a speech given by Woodrow Wilson on the 150th anniversary of the University. It became the unofficial Princeton motto and was expanded for the University's 250th anniversary to "Princeton in the nation's service and in the service of all nations." *Woodrow Wilson, Princeton Class of 1879, served on the faculty and was Princeton's president from 1902–1910.*

- Using the following quotation from "The Moral Obligations of Living in a Democratic Society" as a starting point, tell us about an event or experience that helped you define one of your values or changed how you approach the world.

- "Empathy is not simply a matter of trying to imagine what others are going through, but having the will to muster enough courage to do something about it. In a way, empathy is predicated upon hope." *Cornel West, Class of 1943 University Professor in the Center for African American Studies, Princeton University*

- Using a favorite quotation from an essay or book you have read in the last three years as a starting point, tell us about an event or experience that helped you define one of your values or changed how you approach the world. Please write the quotation at the beginning of your essay.

Rhodes College

What risks have you taken in your life? What were the circumstances and the results? How have you benefited from risk taking?

St. Mary's College of Maryland

St. Mary's College is casting for the incoming class. Send us your audition tape via the Web or DVD. Please provide us with the site for posting. Selection of this option will stand as your college essay. Consider your audience.

The College of New Jersey

Write an essay of no less than 250 words on one of the following:

- Describe a character in fiction, an historical figure, or a creative work (as an art, music, science, etc.) that has had an influence on you, and explain hat influence.

- We are fortunate to live in a society that is increasingly multicultural and diverse. Describe a time in your life when you unexpectedly became more aware of either a difference or an area of common ground that existed between you and another person or persons. How did this experience impact your understanding of yourself, other people, or of the world?

Tufts University

- Which aspects of Tufts' curriculum or undergraduate experience prompt your application? In short: "Why Tufts?" (50-100 words.)

- There is a Quaker saying: "Let your life speak." Describe the environment in which you were raised—your family, home, neighborhood or community—and how it influenced the person you are today.

Sample College Supplement Essay Questions

Tufts University (continued)

- For the second short response we asked you to consider the world around you. Now, consider the world within. Taste in music, food and clothing can make a statement while politics, sports, religion and ethnicity are often defining attributes. Are you a vegetarian? A poet? Do you prefer You Tube or test tubes, Mac or PC? Are you the drummer in an all-girl rock band? Do you tinker? Use the richness of your identity to frame your personal outlook.

University of California

All applicants must respond to two essay prompts. Responses to your two prompts must be a maximum of 1,000 words total. Allocate the word count as you wish. If you choose to respond to one prompt at greater length, we suggest your shorter answer be no less than 250 words.

- Describe the world you come from – for example, your family, community or school- and tell us how your world has shaped your dreams and aspirations.

- Tell us about a personal quality, talent, accomplishment, contribution or experience that is important to you. What about this quality or accomplishment makes you proud and how does it relate to the person you are?

University of Chicago

Find X

University of Georgia

- Think about a recent experience in which you displayed initiative or demonstrated leadership ability. What did you learn about yourself—your strengths, weaknesses and aspirations—and how do you expect to use what you learned in the future?

- Think back to what you were like as a student and as a person in your first year of high school. Consider yourself now. Tell us how you have changed, and why.

- In your opinion, what elements of a person's character define integrity? Provide a personal experience in which you believe you have demonstrated integrity.

- Dr. Martin Luther King, Jr. believed that it was critical for one person to have discovered something in life for which it was worth dying. If you could choose one political, environmental, spiritual, or social issue to fight or, what would it be and why?

University of Notre Dame

- In his autobiography Long Walk to Freedom, Nelson Mandela reflects upon his life and commitment to the antiapartheid movement. He writes: "I learned that courage was not the absence of fear, but the triumph over it." Give a personal how courage has played a role in your life.

Sample College Supplement Essay Questions

University of Notre Dame (continued)

- English poet W. H. Auden wrote, "Those who will not perish in the act; t will not act perish for that reason." At Notre Dame, we value equally intellectual inquiry and social responsibility. Describe a personal experience in which your ideas motivated your actions, or an experience in which your actions changed your ideas.

- Compose a Personal Statement with content of your own choosing. In doing so, feel free to introduce yourself to us in any way you feel appropriate. Whether your essay is autobiographical or imaginative, it should reflect who you are in both form and content.

- leaders, dedicated journalists and demandingteachers, judges and muckrakers, scholars and critics and artists. We have the best schools to train them, but social and private environments have eroded." Do you agree with his assessment or not?

University of Pennsylvania

- Describe the courses of study and the unique characteristics of the University of Pennsylvania that most interest you. Why do these interests make you a good match for Penn?

- Your intellectual abilities, your sense of imagination and your creativity are important to us. With this in mind, please respond to one of the following three requests. Your essay should not exceed one page.

- You have just completed your 300 page autobiography. Please submit page 217.

University of Virginia

We are looking for passionate students to join our diverse community of scholars, researchers, and artists. Limit your answer to a half page or roughly 250 words.

- What work of art, music, science, mathematics, or literature has surprised, unsettled, or challenged you, and in what way.

Answer one of the following questions in a half page or roughly 250 words:

- What is your favorite word and why?

- Describe the world you come from and how that world shaped who you are.

- Discuss your favorite place to get lost.

- In *The Dumbest Generation*, Mark Bauerlein asserts that social media and youth culture undercut the skillsnecessary to be a global citizen when he writes: "We need a steady stream of rising men and women to replenishthe institutions, to become strong military leaders and wise political leaders, dedicated journalists and demandingteachers, judges and muckrakers, scholars and critics and artists. We have the best schools to train them, but social and private environments have eroded." Do you agree with his assessment or not?

Sample College Supplement Essay Questions

Wellesley College

Please limit your response to two well-developed paragraphs.

When choosing a college, you are choosing an intellectual community and a place where you believe that you can live, learn, and flourish. To this end, the Board of Admission is interested in knowing your reasons for applying to Wellesley College and how Wellesley will help you to realize your personal and academic goals.

Williams College

Imagine looking through a window at any environment that is particularly significant to you. Reflect on the scene, paying close attention to the relation between what you are seeing and why it is meaningful to you. *Please limit your statement to 300 words.*

Yale University

You have already told us about yourself in the Common Application, with its list of activities, Short Answer, and Personal Essay. In this required second essay, tell us something that you would like us to know about you that we might not get from the rest of your application – or something that you would like a chance to say more about. Please limit your essay to fewer than 500 words.

Other Commonly Asked Essay Questions

- Imagine you have been given the means and the opportunity, beyond what is available to you now, to develop a talent or new area of interest. What do you choose and why?

- Although it may appear to the contrary, we do know that people have a life beyond what they do to get into college. Tell us about a fun experience you've had outside of your formal classroom and extracurricular activities.

- You might choose to write about time spent with friends, family, or even by yourself.

- If you could travel through time and interview a prominent figure in the arts, politics, religion, or science, whom would you choose, and why?

Sample College Essays

Sample Essay 1

Children dream. I'm not referring to the dreams adults have while they sleep after a long day at work. A child's dream occurs during the day, when the sun shines brightly overhead and the future looms on the horizon. Children possess the freedom to dream of greatness because mistakes or judgments do not frighten them. I steadfastly adhered to the dream of my youth, unafraid of the stigma associated with failure. I invested every ounce of sweat and effort to fuel my passion. My dream evolved into my destiny: to rank among the elite of all baseball players. I clearly remember the day, thirteen years ago, when my father placed a bat in my hand and encouraged me to hit a ball off a tee. To this day I can hear the crash of the bat against the ball and see the image of it soaring through the air. I stood, mesmerized the object I propelled into flight. My fascination commenced a passion for learning how to master the skill of what I then considered "launching balls". Little did I know that my goal would not happen overnight.

I sometimes lose perspective on my journey which presented me with many obstacles, including enduring countless injuries. I recall times I continued playing, injured and in pain, determined to hide my agony in order to remain true to my team, the sport and myself. In my mind I recited over and over again: "never give up." My resolve proved necessary because other players consistently challenged my commitment. During a west coast showdown, my first at-bat during the tournament truly led me to doubt my ability to thrive as a baseball player. The pitcher threw every ball hard, fast and with the most sophisticated stash of off-speed pitches I ever encountered. Unwilling to back down, I found myself engaged in a one-on-one battle of epic proportion. The pitcher - shorter and smaller than me - out powered my hitting ability with his velocity and repertoire of pitches with which I had never before con-tended. The experience humbled me; I realized that one's ability to maintain compo-sure and stay focused during showdowns separate the average from the best. I then knew that prevailing in any endeavor comes only through hard work and dedication to a goal. My journey reached a crossroads that challenged my childhood dream: upon entering high school would I dedicate the next four years to baseball or participate in a variety of sports?

Before I decided, fate intervened: Reggie Smith, one of the greatest baseball players of all time, invited me to fill a coveted spot among his invitation only summer baseball session. I could not mask my excitement and nervousness about this opportunity; I eagerly participated in the batting try-out and resolved to perform at the level expected of an elite player. I hopped in my Dad's car with my batting gloves already strapped around my sweaty and clammy hands. Upon our arrival, I immediately spotted the batting cage where - in a matter of minutes - I would dominate like a blood thirsty gladiator in a coliseum surrounded by rivals. I seized my bat and clenched it with honor and pride, like a knight about to engage in battle. With adrenaline flowing through my veins, I ascended the batting cage. I concentrated on the pitcher and his baseball; no one else existed in my world. I crushed every pitch, no matter how fast or how strong. Nothing could stop me because, with the resolve of a champion, I controlled my destiny and would find a way to succeed.

SAMPLE COLLEGE ESSAYS

Sample Essay 1 continued

History teaches us that Americans demonstrate strength of will and achieve success through perseverance, refusing to allow chains of mediocrity to bind them. I am proud that my optimism has not wavered in the midst of small failures or roadblocks. It has not faltered when others attempted to convince me that the loftiness of my dreams rendered them unattainable. In fact, when faced with skepticism, I strengthen my resolve, not only on the baseball field but also in the classroom. During my freshman year of high school I worked diligently to reach my potential, but my performance on exams did not reflect my effort. The following summer my morale dipped when I learned the reason for my struggle: educational testing revealed that I have a mild reading disorder. Once again I faced a choice: I could muster the enthusiasm to work diligently and achieve my academic goals or take the easy way out by foregoing a foreign language – an area in which my disability renders my capacity to thrive nearly impossible. I found myself on the verge of yielding to the stereotype of another athlete without academic ability. My aspirations proved too great to allow myself to submit to a flaw that I would attempt to overcome. I admitted to myself that I could apply the same tenacity I exhibited on the baseball field to my study of Spanish.

Even though I spent more time working on Spanish than any other class I still earned the lowest grade of my high school career. However, the grade did not matter to me nearly as much as my dignity; if I would not give up on baseball – no matter what the odds or obstacles – then I resolved that I must do the same in other areas of my life. In actuality, my decision had nothing to do with baseball or college credits or others' expectations; my choice stemmed from a commitment to stay true to my character and refuse to back down when I face an obstacle that seems impossible to overcome. I have a message for those who underestimate me: in the face of any hardship, I persevere. Each time I reach the brink of surrender, a fire ignites my soul and sparks a fiery yearning for me to achieve my potential

Today, others consider me a gifted athlete and maintain high expectations for my performance. I consider their respect an honor that I do not take for granted, I never forget where I came from or the sheer fortitude required for me to realize success. The dream I carried in my heart as a child has materialized, but not without the determination of a warrior. As I reflect on my past, I realize that the opportunity to pursue one's passion is the greatest gift a person can receive. My parents supported me, enabling me to become who I am today. I am defined not by my role as a baseball player, but as a person of character and perseverance. My childhood dream compelled me not only to play baseball, but to something greater: the strength to triumph over obstacles, anxiety and pain. I will follow my dreams to my absolute limits of human ability if necessary as long as I remain true to the promptings initiated within my soul.

SAMPLE COLLEGE ESSAYS

Sample Essay 2

I could barely stand the stress; I felt choked by a weight that could crush an ox. My gasps for air came in the form of parties, friends, fashion shows, and anything that allowed me to escape my insufferable home life. My mother's rules lay broken, her hopes and dreams shattered, and her support of me long gone. In the beginning, it was just my mom and me. We were close when I was younger, although she often acted irresponsibly, and for that reason I took on the parental role in the relationship. I became her protector, but in doing so I forgot to protect myself. When she married for a second time, my mother's obliviousness to her neglect of me heightened. No one shielded me from my stepfather's mental abuse; I was frightened and abandoned. His brazenly disdained me, called me names as if he were a child bully, and blatantly favored his own daughter. His screams of fury rung in my ears, and I could only guess that he felt angry about my very existence. Regardless of what fueled his behavior, I did not have the heart to tell my mother. She expected so much out of me and I knew that my complaints would disappoint and upset her. At the same time, she provided neither the guidance nor the structure which I desperately needed. I lost control and there was no one to help me. My mother stopped listening to me, her husband hurt me, and my real father could have been 3000 miles or 1 mile away and it would not have improved his ability to care for me.

Alone, with my goals collecting dust from lack of attention and my home cold with hostility, my life hit reached a low and I doubted anyone could stop me from sinking further. How naive I was. Forty-eight hours and 3,000 miles later, I went from an environment drenched in failure to a new home, school, and friends that could support my ambitions and dreams.

I came home from school in Toronto one Thursday evening and my mother informed me that I would be moving to California to live with my aunt and uncle on Saturday - two days away. I could have easily rebelled and resisted such a drastic measure, but as much as I did not want to outwardly admit it I recognized immediately that I had been craving this opportunity, but had lost hope in its existence. Consequently, I accepted the decision without dispute. I packed up my life, said my goodbyes and dusted off those old hopes and dreams. I looked forward to transforming my potential into real achievement. On the other end of my journey, my aunt and uncle, a new brother and sister (my cousins), and even a dog opened their home and hearts and embraced me. Finally, I lived within a structure that could support me. I had a set time and place for homework, a routine and defined rules. To have only to worry about growing up and not grown-ups themselves was truly a unique experience for me. I have had the luxury for the first time to reflect on my circumstances and learn from them. I feel whole again, and relieved of my past burdens, I can now breathe.

I now know that it is rarely too late to confront a problem. Therefore I strive to always work toward a resolution no matter how complicated the issue may be. Over the past year I have grown to confront my issues before they fester. Avoidance of a problem creates more anxiety and complications. For this reason I take great care to pay attention to everything that happens around me. In order to

SAMPLE COLLEGE ESSAYS

Sample Essay 2 continued

do this I stay organized, focus on each task, and define my direction. I work in a routine manner, so that my positive habit becomes automatic. At one time, I ignored my problems and persuaded myself into thinking they would disappear because they seemed too daunting to overcome. Now I recognize that problems do not just goes away and they must be resolved and now I have to skills to conquer them. I have proven to myself that I am capable of correcting even the most desperate situations. I find comfort in knowing that since my move, I encountered and overcome every, even if I had to ask for help from others, and the support I have has taught me the true value of trust. I have learned to no longer shrink silently, but to speak up and be heard.

In addition to learning to triumph over my fears, I now try to carefully consider how I measure myself. I assess myself by the standards I am working towards and not those I have already surpassed so that I avoid lowering my expectations just to make me feel better. Previously, while living in Toronto, I found solace in knowing that at least academically I performed a bit better than many of my friends. It is obvious to me now that my standards were misguided. I feel ashamed for achieving to the level of my potential and for comparing myself to people were not examples for who I wanted to be. It mistakenly to chose friends who made my shortcomings look better in comparison. I now set my own goals and do not judge myself according to others who do not share my ambition. In the end, I determine the measure of my own success.

By reflecting on my past decisions and what I can do to make better decisions going forward, a simple rule came to mind: Never lead without deliberation nor follow without hesitation. While in Toronto, I followed a path that I never intended because I felt afraid. Many people tell how they got caught up in something and could not find a way out. I am fortunate to have the experience and the strength to take control of my life. I carefully consider what kind of people I fit in with, and the kind of friends I need. I feel proud that my new friends are dedicated to their education, honest and of strong character. I know they will be there for me when I need them. I have also crossed paths people who remind me of my old friends, but my making the distinction, I broke my past patterns and positioned myself in a positive social environment.

I have taken difficult journey from one extreme to another, and as a result I have the self-respect and strength to set goals and understand that diligence necessary to accomplish them. I am applying to this University because I know that this is a school that will support me in my endeavor to succeed. I intend to graduate from high school as a well-rounded person. I reaped wisdom from my experiences and therefore, while I know I will make mistakes, I will strive not to make them in vain by learning from them. In addition, my unconventional experiences enable me to contribute unique points of view. With the ending of high school comes the beginning of adulthood and I enthusiastically embrace this transition. I can say without hesitation that I am whole-heartedly determined in my perseverance to achieve in this next step I am undertaking.

SAMPLE COLLEGE ESSAYS

Sample Essay 3

In June 2010, I will be the first male in my family to graduate from high school. My family history tells a story of underachievement, lack of support and societal challenges that many of my cousins still struggle to overcome. My mother was the only one of eight children to graduate from high school. My older sister became the first of our family to attend college. My dream is to follow in her path.

My goal does not stem from reflecting on a family history of successful doctors and lawyers, but from being raised by a mother who sacrificed more than a child could ever expect so my sister and I can experience opportunities she never had. As a child, I resented my mother for forbidding me to hang out with my cousins after school. Instead, she required me to stay home, complete a list of chores and do homework for hours while she worked full days to support my dreams for the future. Further, because I attended school outside my district, I endured the harsh treatment of classmates. My black skin stood out among the sea of white students and caused me to feel like an outsider.

As I grew older, I witnessed my cousins making bad choices, including dropping out of school. These decisions changed the courses of their lives and marked the beginning of the divergence of our respective journeys. For the first time, I appreciated the effort my mother spent to insure I did not share the same fate. My mother taught me strength of character and the importance of hard work. The discipline and ability to focus that she instilled in me are the main reasons I maintain a 3.0 GPA while also spending four to five hours a day practicing football, basketball or track. Now that I am older and on my way to college, I appreciate all the sacrifices she made to give me this opportunity.

So as I look to my future, I will remember the negative parts of life I've experienced, and embrace the positive. The negative parts of the community around me remind me every day of what I do not want for my life or my future family. Instead, it encourages me to stay focused and work hard in spite of any challenges I may face. I will allow the positive in my world—the love my family has for me and I have for them, the camaraderie I experience every time I step on the football field, the triumph I feel when I know all my hard work studying for a test has paid off—to continue elevating me to the next level. I can't wait to see the joy on my mother's face after she watches me throw my cap in the air at my college graduation; it may not be much to some people, but I know it will be the most meaningful way I have of showing just how thankful I am.

As my graduation day draws closer, I aspire to achieve goals beyond those of my high school accomplishments. While I do not have a solid family history of relatives who rank among the educated elite, I recognize the power of an education. I believe it will enable me to realize more success than those who came before me. I endeavor to serve as a role model for those who will come in the future.

SAMPLE COLLEGE ESSAYS

Sample Essay 4

My limited life experience has taught me how rare it is to meet certain types of people: those who show character by working all their lives to achieve success, and those who take a similar journey to fame and fortune but find that the destination is not what they expected and abandon it in exchange for a more meaningful life. In so doing, the latter group discovers an inner self by living according to their own sense of truth. I have studied many historical figures, but I have yet to discover a book or story that touches me in the way my mother's past experiences have influenced my present existence.

Sharon Mayer sped through the dramatic world of Hollywood and high fashion that most people only read about in magazines: traveling around the world, socializing with the rich and powerful and dining with royalty. My mother married immediately after graduating from high school and soon gave birth to my older sister, Jennifer. A few years later, divorced and raising a child by herself, she built a career in fashion, producing shows for a famous designer, in addition to working with a popular singer on her latest film. Although this lifestyle afforded my mother many material perks, she exchanged her lavish lifestyle for a richer and more meaningful experience when her life took an unexpected and dramatic turn and she became the woman I know today as Sarah Weissman, my mother.

While living glamorously brought my mother fame, inside she felt something missing. At the age of 38, a woman invited my mother to a Torah class in Los Angeles. Always curious, but never a seeker of wisdom and truth - or so she thought - my mother took a leap of faith and accepted the invitation. "By Divine Providence," as my mother relates the story, a spark ignited in her soul, which evolved into a lasting flame, burning brighter each day as she attended classes and explored her Jewish heritage. People struggle to make changes at any stage of life, but at the age of 38, with a teenage daughter to support and a rising career, my mother proved her true strength and remained undaunted in her quest to become the person she had been seeking all along.

As I reflect on my mother's life, I cannot fathom the hardships and challenges she faced as she changed direction and journeyed down a new and uncertain path. It reminds me of when Hashem told Avraham "lech lecha." Similar to Avraham, my mother had no idea where she would end up. In spite of the unknowns, my mother exhibited the will to take a risk because she knew it was right, and she knew it was truth. No one in her family understood her choices and they believed it would be a passing phase. She grew up in a secular home in the San Fernando Valley with no sense of her Jewish identity and no affiliation with any shul or the State of Israel and did not benefit from a day-school education. In contrast, I have enjoyed a privileged childhood through

SAMPLE COLLEGE ESSAYS

Sample Essay 4 continued

immersion in Torah, chesed, strong Jewish communal life, and a deep love and appreciation for the State of Israel.

Casting aside the life to which she had grown accustomed, my mother embraced a mission that took priority over all others. She focused her passion and energy on learning Torah, doing mitzvot, and raising a family according to Jewish values and traditions. She married my father, Peter Weissman, and gave birth to two more daughters; first me, then my younger sister Arianna. My mother never looked back at her old life and instead seeks new ways to help me and my sister learn. My mother's first Torah class profoundly affected her life and started her on the path to the chuppah; she now serves as my guide on that same path. My mother's stories at the Shabbos table and her true love - not only of learning, but of sharing - will remain with me always. While it is sometimes easy to take everything my mother so lovingly offers for granted, I cannot forget that she lived the first part of her life without any Torah, yet she shares with me all the tools she was denied. I marvel at her thirst for knowledge and the thrill that insight into our precious Torah gives her. By sharing my ideas with her I discover new insights for myself, which in turn helps us grow and share together. I, too, aspire to show the same unwavering commitment to growth and learning, not only to make her proud, but also to add meaning to my own life. She insures that my sister and I attend Jewish Orthodox day schools and receive a thorough grounding in Jewish education. She wants us to avoid struggling to find the gift of Judaism and guides us to a meaningful and rewarding life.

My mother inspires me by infusing passion and energy into every endeavor she undertakes. First, she climbed to the top of her field in fashion; she now exhibits the same strength by working to make the world a kinder and better place by organizing fundraising events and banquets for every Torah day school in the city. The high expectations she sets for herself help me prioritize the important aspects of life. "What we value the most is ultimately what we will pursue," my mother constantly reminds me. While my mother encourages me to grow and put other people first, I sometimes find it challenging. However, her passion is as contagious as it is inspiring and as a family we remain dedicated to doing chesed and outreach in our community. I grew up watching my mother volunteer to make a mitzvah meal for a new mom or an ill neighbor. I work diligently to follow her lead, but know that it will not always be easy. My mother's strength reminds me of the power of a Jewish woman. My Mother's namesake is my great-grandmother, Sarah, a widow with six children who lived in Czechoslovakia, and was murdered in the Holocaust. Just as my great-grandmother lived a life deeply committed to her faith and her family, so too does my mother. I am proud that my greatgrandmother's legacy lives on through us and that her DNA resonates not only in my mother's genes, but in mine as well. Even when I am uncertain, I realize that as long as remember where I came from, I will always know my path in life.

Sample College Essays

Sample Essay 4 continued

When I was six years old a fire struck our community; my mother suggested I bake cookies for the firefighters in recognition of their heroism. For my Bat Mitzvah, I collected money for young girl – a victim of bombings in Israel - who desperately needed medication. By connecting with the Kids for Kids program in Israel, I continued helping needy and sick families in Israel. This past summer my efforts culminated when I embraced the role as a volunteer counselor at Bet Elazraki , a foster home in Israel. Day and night I comforted the young 10-12 year old girls, knowing that I could not solve their problems, but that I could at least make their struggle bearable. For the first time in my life I understood the meaning of selfless giving and true chesed.

As I embark on a new chapter in my Jewish life, my mother stands with me. My mother offered herself as the greatest role model I can ever hope for by teaching me to live Torah by her example. My mother taught me the true meaning of beautifying every mitzvah and exploring in order to find truth. I remain in awe of her ability to make such a dramatic changes in her life and realize I would not be the young woman I am today without my mother, who has shown me that life spirals upward. I hope I can someday instill the same inspiration in my own children.

SAMPLE COLLEGE ESSAY THAT COLLEGES DO NOT WANT
Why Penn?

I have always had a longing for a business career since I was a little boy. My father's international franchises around Asia certainly initiated my motivation to become a global businessman. Then witnessing my grandfather's substantial enterprise of fossil fuel energy in Southeast Asia provoked my interest in becoming a monopolistic philanthropic tycoon when I become an adult. Seeing the World turn more homogenized every time I travel stirs my ambition for success in finance and corporate executive management. I acknowledge that if I am going to conquer the globalized market one day, I need to immerse myself in a multiracial diverse learning environment. The dynamic modern business world influences my passion and I see Penn as the quintessence of an academic social humanitarian institution that best fit my needs.

The coordinated-dual degree program I want to spend my undergraduate years in is at the Huntsman program. The Huntsman program allows me to master in my target language, which is an invaluable skill that will facilitate my growth after Penn. Furthermore, the Huntsman program gives me the opportunity to study abroad and have real experience with unique cultures. Grasping international studies will build my foundation for research of foreign countries with socioeconomic backgrounds and how the United States can improve its diplomatic relations with them. For instance, I am half Indonesian and a patriotic American and since Indonesia is the largest country with the heaviest Islamic population and I will hypothesize an approach for the United States to build a fruitful economic relationship Indonesia see the best possible future for both countries.

The Huntsman program is the best key to unlocking my potential by thoroughly challenging myself every day. I admire Penn's superior interdisciplinary foundation fostered by one of the greatest figures in American history. Penn's campus possesses a manifold of splendors that I will appreciate and enjoy. I believe I will find my niche in the Huntsman building or the College of Arts and Sciences.

Sample College Essay That Colleges Do Not Want

I admire the ideology of "true learning" at Penn and want to be exposed to the diversity in abstract opinions from each undergraduate classmate.

I am eager to be involved within the energetic Penn community. I will offer my services and school spirited enthusiasm to the admissions office by giving campus tours or participating in info sessions. I want to internationally and domestically represent Penn as an incredible university so that every high school graduate can consider applying and aspiring to be a proud protégés of Benjamin Franklin's philosophy. Moreover, I will perform community service to the greater Philadelphia area because I believe focusing and fixing local issues through volunteer work is more rewarding and pragmatic as a college student. Finally, I want to join the thespian society at Penn. Musicals, Dramas, and Comedies fascinate me and I want to be avidly involved with each production either on or off stage. I will sing for the University choir because I love to perform vocally. I know I will take part in a rich Performing Arts program incorporated with Community Service objectives and a passionate zeal for college life.

Penn has a diverse campus and I am a multiracial individual. The Huntsman program seeks selective students with global perspectives and fortunately I am a global veteran who has left distinct imprints on six continents. I want to experience and engage in Penn's cultured student body. Pick me because I want to stroll up and down Locust Walk with zest and salute the Benjamin Franklin monument. Choose me because I am an exceptional student and a cosmopolitan businessman in the making. Huntsman is my absolute number one choice because ultimately I am a Penn aficionado and I realized I could not fit anywhere else. So please give me Huntsman or give me Penn because I have an insatiable thirst for both.

resumes &
portfolios

HELPFUL HINTS FOR A COLLEGE RESUME

- If the college requests a certain form, you must follow the guidelines.

- Always list the most recent information first. Chronological order is required.

- Omit personal pronouns.

- Use action orientated short statements beginning with a verb to describe qualities, responsibilities, organization purposes, etc.

- Use a simple font and no less than size 10.

- One page is always best. Adjust the spacing and font so that the page is completely filled.

- Individualize your resume when possible.

- Spell and grammar check.

Please note:

To use this resume for a job, you must add your job objectives and list references. To use this resume for letters of recommendation, add your high school GPA and SAT scores.

Sample Resume

YOUR NAME
Address
City, State Zip
Phone
Email

EDUCATION

Beverly Hills High School   XXXXXX City College, City, California
Beverly Hills, California   Courses, Spring 20XX - Spring 20XX
September 2006 - June 2010

ACTIVITIES

ASB (Associated Student Body)   Beverly Hills High School   Senior
Position
- Point 1
- Point 2

Position   Beverly Hills High School   Junior
- Point 1
- Point 2

Sophomore President   Beverly Hills High School   Sophomore
- Point 1
- Point 2

Team Beverly Hills   Beverly Hills, California   Senior
Position
- Chosen from among a substantial applicant pool to represent the youth of Beverly Hills by adult community activities
- Work with Beverly Hills citizens under the coordination of the mayor
- Worked on make Beverly Hills GREEN Campaign

Teen BHEF (Beverly Hills Educational Foundation)   Beverly Hills, California   Sophomore-Present
Position
- Participant on the core committee to assist BHUSD to make and keep education levels high
- Raise money through planning district wide events
- Filter money back into the BHUSD school district
- Invited all incoming freshman to a dance

CASC (California Association of Student Councils)   Los Angeles, California   Sophomore-Present
Member; Region Nine Vice-President
- Organize region cabinet meetings to plan conferences
- Find appropriate space for meetings
- Market leadership conferences to Los Angeles schools and students so they have an opportunity to implement skills in their schools

SAMPLE RESUME

SPORTS

<u>Sport</u>   Beverly Hills High School   Sophomore-Present
Position
• <u>Point 1</u>

WORK EXPERIENCE

<u>Where</u>
•   What you did

<u>Where</u>
•   What you did

VOLUNTEER EXPERIENCE

<u>Name of Institution</u>   Location   Date (right justified)
Volunteer
•   Point 1
•   Point 2

ACADEMIC AWARDS

National Honors Society   Junior
Principals Honor Roll   Year(s)

PERFORMING & VISUAL ARTS

If you are a student with talent in the visual arts, music, dance or theater, you may want to include a sample of your ability to the various colleges to which you are applying. Consider the following in determining what you send:

• Does your Academy or private instructor believe your talent will win a favorable review from a particular college? Which pieces should be used to demonstrate your talent?

• Do you have the time and resources to present your talent in a format that is acceptable to the college (e.g. art in the form of slides not original canvas)?

• Contact each of your respective colleges to learn what supplemental materials they will accept and where to send them (i.e. the admissions office or the music department and/or both).

If you are planning to apply to a conservatory, art institute, or school devoted to the arts (e.g. Julliard or Museum of Fine Arts) or a school for the arts within a larger university (e.g. The Tisch School at NYU or Cornell's College of Architecture, Art and Planning), you should understand how your application will be evaluated. Ask each college:

• How much is your talent used in the decision-making process?

• How do they evaluate your talent (portfolio, audition, and tape)?

• Does each institution look for specific ingredients in talent? What does each college want to see in your portfolio or audition?

• For this year's applicant pool, is the college looking for one type of instrument more than another (e.g. harp players over violinist, or oil painters over graphic designers)?

• How do you make an audition appointment? Who does the actual evaluation? Are there regional auditions available? Can you send a tape?

After learning more about the evaluation process at each college, have a conversation with your college counselor, adviser, and Exeter teacher to determine which schools are a better match for you.

Music Auditions

High School students who wish to pursue a degree in music, whether it is vocal or instrumental, typically must audition. If you're a singer, prepare at least two pieces in contrasting styles. One should be in a foreign language, if possible. Choose from operatic, show music, or art song repertories, and make sure you memorize each piece. If you're an instrumentalist or pianist, be prepared to play scales and arpeggios, at least one etude or technical study, and a solo work. Instrumental audition pieces need not be memorized. In either field, you may be required to do sight- reading.

Performing & Visual Arts

Programs differ, so students are encouraged to call the college and ask for audition information. In general, music departments seek students who demonstrate technical competence and performance achievement.

Admission to music programs varies in degree of competitiveness, so you should audition at a minimum of three colleges and maximum of five to amplify your opportunity. The degree of competitiveness varies also by instrument, especially if a renowned musician teaches a certain instrument. Some colleges offer a second audition if you feel you did not audition to your potential. Ideally, you will be accepted into the music program of your choice, but keep in mind that it's possible to not be accepted. You must then make the decision to either pursue a music program at another college or consider another major at that college.

Dance Auditions

At many four-year colleges, an open class is held the day before auditions. A performance piece that combines improvisation, ballet, modern, and rhythm is taught and then students are expected to perform the piece at auditions. Professors look for coordination, technique, rhythm, degree of movement, and body structure. The dance faulty members also assess your ability to learn and your potential to complete the curriculum. Dance programs vary, so check with the college of your choice for specific information.

Theater Auditions

Most liberal arts colleges do not require that students who audition be accepted into the theater department unless the college offers a Bachelor of Fine Arts (B.F.A.) degree in theater. You should apply to the college of your choice prior to scheduling an audition. You should also consider spending a full day on campus so that you may talk with theater faculty members and students, attend classes, meet with your admission counselor, and tour the facilities.

Although each college and university has different requirements, you should prepare two contrasting monologues taken from plays of your choice if you're auditioning for a B.F.A. acting program. Musical theater requirements generally consist of one up-tempo musical selection and one ballad as well as one monologue from a play or musical of your choice. The total of all your pieces should not exceed 5 minutes. Music for the accompanist, a resume of your theater experience, and photo are also required.

Performing & Visual Arts

Visual Art Portfolios

A portfolio is simply a collection of your best pieces of artwork. The pieces you select to put in your portfolio should demonstrate your interest and aptitude for a serious education in the arts. A well-developed portfolio can help you gain acceptance into a prestigious art college and increase your chances of being awarded a scholarship in national portfolio competition. The pieces you select should show diversity in technique and variety in subject matter. You may show work in any medium (oils, photography, watercolors, pastels, etc.) and in either back-and-white or color. Your portfolio can include classroom assignments as well as independent projects. You can also include your sketchbook.

Specialized art colleges request that you submit an average of ten pieces of art, but remember that quality is more important than quantity. The admission office staff will review your artwork and transcripts to assess your skill and potential for success. Usually, you will present your portfolio in person; however, some schools allow students to mail slides if distance is an issue. There is no simple formula for success other than hard work. In addition there is no such thing as a "perfect portfolio," nor any specific style or direction to achieve one.

Tips for Organizing An Art Portfolio

- Try to make your portfolio as clean and organized as possible.

- It is important to protect your work, but make sure the package you select is easy to handle and does not interfere with the viewing of the artwork.

- Drawings that have been rolled up are difficult for the jurors to handle and view. You many shrink-wrap the pieces, but it is not required.

- Avoid loose sheets of paper between pieces.

- If you choose to mount or mat your work (not required), use only neutral gray tones, black or white.

- Never include framed pieces or three smudge

- A slide portfolio should be presented in a standard 8x11 plastic slide sleeve which can be purchased at any photo or camera supply store.

- Be sure paintings are completely dry before you place them in your portfolio.

- Label each piece with your name, address, and high school.

PERFORMING & VISUAL ARTS

Format

Some colleges may differ, but most will be looking for a selection of slides documenting your work, usually no more than 20 submitted in a slide file page. Each slide should be labeled with your name and a number which corresponds to a typed list accompanying your slide. The list should have a title for each slide, identification of the media, an indication of size, and a brief description of the project or work. You should also include a brief (half page, typed) artist's statement which describes your interests and investment in the visual arts. Other formats are possible and may in some cases be advisable depending on the scope and type of your work and the college you are considering. Consult the college counselors and your art teachers.

Procedure

Collect all of your work including sketchbooks, finished pieces, and things you may have done outside of your coursework in High School. You should start collecting your work in your sophomore or junior year. As soon as you start producing it, start keeping track of it. Contact a member of the Visual Arts Department to serve as your mentor for this process. Review your collected works with that faculty member considering which pieces may be most important and representative of your achievements. You should select about twice the number of pieces that you may finally include in your portfolio.

Arrange an appointment with a photographer. The photographer will charge either by the slide or by the time, so the more you ask the photographer to shoot, the more it will cost you. However, it is not always easy to identify which works will look best in slide format. It is best if you can arrange to be with the photographer, at least at the beginning of the session, in order to make clear what you want and to possibly help with the setup. It is your responsibility to be sure the portfolio is accessible to the photographer and is clearly defined as to what you want included. The photographer will arrange for obtaining film and for processing.

Once you have received the slides, arrange to meet with your faculty mentor once again, review the work, and make a selection which seems most appropriate. Your selection should be your choice, but take into account the suggestions offered by the faculty member as they help you to present your talents most effectively. Prepare your slides, the list, and your artist's statement. If you are submitting a portfolio to more than one college, you will need to have duplicates made which should be done once you have made your final selection.

Music Majors and the College Application

Colleges differ in what they require for a musical tape. If you intend to major in music, most colleges, universities, or conservatories will require an audition at their respective school. (If you do not intend to major in music but just wish to showcase past achievements, the tape is very important.) Please check carefully about each school's audition procedure. In most cases, auditions will take place in February or early March.

These are usually done at the school. The earlier you register, the better, as spaces will quickly fill up. The tape should be professionally recorded with high quality equipment. Make sure the equipment you use (i.e. tape recorder, microphones, cassettes) is the best quality available. Record the performance in the best acoustical surroundings. This may vary according to the instrument or voice. If you are unable to record this yourself, please ask a professional to do so. A badly recorded tape is worse than no tape at all.

Choose your pieces wisely. Play pieces that will show your talent in the best light. Highlight your strengths. Choose a variety of pieces to demonstrate different abilities. Pieces from different historical periods, pieces in differing tempi, dynamics, articulations, etc. are good choices. Do not make the tape too long. Leave them wanting more. If a piece has three movements, you may want to tape only one and then add an additional piece contrasting in style.

Send the tape to both the normal college admission office and also to the most appropriate member of that school's music department. Remember that in many cases in addition to selecting a school, you are selecting a teacher. If you are a string player, send the tape to the school's orchestra director or head of the string faculty; a vocalist to the choral director, etc. Enclose a letter and a resume outlining your past musical achievements. Follow this up with a phone call sometime later to that same member of the faculty.

Your resume should outline past musical achievements especially in your high school years. These may be both at your high school and outside of the school. List any awards, competitions, and/or titles you might have. List teachers with whom you have studied. List pieces that you have played or sung. Sometimes it may be a good idea to include programs or reviews of your work. Once again, keep your information brief. Highlights of your accomplishments are enough.

SAMPLE MUSIC RESUME

YOUR NAME
Address | City, State Zip | Phone | Email | Website

___

EDUCATION

Crossroads School for Arts & Science
1714 21st Street
Santa Monica, California
2009- Present

___

MUSICAL BACKGROUND

<u>Musical Recording</u>   November 2010
Solo Pianist
- Recording select pieces in a professional recording studio
- Pieces include: *Rondo Capriccioso* (Mendelssohn), *Prelude and Fugue #13 in f sharp major, BWV 858* (Bach), *Piano Sonata #17 in d minor, Opus 31 #2* (Beethoven)
- Plan to submit or various music festivals

<u>Private Master Instruction</u>   November 2010
Student
- Chosen by regular piano instructor to work with Max Levinson, Convert Pianist and Faculty Member at Boston Conservatory
- Opportunity included a thorough critique of my piano skills and methods for improvement

<u>Piano</u>   Los Angeles, CA   1999-present
Classical Pianist
- Dedicate at least 15 hours a week to practice
- Study under Robert Ward, Master Teacher, Professor of Music, Convert Pianist, Orchestra Conductor

<u>Alpha Walker</u>   Los Angeles, CA   April 2010-present
Assistant Instructor
- Graded music theory exams
- Train students to recognize music scales and intervals in preparation for *Certificate* of Merit exam
- Conducted "ear training" tests for younger students

<u>Chamber Music</u>   Crossroads School   March 2010- present
Student
- Rehearse twice a week in preparation for performance at the Bing Theatre at the Los Angeles County Museum of Art which is broadcast live on classical radio stations KUSC
- Receive coaching lessons from members of the Los Angeles Philharmonic and UCLA Professors of Music

<u>Multiple Performance/Recitals</u>   Los Angeles, California   1998- present
Performer
- Performed in Senior Assisted Home, Long Term Care Home, Senior Day Center

Sample Music Resume

Church Choir   Los Angeles, CA   2008- Present
Pianist
- Perform Ensemble during Sunday Service when asked

Pilgrim Community Orchestra   Los Angeles, CA   2009
Pianist
- Met weekly and rehearsed with amateur musicians

Sharing the Love Concert   Los Angeles, CA   December 2009
Performer
- Participated in a fundraising concert by playing the piano and doing Korean dance to help a 14 year old girl born with cerebral palsy
- Donated $3,000 I earned from babysitting and assisting my piano teacher in Music Theory classes
- Performed for 300 people
- Korean Daily News Performance Hall scheduling practices

Certificate of Merit Branch Honor Recital   2003-2009
Performer
- Classical Pianist

MUSICAL RECOGNITION

Competitons

Southwestern Youth Music Festival (SYMF)
First place winner, Baroque (2004, 2008)
First place winner, Contemporary (2003, 2007, 2008)
Third place winner, Baroque (2006)

Southern California Junior Bach Festival
Second place winner, "Italian Concerto" (2009)
First place winner, "Sinfonia and Invention" (2006)

Certificate of Merit
- Currently preparing for Level 10 evaluation sponsored by the Music Teacher's Association of California
- Earned Level 9 Certificate
- Tests in performance, technique, ear-training and sight reading skills, and understanding of music theory

SAMPLE FILM RESUME

NAME

Street Address, City, State, Zip   Phone Number

EDUCATION

Santa Monica High School, Santa Monica, California
High School Diploma, June 2005   GPA: 3.9

FILM EXPERIENCE

Cruise/Warner Productions   Los Angeles, California   Summer 2005
Intern
- Assist owner of production company with day to day operations
- Work on set

Running With Speakers   Santa Monica High School   Junior - Senior
Member
- Film school wide events, including the high school's version of "American Idol"
- Coordinate the sound, lights and music for events

"When You Say Nothing At All"   Summer 2005
Director, Writer, Editor, Actor, Location Scout, Casting Director, Costume Designer

"Legend of Bloody Mary" Trailer   October - December 2004
Director, Writer, Editor, Actor, Location Scout, Casting Director, Costume Designer
- Accepted into the Santa Monica Film Festival and Malibu Film Festival

"Above the Center" Trailer   April – June 2005
Director, Writer, Editor and Actor
- Developed trailer for a horror/science-fiction movie about the end of the world

Mock Oreo Commercial   May – June 2005
Director, Writer, Editor and Actor
- Produced mock commercial for entertainment

"Edward and Angelica"   December 2004 – January 2005
Writer and Actor
- Starred as both the main male and female characters in comedic film

"I Want to be a Cheerleader" Documentary   February 2005
Subject, Editor
- Utilized actual footage and created a documentary about a girl's quest to become a cheerleader

SAMPLE FILM RESUME

"Who Flew"   October 2004
Production Assistant
- Created scenery and sets for University of Southern California student film

"Acne Stick" Commercial   June 2005
Production Assistant
- Assisted production company on set by editing script and offering suggestions

ACTING EXPERIENCE

Hollywood Kids   August 2004 - present
Actor/Student
- Receive instruction on commercial preparation and auditioning

Lee Strausberg Acting Studio   West Hollywood, California   August 2003 – August 2004
Actor/Student
- Study scripts, analyze characters and learn acting and improvisation techniques

Center Stage Acting Studio   Los Angeles, California   August 2002 – 2004
Actor/Student
- Review scripts and study characters to commit to acting the characters out in scenes using improvisation techniques

"Halloween 9"   September 2004
Finalist
- Tried out and selected as a top 25 finalist for role in film

Santa Monica Playhouse   Santa Monica, California   Summer 2003
Actor
- Played lead of Chakra (joyful goddess) in play titled "Discord on a Sunday Afternoon"
- Developed character and monologues within the script framework

ACADEMIC AWARDS

Delian's	Santa Monica High School	Freshman, Sophomore, Junior
Honor Roll	Santa Monica High School	All semesters grades 9-11
History Day Award	Santa Monica High School	Junior
Creative Writing Award	Santa Monica High School	Sophomore

SAMPLE PORTFOLIO LIST

NAME | Street Address | City | State | Zip | Phone Number | Email

Summer 2010, "El Capitan," color DVD, 3 minutes 16 seconds.
Position: Writer, Director, and Editor.
Captain Morgan thwarts the attempts of student filmmakers who make films about banned subjects. Produced for New York Film Academy summer program four-week workshops. Chosen from among all student films to be showcased during orientation at all upcoming film programs.

Summer 2010, "Misunderstood Assistance," B&W DVD, 1 minute 45 seconds.
Position: Writer, Director, and Editor.
A youthful Darth Vader just wants to help others but the public cannot ignore his reputation as a villain and leaves him feeling alienated.

Summer 2010, "Minus the Joe," B&W DVD, 1 minute 20 seconds.
Position: Writer, Director, and Editor.
An exaggerated depiction on how we appear to the world without our cup o' Joe in the morning.

Summer 2010, "Perfect Stranger," B&W DVD, 2 minutes 14 seconds.
Position: Director of Photography/Cinematographer.
A woman is haunted by the crazy notion that her husband is a wanted killer, which happens to be the case.

Summer 2010, "Lucky Penny," B&W DVD, 1 minute 45 seconds.
Position: Director of Photography/Cinematographer.
A homeless man receives a penny that has magical powers.

Summer 2010, "The Proposal," B&W DVD, 1 minute 37 seconds.
Position: Assistant Camera.
A man proposes to his wife despite a humorous accident.

Summer 2010, "Lost Dreams," B&W DVD, 3 minutes 10 seconds.
Position: Assistant Camera.
A once enthusiastic volleyball star is crippled by an injury that leaves her grieving over her lost hobby.

Summer 2010, "Crossing Over," Color DVD, 4 minutes.
Position: Assistant Camera.
A homosexual teen contemplates whether to approach a man on the street, considering his parents' distain.

interviews &
recommendations

THE COLLEGE INTERVIEW

THE INTERVIEW

The interview serves two purposes. It reinforces your interest in a particular institution and it is an opportunity for the admission staff to clarify the match between their school's offerings and your interests and abilities. Every school treats interviews differently, so it is important to read their literature closely and determine where and when to interview. Your college counselor will guide you.

TYPES OF INTERVIEWS

Personal Interviews

These usually take place on the college campus and are held with a representative of the admission office. The conversation usually last about 30 minutes. Parents are generally not included in the initial conversation but will be approached afterwards to see if they have any questions.

Alumni/ae Interviews

When students are not able to travel to campus for an interview, the university may offer students the chance to interview with an alumnus/a in the student's home area. The local alumni/ae chapter of the university works with the admission office to arrange the interviews. Some universities may ask students to put their request in writing, and other universities will automatically contact you once you have sent in your application. Be sure to check the application materials or call admission offices directly to see about arranging alumni/ae interviews. Alumni/ae interviews are given the same weight as on-campus interviews in the admission process.

Always thank the interviewer in writing for his/her time. In your brief note, you may want to mention one of the topics brought up during your session so that you are certain he/she will recall just who this polite young man or woman is!

Some questions you might be asked during an interview

- What courses have you taken? Why?
- What books did you read this past summer and why did you like them?
- What is your intended program of study?
- What magazines do you regularly read?
- What are your career plans?
- Why are you interested in our school?
- What do you spend your free time doing?
- What is your major extra-curricular interest?
- What do you like about your high school?
- What would you change about your high school?
- What do you think you will contribute to this college environment?

INTERVIEW POLICIES FROM SELECT COLLEGES

Yale is the only Ivy that offers on-campus EVALUATIVE interviews.

Harvard offers on-campus interviews, but they are not added to a student's file.

Neither Stanford nor MIT offers on-campus interviews. However, Stanford plans to offer alumni interviews starting with the 2011-2012 college admissions season.

Columbia and Penn allow legacies (and they count parents OR grandparents as legacies in this sense) to interview on campus.

Brown

Alumni interviews recommended, but not required. Once your application is received, alumni in your area will contact you. If you do want an interview set up the time and place at that point. This applies to international applicants where possible too. No on-campus interviews.

California Institute of Technology

No interviews.

Columbia University

Interviews are not required. Between October and February, a member of Columbia's Alumni Representative Committee will contact you if an interview is available in the area where your high school is located. If you are a legacy you can arrange an on-campus interview. Columbia does not count all graduate schools into the legacy pool. Please note: only the children of Columbia College or the Fu Foundation School of Engineering and Applied Science graduates are considered legacy.

Cornell

Cornell can get sort of confusing because you're applying to a particular college. The College of Agriculture and Life Sciences does not require an interview. The College of Hotel Administration required an interview either on or off-campus. The College of Architecture, Art, and Planning, for architecture requires applicants to interview either on- or off-campus. For art students, an interview is recommended. For College of Arts and Sciences, College of Engineering, College of Human Ecology, and the College of Industrial and Labor Relations, no interviews required. The deadline for interviews for early decision applicants is November 10 and for regular decision is January 31.

Dartmouth

Dartmouth discontinued on-campus interviews in 2007 and now offer off-campus alumni interview. Early decision applicants interview between October and mid-November. Regular applicants interview from December to mid-February.

Interview Policies from Select Colleges

Duke

Interviews are optional. To be eligible for an interview with a Duke alumnus, submit the Student Supplement (Form A) by October 20 for early decision applicants and December 10 for regular applicants.

Georgetown

Interviews with an alumnus are required, unless it's geographically not possible. When your application is received, the Admissions Office will send you the contact information for the alumni interviewer in your area.

Harvard

When and where possible an alumni interview will be arranged. The alumni interviewer will contact you via phone, email, or letter.

MIT

Interview is not required, but strongly recommended. If an interview can be offered to you, the name and contact information for your Educational Counselor who conducts the interview will be in your MyMIT account. For early action, October 20 is the last day to contact the Educational Counselor to set up the interview and November 1 is the last day to have an interview. For regular applicants, December 1 is last day to schedule an interview and December 15 is the last day to have it.

Northwestern

Interviews, which are conducted by alumni, are optional.

NYU

No interviews offered.

Princeton

An alumni interviewer contacts applicants as they receive applications. Interviews are not required, but the school recommends that students accept the invitation for an interview if you get one. Princeton does not offer on-campus interviews.

INTERVIEW POLICIES FROM SELECT COLLEGES

Rice University

Interviews are recommended, but not required. Applicants can choose an on-campus interview with a Rice Senior Interviewer up until December 9. Alternatively, applicants may choose an off-campus interview with an alumnus. Early applicants should request an interview by October 15, complete it by November 1. For interim applicants, request by November 15 and complete by December 11. For regular applicants, request by December 18 and complete by January 22.

Stanford

Interviews are optional. All applicants could be offered an optional alumni interview starting 2011. The dean of undergraduate admission and financial aid indicated that alumni interviews "add texture" to the applicants' portfolios. In about 10% of the cases, the report of the alumni interviewer influenced the decision one way or another.

University of California

No interviews offered at any of the UC campuses.

University of Pennsylvania

Interviews are optional. On-campus interviews are reserved for the children or grandchild of an alumnus; contact the Alumni Council for an interview appointment. For everyone else, off-campus Secondary School Committees contact prospective students after receiving the application. Early decision interviews are conducted between November 1 and December 1. For regular applicants, interviews take place during January and February.

Washington University in Saint Louis

Interviews are encouraged, but not required.

Yale

Interviews are not required, but if an alumnus contacts you then the school strongly encourages to accept. A member of the alumni committee will contact you after you submit your Yale application in the event they can offer you an interview.

RECOMMENDATIONS

Helpful Guidelines

1. Once you have decided whom to ask to write you recommendations, make an appointment with these teachers. Tell them your college choices and what you think is important to convey about you in the recommendation. Always ask if there is anything else he/she needs from you to write an effective recommendation.

2. Don't necessarily choose the teacher with whom you achieve the highest grades. Sometimes teachers in a class where you had to struggle for that "B" can expound more profoundly on your determination to solve a tough problem, on your leadership skills in the class, or your willingness to give it your all. It's often wiser to ask someone who is more familiar with your personal qualities than your GPA.

3. Ask the same two teachers to write all your recommendations. Advise them regarding how many forms they should expect.

4. Some candidates may also wish to have a person outside of school send letters of recommendation to admissions offices. These recommendations should be chosen carefully. Sometimes too many recommendations hinder rather than help an applicant's chances. In most cases, an outside recommendation is useful only if the person writing it knows something about the applicant that is not reflected in the school reports (e.g., special interests developed outside of school)

5. Give the recommender supplemental information (résumé, brag sheet) along with the recommendation form. Any extra info the writer has about you will enable her to write a more thorough letter on your behalf.

6. Always give teachers a minimum of two weeks' before the postmark date to complete the recommendation.

7. If the writer is to send your letter separately, provide a stamped, addressed envelope with a note attached listing a deadline for mailing that is at least twelve days before the application deadline. Politely check with the writer to be certain your letter was mailed (How's my letter coming? Do you need any more information?).

8. Write a brief thank-you note to the writer.

RECOMMENDATIONS

sample letter for to send to your recommender

Dear [teacher name],

I hope you are enjoying a fabulous summer. As I mentioned before school got out, I would very much appreciate it if you could write a letter of recommendation on my behalf for college. I have started my preliminary list of colleges that I am considering, but I have not yet finalized the list.

I am asking you to write my recommendation because I feel that you have a strong grasp of me, both as a student and a person. As you know, I struggled in your class but never hesitated to ask questions, and with your help I achieved A's both semesters. As I reflect on the year, a recall a few examples that I believe (and hope you agree) show that I stand out as a student.

First, when I needed to leave early for winter break [WHY DID YOU LEAVE EARLY? YOU SHOULD REMIND HIM], I came the week prior to my departure early every morning so I could learn the material I would have miss. I did not ignore my responsibility as a student, but instead pro-actively insured that I knew the material before I left.

Also, almost daily I approached you with several problems that I could not solve the previous night and asked for additional help. [TELL WHY YOU THINK THIS MAKES YOU STAND OUT]

Aside from my effort in your class, you also witnessed my involvement in other school activities from sports to ASB elections. [GIVE EXAMPLES]

As I prepare for my final year in high school, I am organizing myself and application so that I can start the year off strong. Therefore, I would appreciate it if you could let me know if you are comfortable writing a college recommendation on my behalf. I know the school year will start off in full swing, so if you are willing to write one for me, I plan to offer you the courtesy of having all my forms to you during the first week of school.

I look forward to hearing from you.

Thank you,

[student name]

california
colleges

HIGHER EDUCATION IN CALIFORNIA

COMMUNITY COLLEGE

Open admissions to any high school graduate or student over the age of 18. The community colleges serve three functions:
- To serve the community by providing technical education in programs such as Horticulture, Welding and Child Care.
- To provide general education (GE) classed in preparation for transfer to California State University (CSU) or the University of California (UC).
- CSU and UC give priority to community college transfer applicants.

CALIFORNIA STATE UNIVERSITY (applications accepted from October 1 through November 30)

- Designed to admit the top 30% of California high school graduates and community college transfers.
- Offers Bachelors and Masters degrees.
- Twenty-three campuses and nine off-campus center from Arcata to San Diego.
- ONLY online applications are accepted at www.csumentor.edu.

ADMISSION IS BASED ON
- High school graduation.
- Completion, with grades C- or better, of each of the UC/CSU approved courses in a comprehensive pattern of college prep subject requirements.
- A qualifying index, based on GPA (10th and 11th grades) and SAT or ACT scores.

UNIVERSITY OF CALIFORNIA (applications due November 1-20)

- Designed to admit the top 12% of California high school graduates and community college transfers.
- Offers Bachelors, Masters and Doctoral degrees.
- Eight campuses.
- ONLY online applications accepted at www.ucop.edu/pathways.

ADMISSION IS BASED ON
- A combination of academic criteria and comprehensive review of extracurricular activities, talents and special circumstances, low income, and the essay.
- GPA based on 10th and 11th grades in IC approved classes in specified subject areas (15 units).
- SAT or ACT scores.
- Number and content of classes completed beyond minimum.
- AP/Honors courses.
- Quality of the senior program.

CALIFORNIA COMMUNITY COLLEGES

Allan Hancock College
American River College
Antelope Valley College
Bakersfield College
Barstow Community College
Berkeley City College
Butte College
Cabrillo College
Canada College
Cerritos College
Cerro Coso Community College
Chabot College
Chaffey College
Citrus College
City College of San Francisco
Coastline Community College
College of Alameda
College of Marin
College of San Mateo
College of the Canyons
College of the Desert
College of the Redwoods
College of the Sequoias
College of the Siskiyous
Columbia College
Compton Community Education Center
Contra Costa College
Copper Mountain College
Cosumnes River College
Crafton Hills College
Cuesta College
Cuyamaca College
Cypress College
De Anza College
Diablo Valley College
East Los Angeles College
El Camino College
Evergreen Valley College
Feather River College
Folsom Lake College
Foothill College
Fresno City College
Fullerton College
Gavilan College
Glendale Community College
Golden West College
Grossmont College
Hartnell College
Imperial Valley College
Irvine Valley College

Lake Tahoe Community College
Laney College
Las Positas College
Lassen Community College
Long Beach City College
Los Angeles City College
Los Angeles Harbor College
Los Angeles Mission College
Los Angeles Southwest College
Los Angeles Trade-Technical College
Los Angeles Valley College
Los Medanos College
Mendocino College
Merced College
Merritt College
MiraCosta College
Mission College
Modesto Junior College
Monterey Peninsula College
Moorpark College
Moreno Valley College
Mt. San Antonio College
Mt. San Jacinto College
Napa Valley College
Norco College
Ohlone College
Orange Coast College
Oxnard College
Palo Verde College
Palomar College
Pasadena City College
Pierce College
Porterville College
Reedley College
Rio Hondo College
Riverside City College
Sacramento City College
Saddleback College
San Bernardino Valley College
San Diego City College
San Diego Mesa College
San Diego Miramar College
San Joaquin Delta College
San Jose City College
Santa Ana College
Santa Barbara City College
Santa Monica College
Santa Rosa Junior College
Santiago Canyon College
Shasta College

CALIFORNIA COMMUNITY COLLEGES

Sierra College
Skyline College
Solano Community College
Southwestern College
Taft College
Ventura College
Victor Valley College
West Hills College - Coalinga
West Hills College - Lemoore
West Los Angeles College
West Valley College
Woodland Community College
Yuba College

CALIFORNIA STATE UNIVERSITIES

The California State University provides high-quality, affordable higher education to meet the changing workforce needs of California, making the CSU indispensable to California's economic prosperity and diverse communities.

The California State University:
- Is the nation's largest university system.
- Has 23 campuses and nine off-campus centers.
- Educates over 412,000 students.
- Employs 43,000 faculty and staff.
- Stretches from Humboldt in the north to San Diego in the south.
- Is renowned for the quality of its teaching and preparing job-ready graduates.

California State University Locations

California Maritime Academy, (Vallejo)
California Polytechnic State University, (San Luis Obispo)
California State Polytechnic University, Pomona, (Pomona)
California State University, Bakersfield, (Bakersfield)
California State University, Channel Islands, (Camarillo)
California State University, Chico, (Chico)
California State University, Dominguez Hills, (Carson)
California State University, East Bay, (Hayward)
California State University, Fresno, (Fresno)
California State University, Fullerton, (Fullerton)
California State University, Long Beach, (Long Beach)
California State University, Los Angeles, (Los Angeles)
California State University, Monterey Bay, (Seaside)
California State University, Northridge, (Northridge)
California State University, Sacramento, (Sacramento)
California State University, San Bernardino, (San Bernardino)
California State University, San Marcos, (San Marcos)
California State University, Stanislaus, (Turlock)
Humboldt State University, (Arcata)
San Diego State University, (San Diego)
San Francisco State University, San Francisco
San Jose State University, (San Jose)
Sonoma State University, (Rohnert Park)

CALIFORNIA STATE UNIVERSITIES

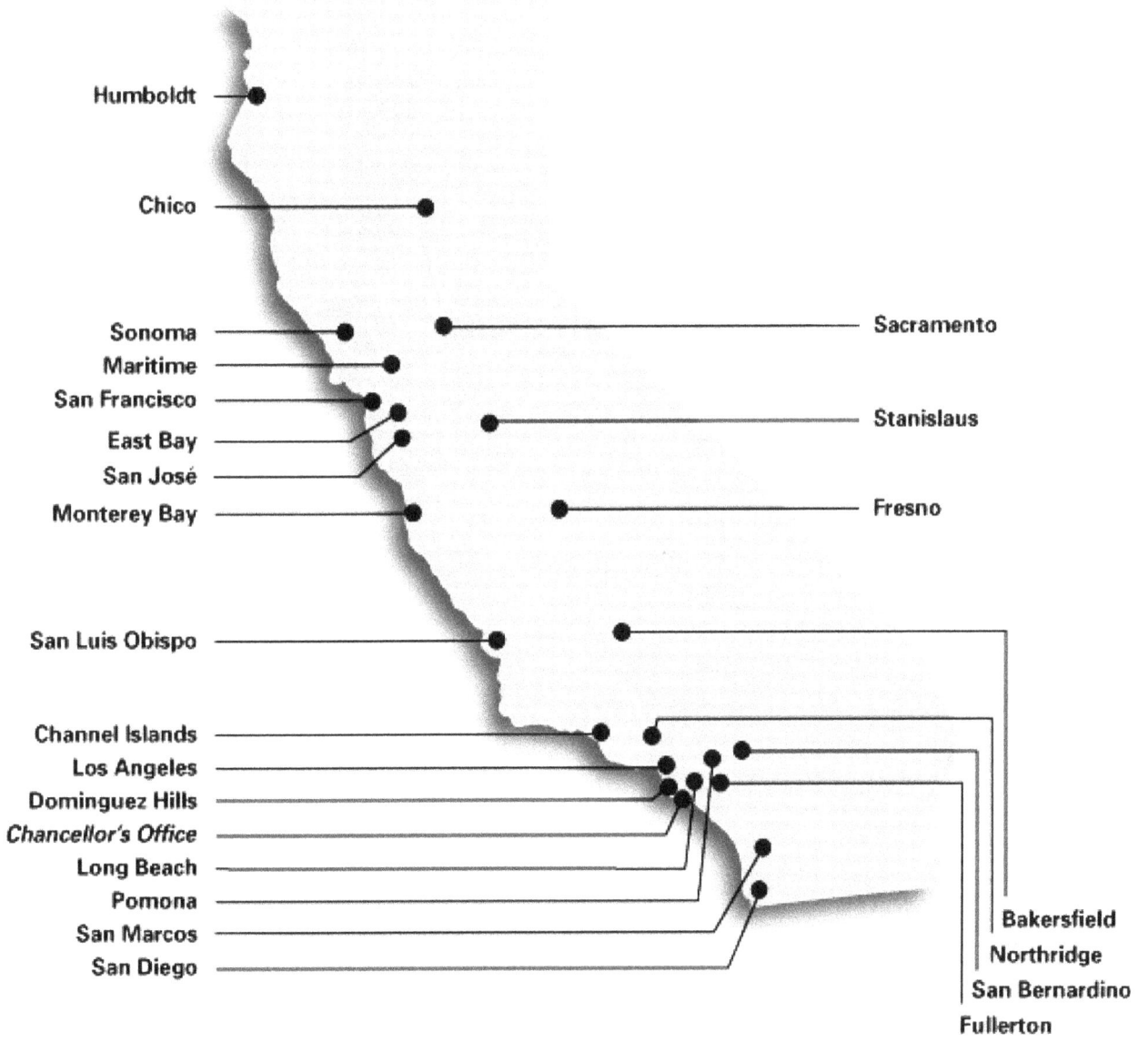

Humboldt

Chico

Sonoma

Maritime

San Francisco

East Bay

San José

Monterey Bay

Sacramento

Stanislaus

Fresno

San Luis Obispo

Channel Islands

Los Angeles

Dominguez Hills

Chancellor's Office

Long Beach

Pomona

San Marcos

San Diego

Bakersfield

Northridge

San Bernardino

Fullerton

CALIFORNIA STATE UNIVERSITY ELIGIBILITY INDEX

GPA	ACT Score	SAT Score	GPA	ACT Score	SAT Score	GPA	ACT Score	SAT Score
			3.0 and above qualifies for any score			*Below 2.0 does not qualify*		
2.99	10	510	2.66	17	780	2.33	23	1040
2.98	10	520	2.65	17	780	2.32	23	1050
2.97	10	530	2.64	17	790	2.31	24	1060
2.96	11	540	2.63	17	800	2.30	24	1060
2.95	11	540	2.62	17	810	2.29	24	1070
2.94	11	550	2.61	18	820	2.28	24	1080
2.93	11	560	2.60	18	820	2.27	24	1090
2.92	11	570	2.59	18	830	2.26	25	1100
2.91	12	580	2.58	18	840	2.25	25	1100
2.90	12	580	2.57	18	850	2.24	25	1110
2.89	12	590	2.56	18	860	2.23	25	1120
2.88	12	600	2.55	19	860	2.22	25	1130
2.87	12	610	2.54	19	870	2.21	26	1140
2.86	13	620	2.53	19	880	2.20	26	1140
2.85	13	620	2.52	19	890	2.19	26	1150
2.84	13	630	2.51	20	900	2.18	26	1160
2.83	13	640	2.50	20	900	2.17	26	1170
2.82	13	650	2.49	20	910	2.16	27	1180
2.81	14	660	2.48	20	920	2.15	27	1180
2.80	14	660	2.47	20	930	2.14	27	1190
2.79	14	670	2.46	21	940	2.13	27	1200
2.78	14	680	2.45	21	940	2.12	27	1210
2.77	14	690	2.44	21	950	2.11	28	1220
2.76	15	700	2.43	21	960	2.10	28	1220
2.75	15	700	2.42	21	970	2.09	28	1230
2.74	15	710	2.41	22	980	2.08	28	1240
2.73	15	720	2.40	22	980	2.07	28	1250
2.72	15	730	2.39	22	990	2.06	29	1260
2.71	16	740	2.38	22	1000	2.05	29	1260
2.70	16	740	2.37	22	1010	2.04	29	1270
2.69	16	750	2.36	23	1020	2.03	29	1280
2.68	16	760	2.35	23	1020	2.02	29	1290
2.67	16	770	2.34	23	1030	2.01	30	1300
						2.00	30	1300

California State University Acceptance & Enrollment Rates

Campus	Total Freshman Applications	Total Freshman Accepted	Acceptance Rate	Total Freshman Enrolled	Enrollment Rate
California Maritime Academy	587	457	77.85%	150	32.82%
California Polytechnic State University-San Luis Obispo	31,489	11,737	37.27%	3,847	32.78%
California State Polytechnic University-Pomona	20,759	12,731	61.33%	2,913	22.88%
CSU-Bakersfield	4,353	3,111	71.47%	1,063	34.17%
CSU-Channel Islands	5,202	3,534	67.94%	499	14.12%
CSU-Chico	13,885	11,298	81.37%	2,505	22.17%
CSU-Dominguez Hills	9,728	5,737	58.97%	1,135	19.78%
CSU-East Bay	8,712	6,387	73.31%	1,445	22.62%
CSU-Fresno	14,025	10,090	71.94%	2,764	27.39%
CSU-Fullerton	30,612	16,865	55.09%	4,065	24.10%
CSU-Long Beach	45,782	14,543	31.77%	3,551	24.42%
CSU-Los Angeles	21,394	14,382	67.22%	2,019	14.04%
CSU-Monterey Bay	9,938	8,099	81.5%	949	11.72%
CSU-Northridge	20,657	14,984	72.54%	4,203	28.05%
CSU-Sacramento	16,535	13,301	80.44%	3,076	23.13%
CSU-San Marcos	9,735	6,953	71.42%	1,567	22.54%
CSU-Stanislaus	4,421	1,618	36.6%	966	59.7%
Humboldt State University	9,427	7,924	84.06%	1,387	17.5%
San Diego State University	41,861	15,223	36.37%	4,223	27.74%
San Francisco State University	28,263	20,465	72.41%	4,032	19.7%
San Jose State University	21,833	16,250	74.43%	2,764	17.01%
Sonoma State University	11,245	8,690	77.28%	1,488	17.12%

UNIVERSITY OF CALIFORNIA MAP

UC Davis

UC Berkeley

UC San Francisco

UC Merced

UC Santa Cruz

UC Santa Barbara

UC Riverside

UC Los Angeles

UC Irvine

UC San Diego

University of California Admission Policies

U.C.'s Freshman Admission Requirements for Fall 2012

All California high school seniors who fulfill the following three requirements will be entitled to a comprehensive review of their applications at each UC campus to which they apply. They must:

- ✓ Complete 15 UC required college-preparatory (a-g) courses, with 11 completed prior to the start of 12th grade

- ✓ Maintain a GPA of 3.0 or better (weighted by honors/AP bonus points) in these courses

- ✓ Take the ACT with Writing or SAT Reasoning Test

Students' qualifications will be assessed using campus-based review processes, which emphasize academic achievement but also account for a wide range of personal accomplishments and educational contexts.

Differences between the pre-2012 policies & 2012 policies

Fundamentally, the new policy will not change the way students prepare for UC. Students will still need to complete the same number of "a-g" courses and earn the same minimum GPA.

1. Two SAT Subject Tests will no longer be required for admission. However, students can still choose to submit their scores for consideration as part of their application, just as they do now with AP and IB scores. The Subject Tests may also be recommended for certain majors.

2. The share of students who are guaranteed admission based on their rank in their own high school class will grow (9 percent versus 4 percent).

3. Fewer students overall will receive an admission guarantee (10 percent of high school graduates vs. 12.5 percent now), but nearly all students who would have received this guarantee under current policy will be entitled to a full review by their campuses of choice under the new policy.

4. Under the new policy, students who become eligible by examination will not be guaranteed admission. They will, however, be entitled to a full review of their application. Students who take this path must complete two SAT Subject Tests in two different subject area

SAT Subject Tests

SAT Subject Tests will no longer be required for admission. Students may submit scores if they wish to showcase academic mastery, just as scores on Advanced Placement and International Baccalaureate tests show ability and subject mastery.

University of California - Eligibility

State Wide Context

To determine whether California students rank in the top 9 percent statewide, the University uses an admissions index.

Local Context

The University will identify the top 9 percent of students in each participating high school on the basis of GPA for all UC approved coursework completed in grades 10 and 11. Students must submit UC undergraduate application during the filing period and complete remaining requirements as noted above.

Qualifying by Examination

Under the new policy, students who qualify for admission by examination will not be guaranteed admission. They will, however, be entitled to a full review of their application.

Students who take this path must complete two SAT Subject Tests in two different subject areas. Students must achieve a minimum UC Score Total of 410 and a minimum UC Score of 63 on each component of the ACT or SAT Reasoning Test and on each of two SAT Subject Tests.

Non-Resident Applicants

Nonresident applicants must meet the same requirements as California-resident students but with a minimum GPA of 3.4. Nonresidents are not guaranteed admission.

Who receives guaranteed admission

Within this pool of applicants, two categories of students will be guaranteed admission somewhere in the UC system:

- ✓ Those who fall in the top 9 percent of all high school graduates statewide

- ✓ Those who rank in the top 9 percent of their own high school graduating class

Freshman applicants deemed to be in one of these groups who are not admitted to any campus where they apply will be offered admission at a campus with available space.

Students must complete the University's course and test-taking requirements by the end of their senior year in high school to be considered fully qualified to enroll.

ELIGIBILITY IN THE LOCAL CONTEXT

California Students

If you're a state resident who has met the minimum requirements and aren't admitted to any UC campus to which you apply, you'll be offered a spot at another campus if space is available, provided:

- You rank in the top 9% of California high school students, according to our admissions index, or
- You rank in the top 9% percent of your graduating class at a participating high school. We refer to this as "Eligible in the Local Context" (ELC).

The UC uses an admissions index to determine if a student falls in the top 9% of California high school graduates. If you do and you're not admitted to any UC campus to which you apply, you'll be offered a spot at another campus if space is available.

Here's how to calculate if you'll be in the top 9 percent:

(1) Calculate your grade point average (GPA)

- Convert the grades earned in all college-preparatory courses ("a-g" courses) taken in 10th and 11th grades, including summer sessions: A=4, B=3, C=2, D=1. (Pluses and minuses don't count.)

- Give yourself an extra point for each honors-level course, up to eight semesters.
  Honors courses are Advanced Placement courses, Higher Level and designated Standard Level International Baccalaureate courses, transferable community college courses and UC certified honors courses that appear on your school's course list. A grade of D in an honors course does not earn an extra point. No more than two yearlong UC approved honors-level courses taken in the 10th grade may be given extra points.

(2) Convert your test scores to a UC Score total

 If you take the ACT With Writing exam:

Use your highest ACT composite and combined English with writing scores from a single sitting. (That means if you take the test more than once, you can't use the composite score from one exam and the English with writing score from another.)

Find your composite score on the conversion table below and note the corresponding UC Score. Find your English with writing score on the table and note the corresponding UC Score.

Your UC Score from the ACT composite may meet the minimum, but you also need to take the English with writing test. Add the two UC Scores together to get your UC Score total.

UNIVERSITY OF CALIFORNIA ACT TEST SCORE TRANSLATION

Composite	UC Score	English with writing	UC Score
36	200	36	100
35	196	35	100
34	191	34	97
33	186	33	94
32	182	32	92
31	178	31	89
30	174	30	87
29	170	29	85
28	166	28	83
27	162	27	81
26	159	26	79
25	155	25	77
24	151	24	75
23	147	23	73
22	143	22	71
21	139	21	69
20	135	20	67
19	131	19	65
18	127	18	63
17	123	17	62
16	119	16	60
15	114	15	58
14	109	14	56
13	104	13	54
12	99	12	53
11	93	11	51
10	89	10	49
9	86	9	47
8	84	8	45
7	82	7	43
1 to 6	80	1 to 6	40

UNIVERSITY OF CALIFORNIA SAT TEST SCORE TRANSLATION

Critical Reading + Math	UC Score	Critical Reading + Math	UC Score	Writing	UC Score
1600	200	990	139	800	100
1590	199	980	138	790	99
1580	198	970	137	780	98
1570	197	960	136	770	97
1560	196	950	135	760	96
1550	195	940	134	750	95
1540	194	930	133	740	94
1530	193	920	132	730	93
1520	192	910	131	720	92
1510	191	900	130	710	91
1500	190	890	129	700	90
1490	189	880	128	690	89
1480	188	870	127	680	88
1470	187	860	126	670	87
1460	186	850	125	660	86
1450	185	840	124	650	85
1440	184	830	123	640	84
1430	183	820	122	630	83
1420	182	810	121	620	82
1410	181	800	120	610	81
1400	180	790	119	600	80
1390	179	780	118	590	79
1380	178	770	117	580	78
1370	177	760	116	570	77
1360	176	750	115	560	76
1350	175	740	114	550	75
1340	174	730	113	540	74
1330	173	720	112	530	73
1320	172	710	111	520	72
1310	171	700	110	510	71

UNIVERSITY OF CALIFORNIA SAT TEST SCORE TRANSLATION

Critical Reading + Math	UC Score	Critical Reading + Math	UC Score	Writing	UC Score
1290	169	680	108	490	69
1280	168	670	107	480	68
1270	167	660	106	470	67
1260	166	650	105	460	66
1250	165	640	104	450	65
1240	164	630	103	440	64
1230	163	620	102	430	63
1220	162	610	101	420	62
1210	161	600	100	410	61
1200	160	590	99	400	60
1190	159	580	98	390	59
1180	158	570	97	380	58
1170	157	560	96	370	57
1160	156	550	95	360	56
1150	155	540	94	350	55
1140	154	530	93	340	54
1130	153	520	92	330	53
1120	152	510	91	320	52
1110	151	500	90	310	51
1100	150	490	89	300	50
1090	149	480	88	290	49
1080	148	470	87	280	48
1070	147	460	86	270	47
1060	146	450	85	260	46
1050	145	440	84	250	45
1040	144	430	83	240	44
1030	143	420	82	230	43
1020	142	410	81	220	42
1010	141	400	80	210	41
1000	140			200	40

University of California Required Courses

Coursework Requirements

Freshman applicants will be required to complete a minimum of 15 yearlong "a-g" courses in grades 9–12, as they are now. Seven of these courses must be taken in the last two years of high school.

Eleven of the 15 required courses must be completed by the end of 11th grade in order for applicants to receive a review of their application. No particular course pat-tern is required to apply for admission. Courses completed in the summer after 11th grade will be counted.

To be considered for a guarantee in the local context, students must complete 11 specific year long courses by the end of junior year (including summer): one year of history/social science, two years of English, two years of mathematics, one year of laboratory science, one year of language other than English and four courses selected from among the "a-g" subject requirements.

All applicants should be reminded that admission to the University of California is competitive, and most applicants present more than the minimum requirements when applying for admission. For example, students who were offered admission for the fall 2010 term completed, on average, 23 year-long courses, or nearly six academic courses per year.

Applicants present more than the minimum requirements when applying for admission. For example, students who were offered admission for the fall 2010 term completed, on average, 23 year-long courses, or nearly six academic courses per year.

Following is the minimum expected coursework for each UC applicant:

  a. History/social science: 2 years

  b. English: 4 years

  c. Mathematics: 3 years

  d. Laboratory science: 2 years

  e. Language other than English: 2 years

  f. Visual and performing arts: 1 year

  g. College-preparatory elective: 1 year
     (chosen from the subjects listed above or another course approved by the university)

Earn a grade point average (GPA) of 3.0 or better (3.4 if you're a nonresident) in these courses with no grade lower than a C.

University of California Acceptance & Enrollment Rates

Campus	Total Freshman	Total Freshman Accepted		Total Freshman Enrolled	Enrollment Rate
UC Berkeley	48,682	10,524	21.62%	4,356	41.39%
UC Davis	42,388	20,078	47.37%	4,414	21.98%
UC Irvine	44,126	19,482	44.15%	4,030	20.69%
UC Los Angeles	55,694	12,178	21.87%	4,472	36.72%
UC Merced	20,851	19,044	91.33%	1,127	5.92%
UC Riverside	31,884	26,707	83.76%	4,299	16.1%
UC San Diego	47,060	17,042	36.21%	3,749	22%
UC Santa Barbara	44,736	21,539	48.15%	4,587	21.3%
UC Santa Cruz	27,247	17,316	63.55%	3,215	18.57%

UNIVERSITY OF CALIFORNIA, BERKELEY, ADMISSIONS STATS FALL 2010

Admit Rate

By Percentage (Admits/Applicants) GPA range

GPA range	Admit Rate
4.00 and above	50.9% (11,099/21,826)
3.70–3.99	9.7% (1,217/12,556)
3.30–3.69	3.1% (293/9,586)
3.00–3.29	1.8% (57/3,159)
below 3.00	2.7% (46/1,683)

act composite range

31–36	48.1% (2,752/5,722)
26–30	21.4% (1,452/6,777)
21–25	12.9% (485/3,758)
16–20	8.4% (108/1,279)
below 16	3.4% (7/208)

sat critical reading range

700–800	55.5% (5,140/9,253)
600–690	27.7% (4,841/17,447)
500–590	13.5% (1,678/12,390)
400–490	7.7% (412/5,339)
below 400	2.6% (28/1,061)

sat mathematics range

700–800	42.3% (7,164/16,941)
600–690	22.1% (3,473/15,700)
500–590	13.3% (1,158/8,734)
400–490	8.3% (279/3,360)
below 400	3.3% (25/755)

sat writing range

700–800	53.0% (6,327/11,928)
600–690	24.3% (4,050/16,645)
500–590	12.2% (1,386/11,375)
400–490	6.7% (313/4,662)
below 400	2.6% (23/880)

admit rate 25.8%

Admits	13,024
Applicants	50,385

25.8%

ELC Student Admit Rate	59.1%
California Residents	73.3%
(% of admits)	

AVERAGES

High School GPA	4.15
ACT Composite Score	30
SAT Critical Reading	672
SAT Mathematics	700
SAT Writing	688

"a-g" courses completed (7th–12th grades, by semester)

50+	32.2% (5,592/17,345)
40–49	21.4% (4,519/21,127)
30–39	10.6% (295/2,790)
	11.1% (12/108)

honors courses completed (10th–12th grades, by semester)

15+	38.7% (8,118/20,999)
10–14	13.6% (1,370/10,049)
5–9	6.8% (335/4,935)
	5.3% (132/2,489)

University of California, Davis, Admissions Stats Fall 2010

Admit Rate

By Percentage (Admits/Applicants) GPA range

4.00 and above	86.4% (11,984/13,866)
3.70–3.99	47.5% (5,044/10,627)
3.30–3.69	21.8% (2,516/11,555)
3.00–3.29	7.2% (326/4,541)
below 3.00	1.8% (40/2,255)

act composite range

31–36	82.2% (2,561/3,116)
26–30	52.3% (3,302/6,313)
21–25	32.9% (1,520/4,620)
16–20	25.3% (427/1,686)
below 16	12.3% (34/277)

sat critical reading range

700–800	84.8% (3,923/4,626)
600–690	61.9% (8,011/12,934)
500–590	36.8% (4,916/13,375)
400–490	25.8% (1,754/6,808)
below 400	14.2% (204/1,434)

sat mathematics range

700–800	76.1% (6,790/8,922)
600–690	52.2% (7,661/14,682)
500–590	31.7% (3,298/10,391)
400–490	22.6% (968/4,286)
below 400	10.2% (91/896)

sat writing range

700–800	84.0% (4,978/5,924)
600–690	58.0% (7,559/13,042)
500–590	35.8% (4,619/12,903)
400–490	24.4% (1,489/6,101)
below 400	13.5% (163/1,207)

admit rate **46.4%**

Admits	20,116
Applicants	43,324

ELC Student Admit Rate	99.0%
California Residents	91.5%
(% of admits)	

AVERAGES

High School GPA	3.99
ACT Composite Score	28
SAT Critical Reading	620
SAT Mathematics	656
SAT Writing	632

"a-g" courses completed (7th–12th grades, by semester)

50+	60.7% (6,784/11,183)
40–49	41.0% (8,976/21,897)
30–39	25.0% (824/3,299)
	17.1% (13/76)

honors courses completed (10th–12th grades, by semester)

15+	68.5% (8,705/12,703)
10–14	46.8% (5,122/10,941)
5–9	26.0% (1,815/6,979)
	13.9% (553/3,988)

University of California, Irvine, Admissions Stats Fall 2010

Admit Rate

By Percentage (Admits/Applicants) GPA range

GPA range		
4.00 and above	91.7%	(11,743/12,812)
3.70–3.99	61.6%	(7,006/11,377)
3.30–3.69	14.0%	(1,776/12,726)
3.00–3.29	1.5%	(85/5,520)
below 3.00	0.9%	(25/2,836)

act composite range

31–36	84.4%	(2,195/2,602)
26–30	60.5%	(3,445/5,693)
21–25	37.5%	(1,919/5,111)
16–20	21.5%	(490/2,277)
below 16	9.8%	(34/347)

sat critical reading range

700–800	82.2%	(3,093/3,761)
600–690	63.7%	(7,805/12,258)
500–590	42.3%	(6,365/15,042)
400–490	24.5%	(2,113/8,636)
below 400	11.3%	(216/1,909)

sat mathematics range

700–800	74.9%	(6,645/8,871)
600–690	54.1%	(7,805/14,426)
500–590	34.1%	(3,936/11,558)
400–490	19.9%	(1,107/5,560)
below 400	8.3%	(99/1,191)

sat writing range

700–800	84.2%	(4,436/5,267)
600–690	61.7%	(7,699/12,475)
500–590	38.6%	(5,626/14,576)
400–490	21.5%	(1,671/7,767)
below 400	10.5%	(160/1,521)

admit rate **45.5%**

Admits	20,798
Applicants	45,738

ELC Student Admit Rate	97.3%
California Residents (% of admits)	92.2%

AVERAGES

High School GPA	3.99
ACT Composite Score	27
SAT Critical Reading	605
SAT Mathematics	650
SAT Writing	622

"a-g" courses completed (7th–12th grades, by semester)

50+	57.7%	(6,191/10,729)
40–49	42.9%	(10,197/23,757)
30–39	20.0%	(826/4,126)
	16.4%	(10/61)

honors courses completed (10th–12th grades, by semester)

15+	70.7%	(9,929/14,039)
10–14	45.5%	(5,146/11,318)
5–9	21.2%	(1,526/7,210)
	8.2%	(348/4,229)

University of California, Los Angeles, Admissions Stats Fall 2010

Admit Rate

By Percentage (Admits/Applicants) GPA range

4.00 and above	48.9% (10,807/22,110)
3.70–3.99	9.4% (1,381/14,632)
3.30–3.69	3.3% (409/12,558)
3.00–3.29	2.1% (98/4,573)
below 3.00	2.7% (66/2,461)

act composite range

	49.0% (2,605/5,316)
31–36	18.8% (1,502/7,977)
26–30	10.9% (561/5,125)
21–25	7.4% (152/2,065)
16–20	2.6% (10/378)
below 16	

sat critical reading range

	55.1% (4,417/8,023)
700–800	28.5% (5,186/18,224)
600–690	13.0% (2,071/15,905)
500–590	6.9% (537/7,817)
400–490	1.3% (21/1,667)
below 400	

	45.1% (7,097/15,751)
700–800	19.7% (3,527/17,914)

sat mathematics range

600–690	10.6% (1,233/11,606)
500–590	6.6% (341/5,155)
400–490	2.8% (34/1,210)
below 400	

	52.8% (5,707/10,806)
	24.8% (4,433/17,884)
700–800	11.4% (1,689/14,812)

sat writing range

600–690	5.6% (384/6,799)
500–590	1.4% (19/1,335)
400–490	
below 400	

admit rate 22.8%

Admits	13,130
Applicants	57,662

22.8%

ELC Student Admit Rate	59.9%
California Residents	76.0%
(% of admits)	

AVERAGES

High School GPA	4.14
ACT Composite Score	30
SAT Critical Reading	660
SAT Mathematics	697
SAT Writing	678

"a-g" courses completed (7th–12th grades, by semester)

50+	29.7% (5,209/17,788)
40–49	18.8% (4,925/26,159)
30–39	9.3% (373/4,019)
	9.6% (11/114)

honors courses completed (10th–12th grades, by semester)

15+	**36.4%** (8,116/22,300)
10–14	**11.2%** (1,404/12,492)
5–9	**5.0%** (335/6,717)
	3.8% (138/3,595)

University of California, Merced, Admissions Stats Fall 2010

Admit Rate –
By Percentage (Admits/Applicants)

GPA		
4.00 and above		99.4% (2,212/2,226)
3.70–3.99		99.0% (4,748/4,797)
3.30–3.69		97.9% (8,968/9,158)
3.00–3.29		89.3% (4,262/4,774)
below 3.00		15.9% (295/1,858)

act composite range

31–36		98.6% (479/486)
26–30		97.0% (2,412/2,487)
21–25		95.5% (3,033/3,177)
16–20		85.1% (1,403/1,649)
below 16		67.0% (217/324)

sat critical reading range

700–800		98.4% (779/792)
600–690		96.6% (4,246/4,396)
500–590		94.7% (7,738/8,168)
400–490		87.6% (4,871/5,559)
below 400		70.3% (985/1,401)

sat mathematics range

700–800		96.4% (1,602/1,661)
600–690		95.6% (5,713/5,976)
500–590		93.6% (6,993/7,472)
400–490		86.7% (3,645/4,205)
below 400		66.5% (666/1,002)

sat writing range

700–800		99.0% (887/896)
600–690		96.9% (4,445/4,588)
500–590		94.7% (7,851/8,291)
400–490		86.6% (4,676/5,401)
below 400		66.7% (760/1,140)

admit rate	89.6%	
Admits	20,528	
Applicants	22,904	

ELC Student Admit Rate	99.5%
California Residents	98.4%
(% of admits)	

AVERAGES

High School GPA	3.55
ACT Composite Score	24
SAT Critical Reading	540
SAT Mathematics	567
SAT Writing	546

"a-g" courses completed (7th–12th grades, by semester)

50+		90.5% (3,666/4,049)
40–49		91.0% (11,627/12,771)
30–39		83.7% (2,445/2,921)
below 30		40.7% (22/54)

honors courses completed (10th–12th grades, by semester)

15+		95.7% (3,411/3,563)
10–14		95.6% (5,362/5,611)
5–9		90.1% (4,782/5,307)
below 5		83.6% (3,234/3,868)

University of California, Riverside, Admissions Stats Fall 2010

Admit Rate

By Percentage (Admits/Applicants)

GPA	Admit Rate
4.00 and above	97.1% (3,441/3,542)
3.70–3.99	94.7% (5,381/5,684)
3.30–3.69	90.0% (8,092/8,994)
3.00–3.29	70.5% (3,503/4,969)
below 3.00	7.1% (222/3,110)

act composite range

31–36	96.6% (648/671)
26–30	93.6% (2,249/2,403)
21–25	88.0% (2,844/3,230)
16–20	72.2% (1,462/2,025)
below 16	47.4% (199/420)

sat critical reading range

700–800	94.5% (938/993)
600–690	92.3% (4,636/5,021)
500–590	86.0% (7,583/8,815)
400–490	74.0% (5,131/6,931)
below 400	52.5% (1,024/1,950)

sat mathematics range

700–800	92.3% (2,700/2,926)
600–690	89.4% (6,247/6,988)
500–590	82.8% (6,281/7,586)
400–490	70.9% (3,438/4,852)
below 400	47.6% (646/1,358)

sat writing range

700–800	97.2% (1,298/1,336)
600–690	92.5% (4,731/5,116)
500–590	85.5% (7,816/9,138)
400–490	71.7% (4,671/6,519)
below 400	49.7% (796/1,601)

admit rate 78.2%

Admits	20,692
Applicants	26,476

ELC Student Admit Rate	99.0%
California Residents	97.0%

(% of admits))

AVERAGES

High School GPA	3.62
ACT Composite Score	24
SAT Critical Reading	542
SAT Mathematics	582
SAT Writing	551

"a-g" courses completed (7th–12th grades, by semester)

50+	79.2% (3,801/4,799)
40–49	80.8% (11,685/14,465)
30–39	66.5% (2,362/3,554)
below 30	19.6% (11/56)

honors courses completed (10th–12th grades, by semester)

15+	91.5% (5,120/5,594)
10–14	88.1% (5,735/6,513)
5–9	75.8% (4,059/5,354)
below 5	60.5% (2,328/3,849)

University of California, San Diego, Admissions Stats Fall 2010

Admit Rate
By Percentage (Admits/Applicants)

4.00 and above	75.3% (13,021/17,300)
3.70–3.99	31.3% (3,901/12,461)
3.30–3.69	8.9% (1,013/11,428)
3.00–3.29	1.2% (49/4,080)
below 3.00	1.7% (35/2,054)

act composite range

31–36	72.0% (3,035/4,214)
26–30	38.8% (2,636/6,802)
21–25	23.6% (1,049/4,450)
16–20	14.5% (230/1,581)
below 16	5.9% (12/202)

sat critical reading range

700–800	73.4% (4,680/6,378)
600–690	48.4% (7,492/15,489)
500–590	27.2% (3,855/14,171)
400–490	17.4% (1,136/6,544)
below 400	5.5% (65/1,190)

sat mathematics range

700–800	65.8% (8,559/13,004)
600–690	37.7% (6,015/15,967)
500–590	21.2% (2,141/10,089)
400–490	11.9% (468/3,946)
below 400	5.9% (45/766)

sat writing range

700–800	74.1% (6,288/8,486)
600–690	44.4% (6,814/15,349)
500–590	24.7% (3,280/13,293)
400–490	13.8% (787/5,710)
below 400	6.3% (59/934)

admit rate 38.1%

Admits	18,330
Applicants	48,114

ELC Student Admit Rate	86.9%
California Residents	84.3%
(% of admits)	

AVERAGES

High School GPA	4.07
ACT Composite Score	29
SAT Critical Reading	639
SAT Mathematics	684
SAT Writing	657

"a-g" courses completed (7th–12th grades, by semester)

50+	46.7% (6,415/13,729)
40–49	34.9% (8,131/23,291)
30–39	14.9% (466/3,135)
below 30	14.1% (11/78)

honors courses completed (10th–12th grades, by semester)

15+	56.9% (10,155/17,839)
10–14	30.3% (3,430/11,308)
5–9	13.6% (826/6,058)
below 5	4.8% (148/3,080)

UNIVERSITY OF CALIFORNIA, SANTA CRUZ, ADMISSIONS STATS FALL 2010

Admit Rate

By Percentage (Admits/Applicants) GPA range

4.00 and above	97.6% (4,750/4,868)
3.70–3.99	92.7% (5,868/6,325)
3.30–3.69	65.4% (5,975/9,139)
3.00–3.29	22.1% (1,026/4,653)
below 3.00	3.8% (92/2,407)

act composite range

31–36	94.5% (1,145/1,211)
26–30	81.5% (3,085/3,787)
21–25	59.3% (1,933/3,262)
16–20	47.3% (612/1,295)
below 16	34.8% (93/267)

sat critical reading range

700–800	91.8% (2,057/2,241)
600–690	79.8% (6,137/7,692)
500–590	62.6% (5,507/8,799)
400–490	48.2% (2,262/4,695)
below 400	34.5% (397/1,152)

sat mathematics range

700–800	89.6% (3,026/3,377)
600–690	76.2% (6,751/8,865)
500–590	58.8% (4,648/7,903)
400–490	46.6% (1,663/3,567)
below 400	31.4% (272/867)

sat writing range

700–800	92.5% (2,365/2,557)
600–690	80.0% (6,205/7,759)
500–590	61.4% (5,477/8,919)
400–490	45.7% (2,016/4,415)
below 400	32.0% (297/929)

admit rate	64.4%
Admits	17,819
Applicants	27,658

ELC Student Admit Rate	97.4%
California Residents	94.5%
(% of admits)	

AVERAGES

High School GPA	3.76
ACT Composite Score	26
SAT Critical Reading	590
SAT Mathematics	611
SAT Writing	598

"a-g" courses completed (7th–12th grades, by semester)

50+	72.2% (4,687/6,493)
40–49	63.2% (9,084/14,375)
30–39	47.4% (1,177/2,485)
below 30	23.8% (10/42)

honors courses completed (10th–12th grades, by semester)

15+	85.6% (4,946/5,781)
10–14	76.8% (5,382/7,010)
5–9	55.5% (3,105/5,591)
below 5	34.3% (1,234/3,598)

University of California, Santa Barbara, Admissions Stats Fall 2010

Admit Rate
By Percentage (Admits/Applicants) GPA range

GPA range	Admit Rate
4.00 and above	91.8% (11,463/12,486)
3.70–3.99	60.5% (7,084/11,717)
3.30–3.69	17.1% (2,302/13,434)
3.00–3.29	2.3% (135/5,748)
below 3.00	1.3% (38/2,858)

act composite range

Range	Admit Rate
31–36	86.0% (2,540/2,955)
26–30	59.6% (4,147/6,956)
21–25	34.7% (1,805/5,200)
16–20	20.8% (443/2,132)
below 16	7.6% (28/370)

sat critical reading range

Range	Admit Rate
700–800	84.0% (3,523/4,192)
600–690	62.7% (8,404/13,394)
500–590	38.7% (5,745/14,841)
400–490	22.4% (1,716/7,668)
below 400	8.9% (145/1,629)

sat mathematics range

Range	Admit Rate
700–800	75.1% (5,790/7,707)
600–690	54.8% (8,288/15,127)
500–590	34.8% (4,221/12,141)
400–490	20.6% (1,132/5,491)
below 400	8.1% (102/1,258)

sat writing range

Range	Admit Rate
700–800	85.4% (4,572/5,351)
600–690	60.2% (8,264/13,730)
500–590	35.9% (5,171/14,407)
400–490	20.3% (1,409/6,941)
below 400	9.0% (117/1,295)

admit rate	45.5%
Admits	21,241
Applicants	46,733
ELC Student Admit Rate	98.0%
California Residents	89.9%
(% of admits)	

AVERAGES

High School GPA	3.98
ACT Composite Score	28
SAT Critical Reading	616
SAT Mathematics	643
SAT Writing	628

"a-g" courses completed (7th–12th grades, by semester)

Range	Admit Rate
50+	52.3% (5,887/11,259)
40–49	44.0% (10,647/24,193)
30–39	30.5% (1,304/4,271)
below 30	24.0% (12/50)

honors courses completed (10th–12th grades, by semester)

Range	Admit Rate
15+	69.5% (9,200/13,240)
10–14	48.5% (5,817/12,002)
5–9	24.9% (1,992/7,987)
below 5	11.3% (514/4,557)

CALIFORNIA PRIVATE COLLEGES

Academy of Art University, San Francisco
Allied American University, Laguna Hills (Online)
American Heritage University of Southern California, San Bernardino, California
American Jewish University, Los Angeles
American Sports University, San Bernardino
Anaheim University, Anaheim (Online)
Antioch University, Culver City
Apollos University, Huntington Beach (Online)
Argosy University, Alameda
Art Center College of Design, Pasadena
The Art Institute of California - San Francisco, San Francisco
Azusa Pacific University, Azusa
Bethany University, Scotts Valley
Biola University, La Mirada
Brooks Institute, Santa Barbara
California Baptist University, Riverside
California Coast University, Santa Ana
California College of the Arts, San Francisco
California College San Diego (CCSD), San Diego
California Institute of the Arts, Valencia
California Institute of Integral Studies, San Francisco
California Institute of Technology, Pasadena
California InterContinental University, Diamond Bar (Online)
California Lutheran University, Thousand Oaks
California Miramar University (formerly Pacific Western University, San Diego
California National University, Northridge
California Pacific University, Escondido
California South Bay University, Sunnyvale
California South University, Irvine, California
California Southern Law School, Riverside
California Southern University, Santa Ana (online)
California Takshila University,Santa Clara,California
California University of Management and Technology, San Jose
California University of Management and Sciences, Anaheim
Capital Bible College, Sacramento
CapStone University, Pasadena (online)
Carnegie Mellon Silicon Valley Campus, Mountain View
Chapman University, Orange
Charles R. Drew University of Medicine and Science, Los Angeles
Claremont Colleges, Claremont
Claremont McKenna College

CALIFORNIA PRIVATE COLLEGES

Harvey Mudd College
Pitzer College
Pomona College
Scripps College
Claremont Graduate University
Cogswell College, Sunnyvale
Concordia University Irvine, Irvine
Culinary Institute of America at Greystone, St. Helena
Dominican University of California, San Rafael
Design Institute of San Diego[3]
Epic Bible College (formerly Trinity Life Bible College), Sacramento
Fresno Pacific University, Fresno
Fuller Theological Seminary, Pasadena
Golden Gate University, San Francisco
Herguan University, Sunnyvale
Holy Names University, Oakland
Hope International University, Fullerton
Hult International Business School, San Francisco
Humphreys College, Stockton
Imago Dei College, Oak Glen
John F. Kennedy University, Pleasant Hill
John Paul the Great Catholic University, San Diego
Laguna College of Art and Design, Laguna Beach
La Sierra University, Riverside
Life Pacific College, San Dimas
Lincoln University, Oakland
Loma Linda University, Loma Linda
Loyola Marymount University, Los Angeles
Master's College, Newhall
Mayfield College, Cathedral City[4]
Menlo College, Atherton
Mills College, Oakland
Monsbey College, Watsonville
Monterey Institute of International Studies, Monterey
Mount St. Mary's College, Los Angeles
National Hispanic University, San Jose
National University, San Diego (La Jolla, San Diego)
NewSchool of Architecture and Design, San Diego
Northern Coastal College, Crescent City
Northwestern Polytechnic University, Fremont
Notre Dame de Namur University, Belmont

CALIFORNIA PRIVATE COLLEGES

Occidental College, Los Angeles
Otis College of Art and Design, Los Angeles
Pacific Oaks College, Pasadena
Pacific Union College, Angwin
Patten College, Oakland
Pepperdine University, Malibu
Point Loma Nazarene University, San Diego
San Francisco Institute of Architecture, Berkeley
Saint Mary's College of California, Moraga
Samuel Merritt University, Oakland
San Diego Christian College, El Cajon
San Joaquin College of Law, Clovis
San Luis Rey College, Oceanside
Santa Clara University, Santa Clara
Silicon Valley University, San Jose
Simpson University, Redding
Soka University of America, Aliso Viejo
Southern California Institute of Architecture, Los Angeles
St. Mary's College of California, Moraga
Stanford University, Stanford
Thomas Aquinas College, Santa Paula
Trinity International University
Touro University, Vallejo
TUI University, Cypress (Online)
University of La Verne, La Verne
University of Northern California, Santa Rosa
University of Northern California, Lorenzo Patiño School of Law, Sacramento
University of Redlands, Redlands
University of the Pacific, Stockton
University of San Diego, San Diego
University of San Francisco, San Francisco
University of Southern California, Los Angeles
University of West Los Angeles
      Inglewood
      Woodland Hills
University of the West, Rosemead
Vanguard University of Southern California, Costa Mesa
Western Institute for Social Research, Berkeley
Westmont College, Santa Barbara
Whittier College, Whittier
William Howard Taft University, Santa Ana

admissions data

COLLEGE/UNIVERSITY YIELDS

By comparing a school's yield, the percentage of applicants accepted by a university who enroll at that institution indicates a school's popularity. In contrast, a very low yield means that the school could be a safety or second choice for many of the applicants.

SCHOOL	Acceptance Rate	Yield
Agnes Scott College (GA)	45%	30%
Albion College (MI)	81%	28%
Allegheny College (PA)	57%	24%
Amherst College (MA)	18%	40%
Augustana College (IL)	73%	32%
Austin College (TX)	71%	28%
Bard College (NY)	27%	36%
Barnard College (NY)	29%	43%
Bates College (ME)	30%	34%
Beloit College (WI)	60%	25%
Bennington College (VT)	62%	32%
Berea College (KY)	29%	73%
Berry College (GA)	70%	42%
Birmingham-Southern College (AL)	66%	30%
Bowdoin College (ME)	19%	42%
Bryn Mawr College (PA)	45%	37%
Bucknell University (PA)	30%	33%
Calvin College (MI)	95%	48%
Carleton College (MN)	30%	35%
Central College (IA)	79%	28%
Centre College (KY)	61%	24%
Claremont McKenna College (CA)	16%	40%
Coe College (IA)	64%	28%
Colby College (ME)	32%	31%
Colgate University (NY)	26%	33%
College of St. Benedict (MN)	75%	43%
College of the Holy Cross (MA)	33%	31%
College of Wooster (OH)	74%	23%
Colorado College	32%	34%

COLLEGE/UNIVERSITY YIELDS

SCHOOL	Acceptance Rate	Yield
Connecticut College	35%	30%
Cornell College (IA)	45%	26%
Davidson College (NC)	28%	41%
Denison University (OH)	39%	29%
DePauw University (IN)	69%	27%
Dickinson College (PA)	42%	25%
Drew University (NJ)	61%	16%
Earlham College (IN)	69%	25%
Franklin and Marshall College (PA)	37%	30%
Furman University (SC)	56%	32%
Gettysburg College (PA)	36%	32%
Goucher College (MD)	66%	17%
Grinnell College (IA)	50%	28%
Gustavus Adolphus College (MN)	71%	29%
Hamilton College (NY)	28%	34%
Hampden-Sydney College (VA)	67%	34%
Hampshire College (MA)	55%	28%
Hanover College (IN)	66%	19%
Harvey Mudd College (CA)	28%	28%
Haverford College (PA)	25%	36%
Hendrix College (AR)	83%	34%
Hillsdale College (MI)	64%	42%
Hobart and William Smith Colleges (NY)	55%	27%
Hollins University (VA)	88%	37%
Hope College (MI)	83%	35%
Illinois Wesleyan University	57%	32%
Juniata College (PA)	67%	29%
Kalamazoo College (MI)	63%	28%
Kenyon College (OH)	29%	34%
Knox College (IL)	61%	21%
Lafayette College (PA)	35%	27%
Lake Forest College (IL)	61%	26%
Lawrence University (WI)	56%	25%

COLLEGE/UNIVERSITY YIELDS

SCHOOL	Acceptance Rate	Yield
Lewis and Clark College (OR)	56%	17%
Linfield College (OR)	80%	29%
Luther College (IA)	83%	39%
Lyon College (AR)	69%	24%
Macalester College (MN)	41%	24%
Middlebury College (VT)	21%	44%
Millsaps College (MS)	77%	31%
Mount Holyoke College (MA)	52%	31%
Muhlenberg College (PA)	37%	32%
New College of Florida	57%	34%
Oberlin College (OH)	31%	34%
Occidental College (CA)	44%	20%
Ohio Wesleyan University	66%	23%
Pitzer College (CA)	26%	25%
Pomona College (CA)	16%	39%
Presbyterian College (SC)	71%	36%
Randolph College (VA)	83%	18%
Reed College (OR)	34%	30%
Rhodes College (TN)	51%	24%
Scripps College (CA)	43%	27%
Sewanee--University of the South (TN)	64%	26%
Siena College (NY)	54%	25%
Skidmore College (NY)	37%	28%
Smith College (MA)	52%	38%
Southwestern University (TX)	67%	29%
Spelman College (GA)	33%	30%
St. John's College (NM)	79%	49%
St. John's University (MN)	74%	46%
St. Lawrence University (NY)	44%	31%
St. Mary's College (IN)	81%	46%
St. Mary's College of Maryland	55%	36%
St. Michael's College (VT)	69%	22%
St. Olaf College (MN)	54%	34%

COLLEGE/UNIVERSITY YIELDS

SCHOOL	Acceptance Rate	Yield
Stonehill College (MA)	52%	22%
Susquehanna University (PA)	86%	29%
Swarthmore College (PA)	18%	39%
Sweet Briar College (VA)	81%	40%
Thomas Aquinas College (CA)	60%	76%
Transylvania University (KY)	80%	31%
Trinity College (CT)	34%	28%
Union College (NY)	43%	27%
United States Military Academy (NY)	15%	78%
United States Naval Academy (MD)	12%	85%
University of Puget Sound (WA)	66%	18%
University of Richmond (VA)	40%	31%
Ursinus College (PA)	53%	17%
Vassar College (NY)	29%	37%
Virginia Military Institute	54%	50%
Wabash College (IN)	47%	37%
Washington and Jefferson College (PA)	34%	16%
Washington and Lee University (VA)	27%	45%
Washington College (MD)	64%	24%
Wellesley College (MA)	36%	41%
Wesleyan University (CT)	27%	35%
Westminster College (PA)	71%	33%
Westmont College (CA)	73%	32%
Wheaton College (IL)	55%	49%
Wheaton College (MA)	37%	30%
Whitman College (WA)	48%	29%
Willamette University (OR)	77%	19%
Williams College (MA)	18%	45%
Wofford College (SC)	53%	31%

LIBERAL ARTS COLLEGES LOCATED NEAR CITIES

East Coast
• Babson College, Babson Park, MA
• Barnard College, New York City
• Bryn Mawr College, Bryn Mawr, PA (Philadelphia)
• Drew University, Madison, NJ (near New York City)
• Goucher College, Towson, MD (Baltimore suburb)
• Haverford College, Haverford, PA
• Providence College, Providence, RI
• Sarah Lawrence College, Bronxiville, NY (New York City)
• Simmons College, Boston, MA
• Swarthmore College, Swarthmore, PA
• Trinity College, Hartford, CT
• Wellesley College, Wellesley, MA
• Wheaton College, Norton, MA (near Providence, RI)

Midwest
• Lake Forest College, Lake Forest, IL (Chicago suburb)
• Macalester College, St. Paul, MN

South
• Eckerd College, St. Petersburg, FL
• Morehouse College, Atlanta, GA
• Rhodes College, Memphis, TN
• Spelman College, Atlanta, GA

West
• Colorado College, Colorado Springs, CO
• Lewis & Clark College, Portland, OR
• Mills College, Oakland, CA
• Occidental College, Los Angeles, CA
• Reed College, Portland, OR
• St. John's College, Santa Fe, NM
• St. Mary's College of California, Moraga, CA (San Francisco Bay)
• Westminister College, Salt Lake City, UT
• Westmont College, Santa Barbara, CA
• Whittier College, Whittier, CA (Los Angeles suburb)

AMERICA'S BEST UNIVERSITIES

Rank School (State) (*Public)	Average freshman retention rate	% of classes under 20 ('09)	% of classes of 50 or more ('09)	Student faculty ratio ('09)	SAT/ACT 25th-75th percentile ('09)	Acceptance rate ('09)	Average alumni giving rate
1. Harvard University (MA)	97%	80%	8%	7/1	1380-1570	7%	37%
2. Princeton University (NJ)	98%	73%	11%	6/1	1390-1580	10%	60%
3. Yale University (CT)	99%	79%	7%	6/1	1400-1580	8%	38%
4. Columbia University (NY)	99%	79%	7%	6/1	1370-1550	10%	34%
5. Stanford University (CA)	98%	68%	12%	6/1	1340-1540	8%	34%
5. University of Pennsylvania	98%	72%	7%	6/1	1350-1530	18%	37%
7. California Institute of Technology	98%	64%	9%	3/1	1460-1570	15%	35%
7. Massachusetts Inst. of Technology	98%	65%	13%	7/1	1370-1560	11%	36%
9. Dartmouth College (NH)	98%	64%	9%	8/1	1340-1550	13%	49%
9. Duke University (NC)	97%	71%	6%	8/1	1340-1530	19%	38%
9. University of Chicago	98%	78%	4%	6/1	1370-1560	27%	32%
12. Northwestern University (IL)	97%	73%	7%	7/1	1360-1530	27%	31%
13. Johns Hopkins University (MD)	97%	67%	11%	10/1	1300-1500	27%	33%
13. Washington University in St. Louis	97%	70%	10%	7/1	1390-1530	22%	31%
15. Brown University (RI)	97%	70%	10%	9/1	1320-1530	11%	37%
15. Cornell University (NY)	96%	56%	18%	11/1	1290-1500	19%	31%
17. Rice University (TX)	97%	65%	8%	6/1	1320-1530	22%	33%
17. Vanderbilt University (TN)	96%	65%	8%	8/1	30-34	20%	24%
19. University of Notre Dame (IN)	98%	54%	9%	12/1	31-34	29%	44%
20. Emory University (GA)	95%	64%	9%	7/1	1300-1480	30%	36%
21. Georgetown University (DC)	96%	61%	4%	10/1	1300-1500	20%	27%
22. University of California-Berkeley*	97%	60%	15%	16/1	1230-1470	22%	13%
23. Carnegie Mellon University (PA)	95%	62%	11%	12/1	1290-1500	36%	18%
23. Univ. of Southern California	96%	63%	11%	9/1	1270-1450	24%	43%
25. Univ. of California-Los Angeles*	97%	52%	22%	17/1	1170-1410	22%	13%
25. University of Virginia*	97%	52%	15%	16/1	1230-1440	32%	22%
25. Wake Forest University (NC)	94%	57%	3%	11/1	1180-1390	38%	30%
28. Tufts University (MA)	96%	71%	5%	9/1	1360-1500	27%	21%
29. University of Michigan-Ann Arbor*	96%	46%	17%	15/1	27-31	50%	16%
30. U. of North Carolina-Chapel Hill*	97%	39%	12%	14/1	1210-1410	32%	22%
31. Boston College	95%	47%	8%	13/1	1250-1430	30%	26%
31. College of William and Mary (VA)*	95%	48%	7%	12/1	1240-1450	34%	22%
33. New York University	92%	60%	12%	11/1	1210-1430	38%	9%
34. Brandeis University (MA)	94%	61%	9%	9/1	1260-1460	40%	30%
35. Georgia Institute of Technology*	93%	38%	24%	20/1	1230-1430	59%	28%
35. Univ. of California-San Diego*	94%	40%	32%	19/1	1150-1380	38%	6%
37. Lehigh University (PA)	94%	49%	10%	10/1	1220-1340	33%	22%
37. University of Rochester (NY)	95%	59%	13%	10/1	1230-1410	39%	18%
39. University of California-Davis*	91%	35%	25%	16/1	1080-1320	46%	10%
39. Univ. of California-Santa Barbara*	91%	47%	18%	17/1	1090-1330	48%	17%
41. Case Western Reserve Univ. (OH)	91%	61%	10%	9/1	1240-1440	70%	20%
41. Rensselaer Polytechnic Inst. (NY)	93%	53%	10%	16/1	1270-1450	43%	16%
41. University of California-Irvine*	94%	45%	20%	19/1	1090-1320	44%	9%
41. University of Washington*	93%	33%	18%	12/1	1100-1330	58%	16%
45. University of Texas-Austin*	92%	36%	23%	17/1	1100-1360	45%	15%
45. Univ. of Wisconsin-Madison*	94%	44%	19%	17/1	26-30	57%	12%
47. Pennsylvania State U.-University Park*	93%	31%	19%	17/1	1090-1300	52%	22%
47. Univ. of Illinois-Urbana-Champaign*	93%	38%	20%	16/1	26-31	65%	13%
47. University of Miami (FL)	90%	52%	7%	11/1	1170-1380	44%	18%
50. Yeshiva University (NY)	91%	65%	1%	7/1	1100-1370	63%	22%

AMERICA'S BEST UNIVERSITIES

Rank School (State) (*Public)	Average freshman retention rate	% of classes under 20 ('09)	% of classes of 50 or more ('09)	SAT/ACT 25th-75th percentile ('09)	Acceptance rate ('09)	Average alumni giving rate
51. George Washington University (DC)	91%	56%	10%	1200-1380	37%	9%
51. Tulane University (LA)	89%	65%	7%	29-32	26%	19%
53. Pepperdine University (CA)	89%	65%	3%	1110-1340	41%	11%
53. University of Florida*	95%	40%	22%	1140-1360	42%	16%
55. Syracuse University (NY)	91%	63%	8%	1050-1270	60%	17%
56. Boston University[1]	91%	56%	10%	1180-1360	54%	8%
56. Fordham University (NY)	90%	50%	1%	1140-1340	50%	23%
56. Ohio State University-Columbus*	93%	32%[2]	20%	25-30	76%	15%
56. Purdue Univ.-West Lafayette (IN)*	86%	38%	16%	1040-1280	73%	21%
56. Southern Methodist University (TX)	88%	59%	9%	1140-1340	53%	18%
56. University of Georgia*	94%	36%	13%	1130-1330	54%	13%
56. Univ. of Maryland–College Park*	93%	34%	15%	1200-1390	42%	10%
63. Texas A&M Univ.-College Station*	92%	22%	22%	1100-1310	67%	17%
64. Clemson University (SC)*	91%	43%	13%	1130-1310	63%	28%
64. Rutgers, State U. of N.J.-New Brunswick*	91%	42%	19%	1090-1310	61%	13%
64. Univ. of Minnesota-Twin Cities*	88%	40%	17%	24-29	50%	14%
64. University of Pittsburgh*	91%	40%	18%	1160-1360	59%	14%
64. Worcester Polytechnic Inst. (MA)	93%	67%	9%	1190-1380	63%	16%
69. Northeastern University (MA)	91%	61%	7%	1200-1370	41%	10%
69. University of Connecticut*	93%	43%	18%	1120-1310	50%	18%
69. Virginia Tech*	91%	24%	21%	1110-1310	67%	17%
72. Colorado School of Mines*	86%	46%	13%	26-30	63%	24%
72. Univ. of California-Santa Cruz*	89%	46%	23%	1030-1270	64%	10%
72. University of Iowa*	83%	50%	10%	23-28	83%	12%
75. Brigham Young Univ.-Provo (UT)	84%	47%	11%	25-30	69%	18%
75. Indiana University-Bloomington*	89%	32%	19%	1060-1290	73%	16%
75. Marquette University (WI)	90%	39%	11%	24-29	66%	17%
75. University of Delaware*	91%	40%	12%	1060-1280	57%	10%
79. American University (DC)	88%	45%	3%	1170-1370	53%	12%
79. Baylor University (TX)	85%	48%	9%	1080-1290	50%	16%
79. Miami University-Oxford (OH)*	90%	32%	12%	24-29	79%	17%
79. Michigan State University*	91%	24%	22%	23-27	73%	15%
79. SUNY Col. of Envir. Science and Forestry	86%	77%	7%	1070-1260	43%	27%
79. University of Alabama*	85%	43%	16%	21-28	57%	31%
85. Auburn University (AL)*	86%	25%	16%	23-29	80%	32%
86. Binghamton University-SUNY*	90%	40%	15%	1200-1380	33%	9%
86. Clark University (MA)	89%	57%	5%	1080-1290	64%	16%
86. Drexel University (PA)	84%	65%	4%	1110-1300	55%	16%
86. Stevens Institute of Technology (NJ)	90%	43%	8%	1170-1360	51%	22%
86. St. Louis University	84%	55%	6%	24-30	71%	14%
86. University of Colorado-Boulder*	84%	47%	13%	24-29	84%	9%
86. University of Denver	87%	62%	5%	24-29	70%	7%
93. University of Tulsa (OK)	87%	70%	1%	25-32	50%	23%
94. Iowa State University*	84%	33%	19%	22-28	85%	16%
94. University of California-Riverside*	86%	39%	20%	930-1190	78%	6%
94. University of Missouri*	85%	44%	15%	23-28	83%	18%
94. University of San Diego	86%	42%	0.2%	1115-1300	49%	8%
94. University of Vermont*	85%	47%	13%	1090-1280	71%	16%
99. SUNY-Stony Brook*	89%	33%	23%	1100-1290	40%	12%
99. Texas Christian University	85%	42%	8%	1050-1280	59%	19%
99. University of Dayton (OH)	87%	35%	4%	23-28	73%	21%
99. Univ. of Massachusetts-Amherst*	85%	35%	18%	1060-1280	67%	12%
99. University of the Pacific (CA)	83%	63%	4%	1050-1320	42%	9%
104. Florida State University*	89%	36%	16%	1110-1290	61%	20%
104. Howard University (DC)	86%	63%	4%	900-1320	54%	8%
104. Samford University (AL)	84%	65%	2%	21-28	84%	11%
104. University of Kansas*	80%	39%	12%	22-27	91%	19%
104. University of Nebraska-Lincoln*	84%	38%	14%	22-29	63%	22%
104. University of New Hampshire*	87%	41%	16%	1030-1240	72%	10%
104. University of Tennessee*	84%	31%	9%	24-29	73%	11%
111. Illinois Institute of Technology	87%	55%	6%	25-31	60%	9%
111. North Carolina State U.-Raleigh*	90%	29%	20%	1080-1280	55%	11%
111. University of Oklahoma*	84%	46%	11%	23-29	93%	19%
111. University of Oregon*	83%	37%	17%	990-1225	80%	13%
111. University of South Carolina*	87%	41%	11%	1090-1290	64%	18%

AMERICA'S BEST UNIVERSITIES

Rank School (State) (*Public)	Average freshman retention rate	% of classes under 20 ('09)	% of classes of 50 or more ('09)	SAT/ACT 25th-75th percentile ('09)	Accept-ance rate ('09)	Average alumni giving rate
179. University of Central Florida*	85%	27%	25%	1090-1270	47%	13%
179. Western Michigan University*	74%	37%	11%	20-25	83%	8%
183. Kent State University (OH)*	74%	46%	8%	20-25	72%	4%
183. Montana State University*	72%	43%	13%	21-27	64%	10%
183. San Diego State University*	82%	19%	25%	910-1170	36%	3%
183. Southern Illinois U.-Carbondale*	68%	50%	5%	19-24	69%	6%
183. St. Mary's Univ. of Minnesota	75%	52%	0%	19-26	72%	18%
183. University of Hartford (CT)	73%	69%	1%	900-1120	68%	7%
183. Univ. of Massachusetts-Lowell*	78%	37%	6%	980-1180	73%	8%
183. University of South Florida*	84%	24%	15%	1050-1260	48%	14%
191. Andrews University (MI)	80%	59%	8%	19-25	49%	10%
191. North Dakota State University*	80%	42%	12%	20-26	79%	15%
191. University of Colorado-Denver*	71%	29%	11%	20-25	61%	4%
191. University of Montana*	72%	45%	11%	20-26	83%	15%
191. University of Nevada-Reno*	78%	38%	15%	935-1180	88%	10%
191. U. of North Carolina-Charlotte*	77%	29%	21%	960-1140	76%	5%
191. U. of North Carolina-Greensboro*	76%	40%	14%	930-1130	73%	6%

AMERICA'S TOP LIBERAL ARTS COLLEGES

Rank School (State) (*Public)	Undergraduate academic reputation index (100=highest)	Average freshman retention rate	% of classes under 20 ('09)	% of classes of 50 or more ('09)	Student/ faculty ratio ('09)	SAT/ACT 25th-75th percentile ('09)	Acceptance rate ('09)	Average alumni giving rate
1. Williams College (MA)	93	97%	74%	4%	7/1	1310-1530	20%	58%
2. Amherst College (MA)	93	98%	75%	3%	8/1	1310-1530	16%	60%
3. Swarthmore College (PA)	92	97%	78%	2%	8/1	1340-1530	17%	46%
4. Middlebury College (VT)	87	96%	69%	3%	9/1	1288-1470	20%	60%
4. Wellesley College (MA)	91	95%	68%	1%	8/1	1280-1470	35%	46%
6. Bowdoin College (ME)	87	98%	70%	1%	9/1	1320-1500	19%	51%
6. Pomona College (CA)	86	98%	67%	2%	7/1	1400-1550	16%	49%
8. Carleton College (MN)	85	97%	61%	1%	9/1	1320-1500	31%	61%
9. Davidson College (NC)	84	96%	72%	0%	11/1	1260-1440	26%	54%
8. Haverford College (PA)	81	96%	76%	2%	8/1	1300-1480	25%	45%
11. Claremont McKenna College (CA)	83	96	76%	1%	9/1	1310-1510	16%	38%
12. Vassar College (NY)	86	96%	67%	1%	8/1	1300-1470	25%	31%
12. Wesleyan University (CT)	85	95%	67%	5%	9/1	1290-1500	22%	50%
14. Smith College (MA)	87	91%	67%	5%	9/1	1190-1400	47%	40%
14. Washington and Lee University (VA)	78	94%	72%	0%	9/1	1320-1470	19%	47%
16. United States Military Academy (NY)*	85	91%	96%	0%	7/1	1140-1330	15%	28%
16. United States Naval Academy (MD)*	87	97%	59%	0.1%	9/1	1140-1350	10%	21%
18. Grinnell College (IA)	85	94%	64%	0%	9/1	1220-1460	34%	42%
18. Hamilton College (NY)	83	95%	73%	1%	10/1	1310-1470	30%	49%
18. Harvey Mudd College (CA)	85	94%	59%	7%	8/1	1420-1560	34%	34%
21. Bates College (ME)	84	95%	64%	3%	10/1	1260-1410	27%	42%
21. Colgate University (NY)	83	94%	62%	3%	10/1	1270-1440	32%	39%
23. Colby College (ME)	82	94%	64%	3%	10/1	1270-1440	34%	43%
23. Oberlin College (OH)	83	94%	72%	3%	9/1	1300-1470	34%	36%
23. Scripps College (CA)	78	92%	81%	1%	10/1	1260-1430	33%	45%
26. Barnard College (NY)	81	95%	71%	7%	9/1	1250-1440	31%	27%
26. Colorado College	77	95%	60%	0%	10/1	1240-1420	32%	25%
26. Macalester College (MN)	81	93%	67%	1%	11/1	1290-1450	46%	39%
26. Mount Holyoke College (MA)	83	92%	62%	5%	9/1	1210-1450	58%	38%
30. Bryn Mawr College (PA)	82	93%	72%	4%	8/1	1180-1380	49%	40%
30. Bucknell University (PA)	79	95%	56%	2%	10/1	1230-1400	30%	35%
32. College of the Holy Cross (MA)	75	95%	53%	2%	11/1	1210-1370	36%	51%
32. Kenyon College (OH)	78	93%	70%	2%	10/1	1230-1400	39%	39%
32. Sewanee–University of the South (TN)	77	89%	72%	1%	10/1	1150-1360	68%	41%
32. University of Richmond (VA)	76	91%	66%	0%	8/1	1170-1350	39%	25%
36. Occidental College (CA)	78	92%	66%	1%	9/1	1200-1380	43%	37%
36. Trinity College (CT)	75	91%	66%	3%	9/1	1200-1370	41%	48%
38. Bard College (NY)	72	86%	77%	0%	10/1	1330-1420	33%	43%
38. Lafayette College (PA)	72	94%	57%	3%	11/1	1170-1380	42%	32%
38. Whitman College (WA)	71	94%	67%	1%	10/1	1240-1430	44%	41%
41. Connecticut College	73	90%	64%	2%	9/1	25-30	37%	36%
41. Franklin and Marshall College (PA)	71	92%	57%	1%	10/1	1230-1370	48%	35%
41. Furman University (SC)	73	92%	57%	0.2%	11/1	1180-1370	68%	35%
41. Skidmore College (NY)	74	94%	72%	1%	9/1	1150-1350	42%	29%
41. Union College (NY)	69	92%	70%	1%	10/1	1210-1370	41%	35%
46. Pitzer College (CA)	76	91%	67%	1%	11/1	1196-1373	20%	26%
47. Centre College (KY)	72	91%	58%	0%	11/1	26-30	69%	57%
47. Dickinson College (PA)	72	92%	71%	0%	10/1	1190-1370	49%	36%
47. Gettysburg College (PA)	69	91%	69%	0.2%	11/1	1220-1380	40%	38%
47. Rhodes College (TN)	75	88%	76%	1%	10/1	26-30	42%	35%

AMERICA'S TOP LIBERAL ARTS COLLEGES

Rank School (State) (*Public)	% of classes under 20 ('09)	% of classes of 50 or more ('09)	SAT/ACT 25th-75th percentile ('09)	Accept-ance rate ('09)	Average alumni giving rate
51. Denison University (OH)	65%	0%	27-30	50%	36%
51. DePauw University (IN)	61%	0%	1080-1320	66%	34%
51. St. Olaf College (MN)	60%	4%	26-31	57%	29%
54. Reed College [10] (OR)	72%	4%	1280-1470	41%	27%
55. Beloit College (WI)	70%	0.3%	25-30	73%	36%
55. St. Lawrence University (NY)	64%	1%	1140-1290	39%	33%
55. Wheaton College (IL)	57%	4%	27-31	71%	31%
58. Wabash College (IN)	78%	3%	1030-1260	49%	39%
59. Spelman College (GA)	63%	4%	950-1128	40%	30%
59. Wheaton College (MA)	68%	4%	1130-1350	59%	32%
59. Willamette University (OR)	69%	0%	1120-1320	60%	25%
62. Illinois Wesleyan University	63%	1%	26-30	54%	20%
62. Southwestern University (TX)	80%	0.2%	1140-1350	63%	27%
62. St. John's University (MN)	53%	0.4%	23-29	84%	33%
62. Virginia Military Institute*	72%	0%	1050-1220	56%	37%
62. Wofford College (SC)	62%	1%	1140-1350	58%	35%
67. Agnes Scott College (GA)	76%	0%	1010-1270	46%	42%
67. Berea College (KY)	62%	0%	21-26	19%	22%
67. Hobart and William Smith Col. (NY)	64%	1%	1150-1310	56%	31%
67. Lawrence University (WI)	75%	2%	27-31	69%	43%
71. College of Wooster (OH)	64%	0.3%	24-29	59%	28%
71. Kalamazoo College (MI)	63%	1%	26-30	73%	33%
71. Thomas Aquinas College (CA)	100%	0%	1160-1370	78%	53%
71. Ursinus College (PA)	75%	1%	1140-1350	57%	29%
75. Earlham College (IN)	61%	5%	1090-1330	76%	29%
75. Knox College (IL)	66%	0.4%	26-31	74%	39%
75. Lewis & Clark College (OR)	66%	1%	1220-1390	65%	18%
75. Muhlenberg College (PA)	64%	1%	1120-1320	45%	24%
79. Drew University (NJ)	71%	2%	1010-1248	74%	25%
79. Gustavus Adolphus College (MN)	52%	2%	24-29	74%	29%
81. Austin College (TX)	59%	4%	1130-1350	80%	N/A
81. College of St. Benedict (MN)	53%	0.4%	23-28	85%	29%
81. Cornell College (IA)	62%	0%	24-29	44%	30%
81. Hendrix College (AR)	60%	1%	27-32	80%	27%
81. Juniata College (PA)	76%	1%	1100-1310	72%	33%
81. Luther College (IA)	53%	2%	23-29	70%	28%
81. University of Puget Sound (WA)	54%	0%	1130-1340	63%	18%
88. Augustana College (IL)	61%	1%	23-29	73%	31%
88. Hillsdale College (MI)	77%	0.4%	26-30	62%	26%
88. Hope College (MI)	53%	2%	23-29	84%	28%
88. St. Mary's College of Maryland*	65%	1%	1130-1340	57%	14%
88. Transylvania University (KY)	57%	0%	23-29	81%	45%
93. Allegheny College (PA)	60%	1%	1110-1310	66%	25%
93. Birmingham-Southern Col. (AL)	63%	1%	23-28	59%	24%
93. Millsaps College (MS)	66%	0.4%	23-29	74%	24%
93. St. Mary's College (IN)	57%	2%	23-28	86%	31%
93. St. Michael's College (VT)	59%	1%	1040-1250	81%	20%
93. Washington College (MD)	67%	1%	1030-1230	72%	18%
99. New College of Florida*	64%	3%	1220-1410	53%	17%
99. Westmont College (CA)	61%	4%	1050-1300	80%	31%
101. Calvin College (MI)	39%	1%	23-29	93%	29%
101. Coe College (IA)	76%	1%	23-28	65%	23%
101. Sweet Briar College (VA)	91%	0%	940-1148	82%	35%
101. Washington and Jefferson Col. (PA)	70%	0%	1030-1230	42%	23%
105. Hollins University (VA)	86%	0%	960-1230	90%	31%
105. Lake Forest College (IL)	63%	0.4%	23-28	69%	25%
105. Linfield College (OR)	68%	1%	970-1200	82%	15%
105. Ohio Wesleyan University	68%	0%	23-29	64%	24%
105. Ripon College (WI)	59%	2%	22-27	79%	37%
105. Stonehill College (MA)	42%	0.4%	1120-1280	56%	20%
111. Albion College (MI)	57%	1%	22-28	79%	26%
111. Goucher College (MD)	74%	1%	1060-1300	73%	23%
111. Hampden-Sydney College (VA)	70%	0%	1000-1210	56%	30%
114. Hanover College (IN)	81%	0.4%	990-1220	61%	29%
114. Randolph College (VA)	92%	0%	1000-1220	81%	22%

114. Siena College (NY)
114. Susquehanna University (PA)
114. Wittenberg University (OH)
119. Hampshire College (MA)
119. Presbyterian College (SC)
119. Westminster College (PA)
122. Bennington College (VT)
122. Berry College (GA)
122. Fisk University (TN)
122. McDaniel College (MD)
122. St. Anselm College (NH)
127. Grove City College (PA)
127. Morehouse College (GA)
127. Principia College (IL)
127. St. Norbert College (WI)
131. College of the Atlantic (ME)
131. Gordon College (MA)
131. Moravian College (PA)
131. Randolph-Macon College (VA)
131. Russell Sage College (NY)
131. William Jewell College (MO)
137. Alma College (MI)
137. Bethel College (KS)
137. Concordia College–Moorhead (MN)
137. Eckerd College (FL)
137. Goshen College (IN)
137. Houghton College (NY)
137. Whittier College (CA)
144. Baker University (KS)
144. Central College (IA)
144. Emory and Henry College (VA)
144. Lycoming College (PA)
144. Lyon College (AR)
144. Millikin University (IL)
144. Simpson College (IA)
144. Wells College (NY)
152. Doane College (NE)
152. Hiram College (OH)
152. Nebraska Wesleyan University
152. St. Vincent College (PA)
152. University of Minnesota-Morris*
152. Wartburg College (IA)
158. Illinois College
158. Roanoke College (VA)
158. U. of North Carolina-Asheville*
158. Wesleyan College (GA)
162. Asbury University (KY)
162. Bethany College (WV)
162. Clarke University (IA)
162. Georgetown College (KY)
166. Albright College (PA)
166. Guilford College (NC)
166. Oglethorpe University (GA)
166. Salem College[1] (NC)
166. St. John's College[1] (MD)
166. Tougaloo College (MS)
166. University of Mount Union (OH)
166. Westminster College (MO)
174. College of Idaho (ID)
174. Hartwick College (NY)
174. Hastings College (NE)
174. Maryville College (TN)
174. Merrimack College (MA)
174. Monmouth College (IL)
180. Meredith College (NC)

AMERICA'S SECOND-TIER LIBERAL ARTS COLLEGES

Albertus Magnus College (CT)
Allen University (SC)
Atlantic Union College (MA)
Bennett College (NC)
Bloomfield College (NJ)
Brevard College (NC)
Brigham Young University-Hawaii[1]
California State U.-Monterey Bay*
Cedar Crest College (PA)
Centenary College of Louisiana[1]
Christopher Newport Univ. (VA)*
Coastal Carolina University (SC)*
Colorado State University-Pueblo*
Concordia College[1] (NY)
Dillard University (LA)
Evangel University (MO)
Ferrum College (VA)
Fort Lewis College (CO)*
Franklin Pierce University (NH)
Green Mountain College (VT)
Greensboro College[1] (NC)
Huntingdon College (AL)
Huston-Tillotson University[1] (TX)
Jarvis Christian College (TX)
Johnson C. Smith University (NC)
Judson College[1] (AL)
Kentucky Wesleyan College
Lambuth University[1] (TN)
Lane College (TN)
Lindsey Wilson College (KY)
Marlboro College[1] (VT)
Marymount Manhattan College (NY)
Massachusetts Col. of Liberal Arts*
McPherson College (KS)
Mesa State College (CO)*
Metropolitan State Col. of Denver*
North Greenville University (SC)
Olivet College (MI)
Paine College (GA)
Peace College (NC)
Pine Manor College (MA)
Rust College (MS)
Sierra Nevada College (NV)
Simpson University (CA)
St. Andrews Presbyterian Col. (NC)
Stephens College (MO)

Sterling College (KS)
SUNY College-Old Westbury*
Talladega College[1] (AL)
Texas Lutheran University
Thiel College (PA)
University of Hawaii-Hilo[1]*
University of Hawaii-West Oahu*
University of Maine-Machias*
University of Virginia-Wise*
Univ. of Wisconsin-Green Bay*
Univ. of Wisconsin-Parkside*
Virginia Wesleyan College
West Virginia State University[1]*
West Virginia Wesleyan College
Wingate University (NC)

Liberal Arts Colleges with the Lowest Student to Faculty Ratio

Liberal Arts College	Students Per Faculty Member	Undergraduate Enrollment	U.S. News Rank
Pomona College	7	1,550	6
Randolph College	7	488	114
United States Military Academy	7	4,621	16
Williams College	7	2,067	1
Amherst College	8	1,744	2
Brevard College	8	658	RNP*
Bryn Mawr College	8	1,307	30
Harvey Mudd College	8	757	18
Haverford College	8	1,190	9
Principia College	8	527	127
Sierra Nevada College	8	378	RNP
Swarthmore College	8	1,525	3
Sweet Briar College	8	745	101
University of Richmond	8	2,925	32
Vassar College	8	2,452	12
Wellesley College	8	2,324	4

Schools That Offer BA/MD or BS/MD

BA/MD

Drexel University College of Medicine

University of Missouri-Kansas City School of Medicine

BS/MD

Albany Medical School

Baylor College of Medicine

Boston University School of Medicine

Brody School of Medicine at East Carolina University

Drexel University College of Medicine

George Washington University School of Medicine and Health Sciences

Howard University College of Medicine

Jefferson Medical College

Keck School of Medicine of the University of Southern California

Meharry Medical College

Michigan State University College of Human Medicine

Northeastern Ohio Universities College of Medicine

Northwestern University, The Feinberg School of Medicine

Ponce School of Medicine

Stony Brook University Health Sciences Center School of Medicine

Temple University School of Medicine

The Ohio State University College of Medicine

Tufts University School of Medicine

University of Florida College of Medicine

UMDNJ- New Jersey Medical School

UMDNJ- Robert Wood Johnson Medical School

University of Alabama School of Medicine

University of California, San Diego, School of Medicine

University of Cincinnati College of Medicine

Schools That Offer BA/MD or BS/MD

BS/MD

University of Connecticut School of Medicine

University of Kentucky College of Medicine

University of Miami Miller School of Medicine at Miami

University of Nevada School of Medicine

University of New Mexico School of Medicine

University of Pittsburgh School of Medicine

University of Rochester School of Medicine and Dentistry

University of South Florida College of Medicine

Virginia Commonwealth University School of Medicine

Warren Alpert Medical School of Brown University

Wayne State University School of Medicine

SCHOOLS WITH STRONG DRAMA PROGRAMS

Boston College
Boston University
University of California at Los Angeles
Carnegie Mellon University
The Catholic University of America
DePaul University
Emerson College
Florida State University
Fordham University
Indiana University
University of Iowa
Ithaca College
University of Minnesota
New York University
Northwestern University
University of North Carolina at Chapel Hill
University of Southern California
Southern Methodist University
Syracuse University
Texas Christian University
University of Washington
Yale University

SCHOOLS WITH STRONG JOURNALISM PROGRAMS

University of Michigan
University of Nebraska
Ohio University
University of Oregon
Pepperdine University
St. Lawrence University
Stanford University
University of Utah
University of Wisconsin

SCHOOLS WITH STRONG BUSINESS PROGRAMS

University of Notre Dame
University of Pennsylvania
University of Virginia
Massachusetts Institute of Technology
University of California Berkeley
University of Michigan - Ann Arbor
University of Texas - Austin
American University
Baylor University
Boston College
Boston University
Carnegie Mellon University
Case Western Reserve University
University of Dayton
Emory University
Fordham University
Georgetown University
Howard University
Ithaca College
Lehigh University
New York University
Pepperdine University
Rensselaer Polytechnic Institute
University of San Francisco
Santa Clara University
University of Southern California
Southern Methodist University
Syracuse University
Tulane University
Wake Forest University
Washington University in St. Louis

SCHOOLS WITH STRONG ART/MUSIC PROGRAMS

Academy of Art University, CA
American Academy of Art, IL
American Conservatory of Music, IN
Art Academy of Cincinnati, OH
Art Center College of Design, CA
Art Center Design College, AZ
Art Institute of Atlanta, GA
Art Institute of California: Orange County
Art Institute of California: San Diego
Art Institute of Charlotte, NC
Art Institute of Colorado, CO
Art Institute of Dallas, TX
Art Institute of Houston, TX
Art Institute of Las Vegas, NV
Art Institute of Philadelphia, PA
Art Institute of Phoenix, AZ
Art Institute of Pittsburgh, PA
Art Institute of Washington, VA
Art Institute of California: San Francisco
Art Institute of Fort Lauderdale, FL
Art Institute of Portland, OR
Art Institute of Seattle, WA
Art Institutes International Minnesota, MN
Atlantic College, PR
Baylor University, TX
Berklee College of Music, MA
Boston College, MA
Boston Conservatory, MA
Boston University, MA
Brooks Institute of Photography, CA
Brooks Institute of Photography: Ventura, CA
California College of the Arts, CA
California Institute of the Arts, CA
Carnegie Mellon University, CA
Case Western Reserve University, OH
Chester College of New England, NH
Cleveland Institute of Art, OH
Cleveland Institute of Music, OH
Cogswell Polytechnical College, CA
College for Creative Studies, MI

Schools with Strong Art/Music Programs

College of Visual Arts, MN
Collins College, AZ
Columbia College Chicago ,IL
Columbia College: Hollywood, CA
Columbus College of Art and Design, OH
Conservatory of Music of Puerto Rico, PR
Converse College, SC
Cooper Union for the Advancement of Science and Art, NY
Corcoran College of Art and Design, DC
Cornish College of the Arts, WA
Creative Center, NE
Curtis Institute of Music, PA
DePaul University, IL
DePauw University, IN
DigiPen Institute of Technology, WA
Eastman School of Music of the University of Rochester, NY
Escuela de Artes Plasticas de Puerto Rico, PR
Ex'pression College for Digital Arts, CA
Fashion Institute of Technology, NY
Five Towns College, NY
Florida State University, FL
Harrington College of Design, IL
Harvard University, MA
Illinois Institute of Art: Chicago, IL
Illinois Institute of Art: Shaumburg , IL
Indiana University, IN
Institute of American Indian Arts, NM
Interior Designers Institute, CA
International Academy of Design and Technology Henderson, NV
International Academy of Design and Technology Chicago, IL
International Academy of Design and Technology Detroit, MI
International Academy of Design and Technology Nashville, TN
International Academy of Design and Technology Schaumburg, IL
International Academy of Design and Technology Tampa, FL
Ithaca College, NY
Johns Hopkins University: Peabody Conservatory of Music, MD
Juilliard School, NY
Kansas City Art Institute, MO
Kendall College of Art and Design of Ferris State University, MI
Laguna College of Art and Design, CA

Schools with Strong Art/Music Programs

Lawrence University, WI
Lyme Academy College of Fine Arts, CT
Maine College of Art, ME
Manhattan School of Music, NY
Mannes College The New School for Music, NY
Maryland Institute College of Art, MD
Massachusetts College of Art, MA
Memphis College of Art, TN
Miami International University of Art and Design, FL
Miami University, OH
Milwaukee Institute of Art and Design, WI
Minneapolis College of Art and Design, MN
Montserrat College of Art, MA
Moore College of Art and Design, PA
New England Conservatory of Music, MA
New England Institute of Art, MA
New York School of Interior Design, NY
New School of Architecture and Design, CA
New York University, NY
North Carolina School of the Arts, NC
Northwest College of Art, WA
Northwestern University, IL
O'More College of Design, TN
Oberlin College, OH
Oregon College of Art and Craft, OR
Otis College of Art and Design, CA
Pacific Northwest College of Art, OR
Paier College of Art, CT
Parsons The New School for Design, NY
Pennsylvania College of Art and Design, PA
Platt College San Diego, CA
Pratt Institute, NY
Rhode Island School of Design, RI
Rhodec International, MA
Ringling School of Art and Design, FL
Rocky Mountain College of Art and Design, CO
San Francisco Art Institute, CA
San Francisco Conservatory of Music, CA
Savannah College of Art and Design, GA
School of the Art Institute of Chicago, IL
School of the Museum of Fine Arts, MA

Schools with Strong Art/Music Programs

School of Visual Arts, NY
Southern California Institute of Architecture, CA
Southern Methodist University, TX
State University of New York Purchase, NY
University of California - Los Angeles, CA
University of Cincinnati, OH
University of Colorado- Boulder, CO
University of Denver, CO
University of Miami, FL
University of Michigan, MI
University of Nebraska- Lincoln, NE
University of Oklahoma, OK
University of Southern California, CA
University of The Arts, PA
Vander Cook College of Music, IL
Vanderbilt University, TN
Westminster Choir College of Rider University, NJ
Westwood College: Northlake, GA
Yale University, CT

Top Schools among Jewish Students

Private

New York University
Yeshiva University
Boston University
Cornell University
George Washington University
Northwestern University
University of Pennsylvania
Syracuse University
Columbia University
Emory University
Washington University
Brandeis University
Harvard University & Radcliffe College
Brown University
Yale University
Tulane University and Newcomb College
Long Island University, Brooklyn Campus
University of Hartford
University of Miami
University of Southern California
Hofstra University
Tufts University
American University
Barnard College
Northeastern University
Vanderbilt University
Oberlin College
University of Denver
University of Rochester
Wesleyan University

Public

University of Maryland
University of Florida
Rutgers University
University of Central Florida
University of Michigan
Pennsylvania State University
University of Wisconsin
York University
Queens College
CUNY, Brooklyn College
Florida International University
Indiana University
University at Albany
University of Texas, Austin
University of South Florida
Binghamton University
University of Arizona
Florida State University
McGill University
Michigan State University
Universite de Montreal
University of Toronto
University of Western Ontario
Arizona State University
University of Illinois at Urbana, Champaign
California State University
San Diego State University
University of California, Los Angeles
University of Massachusetts, Amherst

TOP SCHOOLS AMONG JEWISH ORTHODOX STUDENTS

American Jewish University
American University
Barnard College
Binghamton University
Boston University
Brandeis University
Carnegie Mellon University
University of Chicago
Columbia University
Cornell University
Emory University
University of Florida
Franklin & Marshall College
The George Washington University
Goucher College
Indiana University at Bloomington
John Hopkins University
University of Maryland, Baltimore County
University of Maryland, College Park
University of Massachusetts, Amherst
McGill University
University of Miami
University of Michigan, Ann Arbor
Muhlenberg College
New York University
Penn State University, University Park
University of Pennsylvania
University of Pittsburgh
University of Rochester
Rutgers University, New Brunswick
SUNY Albany
Stern College for Women

BFA Degree in Studio Art - Foreign Language Requirements

Art Colleges/BFA - no foreign language requirement

RISD (Providence, RI)

Cooper Union (NYC)

SAIC (Chicago)

MICA (Baltimore)

SAIB (affil. w/Lesley Univ.,Boston)

SMFA (affil. w/Tufts Univ., Boston)

California College of Art (SF/Oakland)

San Francisco Art Institute (San Francisco)

Otis, Cal Arts & Art Center (LA area, Pasadena)

University of the Arts (Philadelphia)

Massachusettes College of Art (Boston)

Corcoran College (Washington, DC)

Pratt Institute (NYC/Brooklyn)

Parsons New School (NYC)

School of Visual Arts (NYC)

SCAD (Savannah, GA)

Kansas City Art Institute

MCAD (Minneapolis)

Liberal Arts Colleges/BFA- no foreign language required, or foreign language recommended/encouraged only

Boston University

University of Denver

Colorado State University

Univ. of the Pacific (Stockton)

Virginia Commonwealth University

George Mason University (Washington, DC)

Rutgers University (NJ)

University of Southern California

NYU (Steinhart School)

College of Santa Fe

University of Hawaii

Ithaca College (NY)

Alfred University (NY)

Washington University (St. Louis)

Manhattanville College (NY)

James Madison University (VA)

University of Miami (Coral Gables)

BFA Degree in Studio Art - Foreign Language Requirements
Liberal Arts Colleges/BFA
2 years foreign language required; some exceptions

University of Arizona - Per rule allowing for up to 2 "deficiencies" in courses, school will accept 1 year American Sign Language from an accredited college or 1 year foreign language; 2
> years middle school foreign language would have to be certified by Archer as equal to 1 year high school foreign language and may be allowed, per admissions officer.

Arizona State University - 1 "deficiency" allowed in 2 course areas; 1 year high school foreign language
> may be ok as above.

University of Oregon - Exceptions may be granted, per website.

American University (Washington, DC) - Exceptions may be granted on case by case basis,
> per admissions officer.

University of New Mexico - Waivers may be granted based on test scores, other circumstances,
> per website.

Temple University (Philadelphia) - May grant exception if disability is documented, per admissions
> officer.

University of Massachusettes (Amherst & Dartmouth) - Exceptions may be granted per special rules
> for students with disabilities, per admissions officer.

University of Texas (Austin) - Student may explain "special circumstances" and/or make up deficiency
> in college, per website.

Carnegie Mellon University (Pittsburgh) - Will make exception for visual arts applicants w/disabilities,
> per admissions officer (lack of foreign language "absolutely not a problem" for such students).

Liberal Arts Colleges/BFA - 2-3 years foreign language required; few or no other exceptions

California Polytechnic University - 2 years, no exceptions other than American Sign Language,
> per admissions officers.

Sonoma State University (CA) - 2 yrs., may offer limited exceptions, per website.

University of Minnesota, University of Iowa - 2 years, but possibly some limited exceptions,
> per website.

University of Florida, University of Connecticut - 2 years, no exceptions other than American Sign
> Language, per admissions officers.

University of Washington - 2 years, 1 year foreign language may be in middle school, 2nd in high school, no exceptions other than American Sign Language.

University of Colorado - 3 years, no exceptions other than American Sign Language, may make up deficiency in college (ASL offered).

Colleges not on this list: those which appear to offer BA (not BFA) degrees in art (e.g., UC campuses, Claremont schools); have religious affiliations; are for "women-only"; are less-desirably located (e.g., most of South, Midwest, etc.); or have more extensive academic requirements (e.g. Michigan, Wisconsin, Syracuse, Cornell, New Hampshire, Georgia, UNC).

THE 50 MOST STRESSFUL COLLEGES

Rank		Tuition/Year
1	Columbia University	$53,874
2	Stanford University	$52,048
3	Harvard University	$50,723
4	University of Pennsylvania	$51,944
5	Washington University in St. Louis	$53,310
6	University of Chicago	$54,194
7	Massachusetts Institute of Technology	$50,446
8	Vanderbilt University	$52,988
9	Northwestern University	$52,463
10	Yale University	$49,800
11	Johns Hopkins University	$53,190
12	Princeton University	$48,580
13	Dartmouth College	$52,275
14	Duke University	$51,865
15	California Institute of Technology	$47,679
16	Cornell University	$52,316
17	Brown University	$51,360
18	University of Southern California	$52,602
19	Carnegie Mellon University	$52,886
20	Tufts University	$52,866
21	Georgetown University	$52,961
22	University of California- Berkeley	$26,257
23	New York University	$53,592
24	Rice University	$45,521
25	University of Notre Dame	$50,789
26	Boston College	$52,624
27	Emory University	$50,356
28	Wake Forest University	$50,980
29	University of California- Los Angeles	$24,524
30	University of Rochester	$51,922
31	Rensselaer Polytechnic Institute	$52,145
32	Brandeis University	$51,503
33	University of Michigan- Ann Arbor	$21,029
34	Lehigh University	$50,300

THE 50 MOST STRESSFUL COLLEGES

Rank		Tuition/Year
35	University of California- San Diego	$22,840
36	University of Virginia	$19,418
37	Case Western Reserve University	$49,048
38	University of California- Santa Barbara	$24,799
39	University of California- Davis	$24,456
40	Georgia Institute of Technology	$17,462
41	University of Miami	$48,898
42	College of William & Mary	$20,872
43	University of North Carolina- Chapel Hill	$15,971
44	University of Illinois- Urbana-Champaign	$22,810
45	University of Texas- Austin	$19,530
46	University of California- Irvine	$22,632
47	Pennsylvania State University- University Park	$24,304
48	University of Washington	$18,100
49	University of Wisconsin- Madison	$16,418
50	Yeshiva University	$43,955

WAITLIST STATISTICS - 2010

	Applicants	Admitted Students	Admit Rate	Offered Spot on Wait List	Agreed to Be on Wait List	Admitted Off Wait List	Total Admits Who Enrolled (Yield)
American	16,939	7,373	44%	2,025	390	40	21%
Amherst	8,099	1,239	15%	1,098	471	2	40%
Barnard	4,618	1,293	28%	N/A	N/A	54	46%
Bates	4,518	1,416	31%	846	223	83	35%
Boston College	29,933	9,310	31%	6,026	2,686	103	25%
Boston University	38,270	22,143	58%	2,370	1,152	8	19%
Bowdoin	6,018	1,185	20%	N/A	N/A	0	43%
Brown	30,135	2,820	9%	N/A	N/A	N/A	53%
Bucknell	7,178	2,252	31%	1,988	691	79	42%
California Institute of Technology	4,859	610	13%	529	337	7	37%
Carnegie Mellon	15,487	5,164	33%	4,463	563	70	30%
Claremont McKenna	4,264	732	17%	905	384	0	43%
Colby	4,207	1,445	34%	971	510	9	34%
Colgate	7,871	2,596	33%	N/A	N/A	0	34%
College of N.J.	9,956	4,707	47%	1,322	445	28	31%
Columbia	26,178	2,472	9%	N/A	N/A	75	58%
Connecticut College	5,301	1,678	32%	1,387	442	0	30%
Cooper Union	3,354	279	8%	74	70	4	76%
Cornell	36,338	6,673	18%	2,561	1,492	0	49%
Dartmouth	18,778	2,165	12%	1,800	1,100	19	53%
Davidson	4,090	1,214	30%	963	422	14	41%
Dickinson	5,030	2,402	48%	432	432	12	28%
Duke	26,770	4,207	16%	3,381	N/A	200	42%
Elon	9,771	4,737	48%	3,403	1,376	159	29%
Emerson	6,865	3,200	47%	1,337	486	78	27%
Emory	15,550	4,488	29%	3,113	1,092	46	31%

Waitlist Statistics - 2010

	Applicants	Admitted Students	Admit Rate	Offered Spot on Wait List	Agreed to Be on Wait List	Admitted Off Wait List	Total Admits Who Enrolled (Yield)
Fashion Institute of Technology	5,572	1,684	30%	N/A	N/A	N/A	75%
George Washington	21,177	6,666	31%	2,100	700	20	37%
Georgetown	18,077	3,619	20%	2,118	1,181	116	44%
Georgia Tech	13,553	6,976	51%	1,506	873	311	40%
Grinnell	3,200	1,228	38%	769	355	13	34%
Hamilton	4,857	1,431	29%	1,104	530	52	33%
Harvard	30,489	2,184	7%	N/A	N/A	70	76%
Holy Cross	6,911	2,450	35%	1,691	595	18	30%
Johns Hopkins	18,459	3,794	21%	3,727	2,121	33	33%
Juilliard	2,467	187	8%	40	36	5	70%
Kenyon	4,066	1,598	39%	776	271	0	30%
Lafayette	5,822	2,425	42%	1,439	535	28	27%
Lehigh	10,337	3,900	38%	2,437	N/A	15	32%
Macalester	4,317	1,837	43%	583	258	0	29%
M.I.T.	16,632	1,676	10%	722	606	65	64%
Middlebury	7,984	1,375	17%	N/A	N/A	N/A	42%
Muhlenberg	4,569	2,194	48%	1,451	383	16	28%
New York University	38,037	11,327	30%	2,628	1,427	117	35%
Northeastern	37,691	14,286	38%	4,994	2,074	163	20%
Northwestern	27,615	6,380	23%	3,188	1,397	21	33%
Penn State	39,256	19,960	51%	1,315	N/A	680	28%
Pepperdine	7,942	2,187	28%	1,625	800	20	31%
Pomona	6,765	990	15%	500	300	0	41%
Princeton	26,247	2,148	8%	1,451	N/A	N/A	N/A
Purdue	31,002	20,085	65%	571	188	155*	33%
Rensselaer Polytechnic	13,643	5,369	39%	1,561	958	72	22%
Rice	12,392	2,634	21%	2,521	1,444	131	36%
Rutgers, New Brunswick	29,382	17,425	59%	1,652	N/A	176	34%

Waitlist Statistics - 2010

	Applicants	Admitted Students	Admit Rate	Offered Spot on Wait List	Agreed to Be on Wait List	Admitted Off Wait List	Total Admits Who Enrolled (Yield)
Skidmore	6,044	2,846	47%	1,448	468	0	26%
Stanford	32,022	2,340	7%	999	N/A	40	72%
SUNY Binghamton	27,163	10,828	40%	1,376	500	28	20%
SUNY Geneseo	9,885	3,711	38%	1,800	1,025	0	28%
SUNY Stony Brook	27,814	11,374	41%	1,847	726	31	24%
Swarthmore	6,040	974	16%	996	410	7	40%
Syracuse	22,914	13,659	60%	2,449	1,101	8	25%
Texas A.&M.	26,632	15,991	60%	7,700	0	451	51%
Trinity College	4,687	2,023	43%	1,337	516	28	29%
Tufts	15,434	3,756	24%	N/A	N/A	0	36%
Tulane	43,817	11,371	26%	4,800	2,875	44	15%
UC, Berkeley	50,312	12,914	26%	202	121	0	41%
UCLA	57,658	13,088	23%	0	0	0	37%
University of Chicago	19,353	3,623	19%	N/A	N/A	71	39%
University of Colorado, Boulder	21,107	17,423	83%	949	224	0	30%
University of Connecticut	22,138	11,947	54%	3,464	1,198	479	27%
University of Delaware	26,518	12,755	48%	2,215	767	593	27%
University of Florida	27,306	11,464	42%	0	0	0	56%
University of Iowa	17,146	13,871	81%	0	0	0	32%
University of Maryland, College Park	26,125	11,667	45%	1,023	N/A	0	34%

Waitlist Statistics - 2010

	Applicants	Admitted Students	Admit Rate	Offered Spot on Wait List	Agreed to Be on Wait List	Admitted Off Wait List	Total Admits Who Enrolled (Yield)
University of North Carolina, Chapel Hill	23,174	7,461	32%	2,258	1,115	486	54%
University of Pennsylvania	26,939	3,847	14%	3,000	1,800	40	63%
University of Rochester	12,697	4,893	39%	765	495	2	25%
University of Southern California	35,800	8,725	24%	0	0	0	33%
University of Vermont	22,314	15,748	71%	3,176	982	0	16%
University of Virginia	22,516	7,200	32%	3,746	2,100	200	46%
University of Washington	22,840	12,956	57%	2,582	1,447	426	44%
University of Wisconsin, Madison	25,488	14,384	56%	2,500	500	0	43%
Vanderbilt	21,827	3,906	18%	N/A	N/A	166	41%
Vassar	7,822	1,847	24%	1,421	568	0	37%
Virginia Tech	20,083	13,412	67%	2,100	1,350	0	40%
Villanova	14,376	6,478	45%	4,957	2,427	479	26%
Wake Forest	10,563	4,232	40%	N/A	N/A	N/A	29%
Washington & Lee	6,624	1,255	19%	2,148	617	55	38%
Washington University in St. Louis	24,939	5,286	21%	N/A	N/A	0	31%
Wesleyan	10,656	2,190	21%	N/A	N/A	N/A	34%
Wheaton	2,083	1,326	64%	343	250	58	45%
Williams	6,636	1,236	19%	1,125	475	32	45%
Yale	25,869	1,940	7%	932	N/A	N/A	N/A

College Acceptances 2010-2011

	2011 Total Applicants	2011 Number of Students Accepted	2011 Acceptance Rate	2010 Total Applicants	2010 Number of Students Accepted	2010 Acceptance Rate
American	18,733	7,763	41.44%	16,953	7,334	43.26%
Amherst	8,438	1,077	12.76%	8,099	1,240	15.31%
Babson	5,077	1,685	33.19%	4,061	1,606	39.55%
Barnard	5,154	1,284	24.91%	4,618	1,285	27.83%
Bates	5,195	1,396	26.87%	4,518	1,438	31.83%
Boston College	33,000	9,200	27.88%	29,933	9,310	31.10%
Boston University	41,734	19,905	47.69%	38,275	22,187	57.97%
Bowdoin	6,554	1,022	15.59%	6,018	1,183	19.66%
Brandeis	8,915	3,444	38.63%	7,753	2,746	35.42%
Brown	30,946	2,692	8.70%	30,135	2,804	9.30%
Bucknell	7,937	2,161	27.23%	7,178	2,253	31.39%
California Tech.	5,225	628	12.02%	4,859	610	12.55%
Carleton	4,977	1,474	29.62%	4,856	1,496	30.81%
Carnegie Mellon	16,525	5,023	30.40%	15,459	5,135	33.22%
Case Western	13,527	6,526	48.24%	9,472	6,319	66.71%
Claremont McKenna	4,481	619	13.81%	4,264	729	17.10%
Clark	4,113	2,763	67.18%	4,020	2,799	69.63%
Colby	5,175	1,505	29.08%	4,213	1,445	34.30%
Colgate	7,839	2,271	28.97%	7,871	2,596	32.98%
Colorado College	4,915	1,255	25.53%	4,466	1,501	33.61%
College of New Jersey	10,149	4,400	43.35%	9,954	4,500	45.21%
Columbia	34,929	2,419	6.93%	26,178	2,397	9.16%
Connecticut College	5,239	1,737	33.16%	5,301	1,678	31.65%
Cooper Union	3,502	253	7.22%	3,354	280	8.35%
Cornell	36,392	6,534	17.95%	36,338	6,673	18.36%
Curtis Institute of Music	272	8	2.94%	274	10	3.65%
Dartmouth	22,385	2,178	9.73%	18,778	2,165	11.53%
Davidson	4,757	1,192	25.06%	4,066	1,207	29.69%
Dickinson	6,061	2,531	41.76%	5,033	2,405	47.78%
Duke	29,689	3,739	12.59%	26,770	3,372	12.60%

COLLEGE ACCEPTANCES 2010-2011

	2011 Total Applicants	2011 Number of Students Accepted	2011 Acceptance Rate	2010 Total Applicants	2010 Number of Students Accepted	2010 Acceptance Rate
Elon	9,051	5,150	56.90%	9,771	4,770	48.82%
Emerson	7,431	3,599	48.43%	6,861	3,239	47.21%
Emory	17,027	4,410	25.90%	15,550	4,444	28.58%
Fordham	31,653	12,698	40.12%	27,676	14,020	50.66%
George Washington	21,500	6,890	32.05%	21,177	6,666	31.48%
Georgetown	19,275	3,466	17.98%	18,100	3,490	19.28%
Georgia Tech.	14,209	6,807	47.91%	13,564	6,976	51.43%
Grinnell	2,966	1,315	44.34%	3,200	1,228	38.38%
Hamilton	5,264	1,408	26.75%	4,857	1,430	29.44%
Harvard	34,950	2,158	6.17%	30,489	2,184	7.16%
Harvey Mudd	3,144	614	19.53%	2,718	638	23.47%
Haverford	3,476	865	24.88%	3,312	860	25.97%
Holy Cross	7,350	2,445	33.27%	6,911	2,451	35.47%
Johns Hopkins	19,388	3,550	18.31%	18,459	3,787	20.52%
Juilliard	2,543	140	5.51%	2,466	183	7.42%
Kenyon	4,272	1,416	33.15%	4,067	1,598	39.29%
Lafayette	5,710	2,298	40.25%	5,822	2,425	41.65%
Lehigh	11,589	3,816	32.93%	10,328	3,913	37.89%
Macalester	6,109	1,936	31.69%	4,317	1,837	42.55%
M.I.T.	17,909	1,715	9.58%	16,632	1,676	10.08%
Middlebury	8,533	1,514	17.74%	7,984	1,529	19.15%
Muhlenberg	4,872	2,065	42.39%	4,568	2,195	48.05%
New York University	42,242	10,831	25.64%	38,037	11,327	29.78%
Northeastern	43,250	14,840	34.31%	37,690	14,293	37.92%
Northwestern	30,975	5,575	18.00%	27,615	6,379	23.10%
Notre Dame	16,543	3,995	24.15%	14,510	4,009	27.63%
Oberlin	6,982	2,074	29.70%	6,846	2,207	32.24%
Pennsylvania State	42,979	20,053	46.66%	39,098	18,708	47.85%
Pomona College	7,207	979	13.58%	6,764	997	14.74%
Princeton	27,189	2,282	8.39%	26,247	2,311	8.80%

COLLEGE ACCEPTANCES 2010-2011

	2011 Total Applicants	2011 Number of Students Accepted	2011 Acceptance Rate	2010 Total Applicants	2010 Number of Students Accepted	2010 Acceptance Rate
Purdue	29,283	19,360	66.11%	30,707	19,992	65.11%
Rensselaer Polytechnic	14,554	5,601	38.48%	13,464	5,381	39.97%
Rice	13,803	2,568	18.60%	12,393	2,639	21.29%
Sarah Lawrence	2,001	1,211	60.52%	1,925	1,200	62.34%
Skidmore	5,770	2,411	41.79%	6,044	2,846	47.09%
Smith	4,128	1,877	45.47%	4,015	1,881	46.85%
Southern Methodist	12,817	5,503	42.94%	9,007	4,899	54.39%
Stanford	34,348	2,427	7.07%	32,022	2,340	7.31%
SUNY, Binghamton	28,060	11,276	40.19%	27,162	10,833	39.88%
Swarthmore	6,547	977	14.92%	6,041	967	16.01%
Tufts	17,130	3,735	21.80%	15,433	3,757	24.34%
Tulane	37,751	9,376	24.84%	43,816	11,384	25.98%
UCLA	61,513	15,551	25.28%	57,670	13,088	22.69%
University of Chicago	21,773	3,446	15.83%	19,340	3,639	18.82%
University of Colorado, Boulder	20,452	17,249	84.34%	20,998	17,445	83.08%
University of Connecticut	27,149	10,865	40.02%	22,028	10,874	49.36%
University of Delaware	24,469	13,058	53.37%	26,518	12,755	48.10%
University of Florida	29,269	11,423	39.03%	27,999	11,184	39.94%
University of Iowa	18,500	13,969	75.51%	17,220	13,098	76.06%
University of Maryland, College Park	26,195	11,730	44.78%	26,147	11,671	44.64%
University North Carolina, Chapel Hill	23,726	6,965	29.36%	23,271	7,559	32.48%
University of Pennsylvania	31,659	3,880	12.26%	26,940	3,840	14.25%

COLLEGE ACCEPTANCES 2010-2011

	2011 Total Applicants	2011 Number of Students Accepted	2011 Acceptance Rate	2010 Total Applicants	2010 Number of Students Accepted	2010 Acceptance Rate
University of Richmond	9,419	2,989	31.73%	8,661	2,857	32.99%
University of Rochester	14,890	5,012	33.66%	13,851	4,937	35.64%
University of Southern California	37,107	8,449	22.77%	35,794	8,715	24.35%
University of Texas, Austin	32,577	14,865	45.63%	31,022	14,583	47.01%
University of Virginia	24,010	7,750	32.28%	22,512	7,212	32.04%
University of Wisconsin, Madison	28,814	14,341	49.77%	25,522	14,423	56.51%
Vanderbilt	24,756	3,825	15.45%	21,763	3,542	16.28%
Vassar	7,985	1,779	22.28%	7,822	1,846	23.60%
Villanova	15,387	6,561	42.64%	14,361	6,483	45.14%
Virginia Tech.	21,009	13,545	64.47%	19,981	13,389	67.01%
Washington & Lee	6,488	1,127	17.37%	6,627	1,259	19.00%
Washington University in St. Louis	28,826	4,440	15.40%	24,939	5,285	21.19%
Wesleyan University	10,033	2,368	23.60%	10,657	2,190	20.55%
Wheaton	3,272	1,930	58.99%	3,555	2,097	58.99%
William and Mary	12,820	4,433	34.58%	12,539	3,983	31.76%
Williams	7,030	1,199	17.06%	6,633	1,237	18.65%
Yale	27,282	2,006	7.35%	25,869	2,039	7.88%

geographic
locations

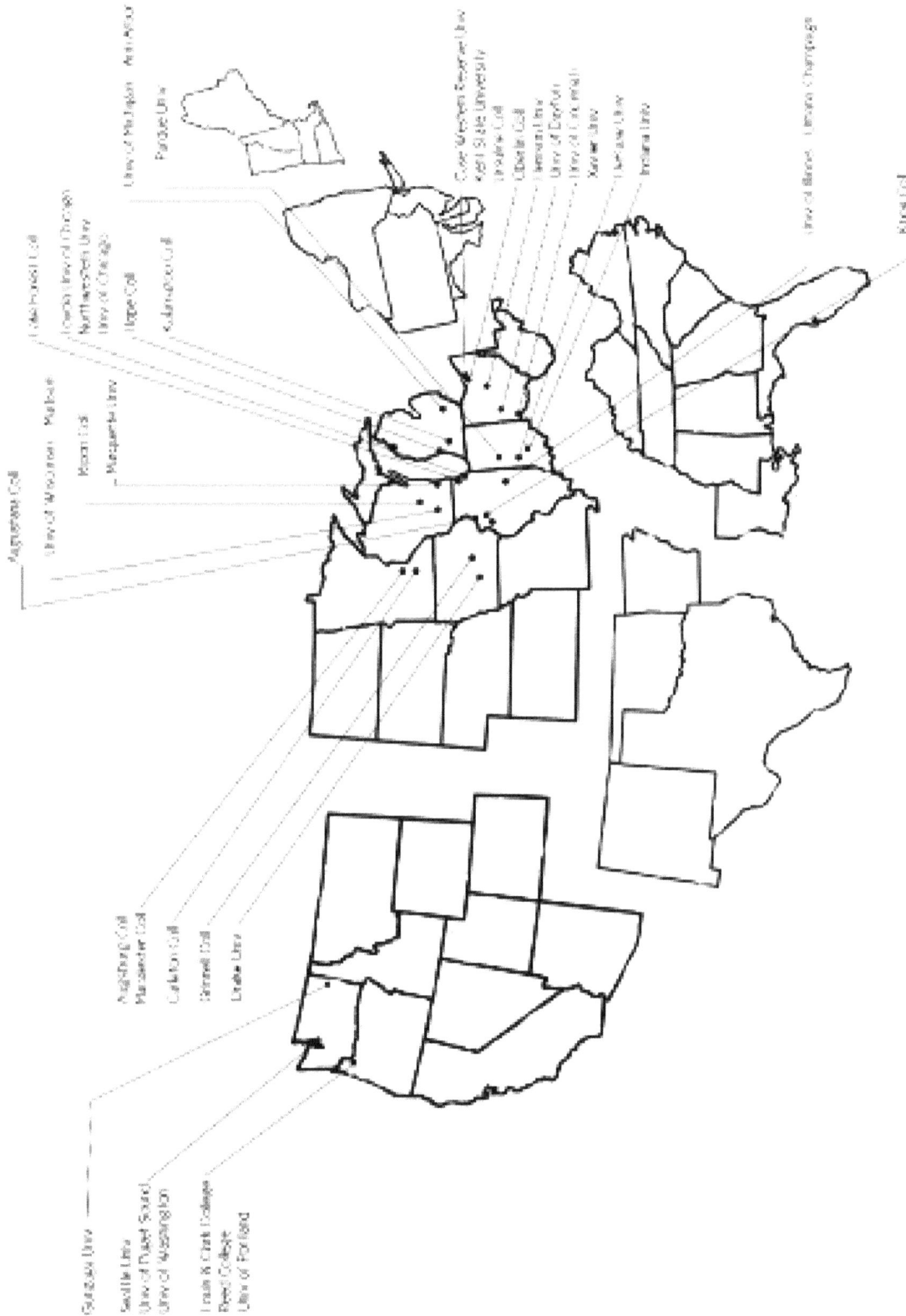

Augustana Coll

Univ of Wisconsin, Madison · Beloit Coll

Ripon Coll

Marquette Univ

Macalester Coll

Univ of Michigan, Ann Arbor

Purdue Univ

Case Western Reserve Univ
Kent State University
Kenyon Coll
Oberlin Coll
Denison Univ
Univ of Dayton
Univ of Cincinnati
Xavier Univ
DePauw Univ
Indiana Univ

Univ of Illinois, Urbana-Champaign

Knox Coll

Macalester Coll
Illinois Inst of Chicago
Northwestern Univ
Univ of Chicago
Ripon Coll
Kalamazoo Coll

Augsburg Coll
Macalester Coll

Carleton Coll

Grinnell Coll

Drake Univ

Gonzaga Univ

Seattle Univ
Univ of Puget Sound
Univ of Washington

Lewis & Clark College
Reed College
Univ of Portland

CALIFORNIA

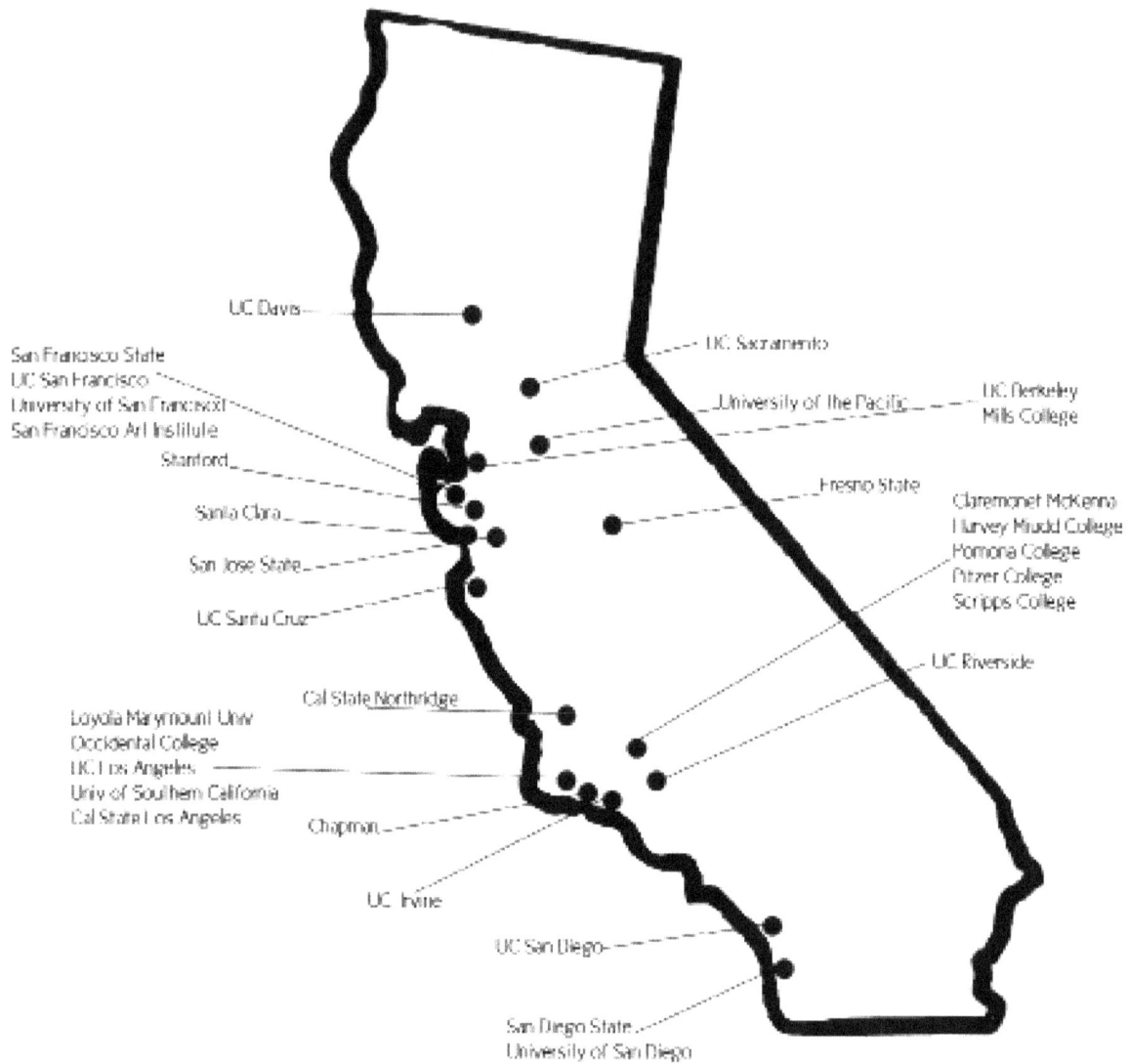

UC Davis

UC Sacramento

San Francisco State
UC San Francisco
University of San Francisco
San Francisco Art Institute

University of the Pacific

UC Berkeley
Mills College

Stanford

Fresno State

Santa Clara

Claremont McKenna
Harvey Mudd College
Pomona College
Pitzer College
Scripps College

San Jose State

UC Santa Cruz

UC Riverside

Cal State Northridge

Loyola Marymount Univ
Occidental College
UC Los Angeles
Univ of Southern California
Cal State Los Angeles

Chapman

UC Irvine

UC San Diego

San Diego State
University of San Diego

FLORIDA

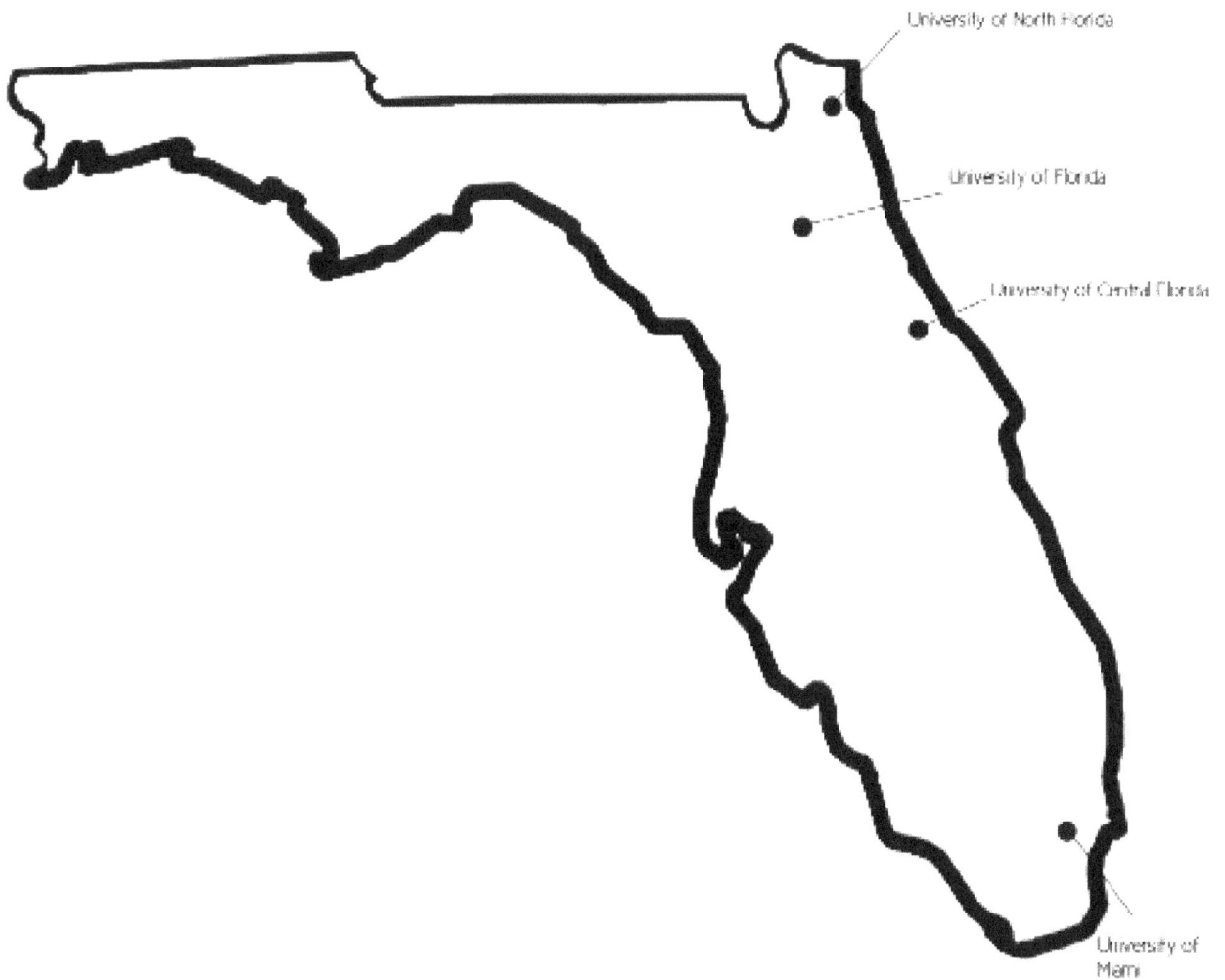

University of North Florida

University of Florida

University of Central Florida

University of Miami

MARYLAND

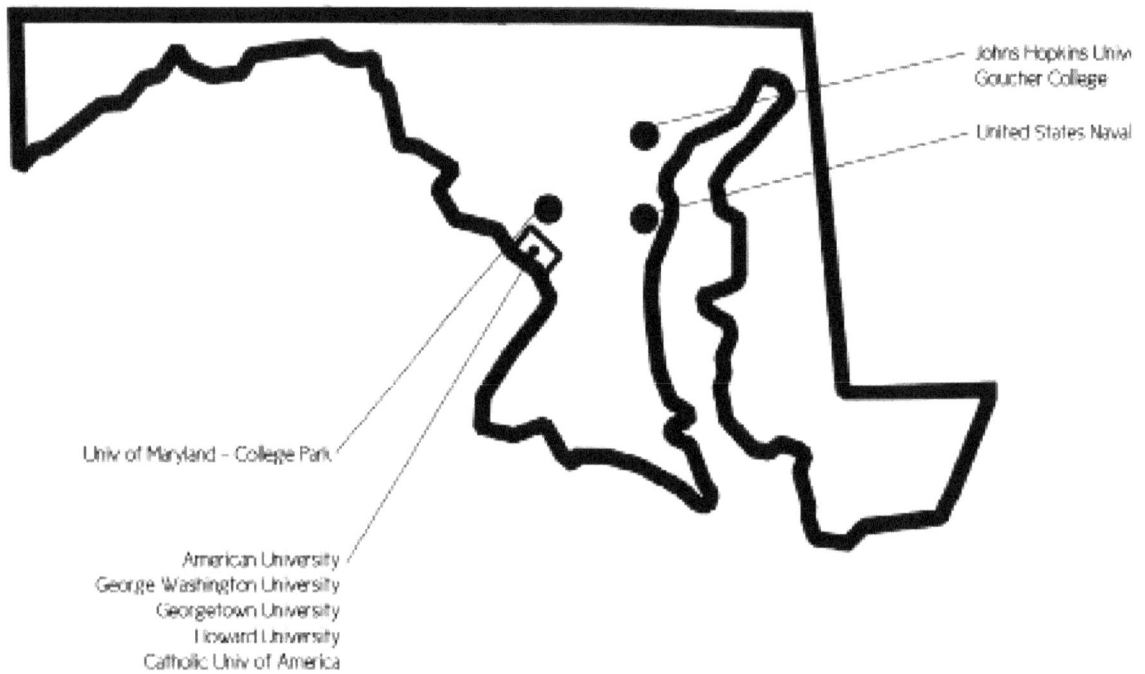

Johns Hopkins Univ
Goucher College

United States Naval

Univ of Maryland – College Park

American University
George Washington University
Georgetown University
Howard University
Catholic Univ of America

MASSACHUSETTS

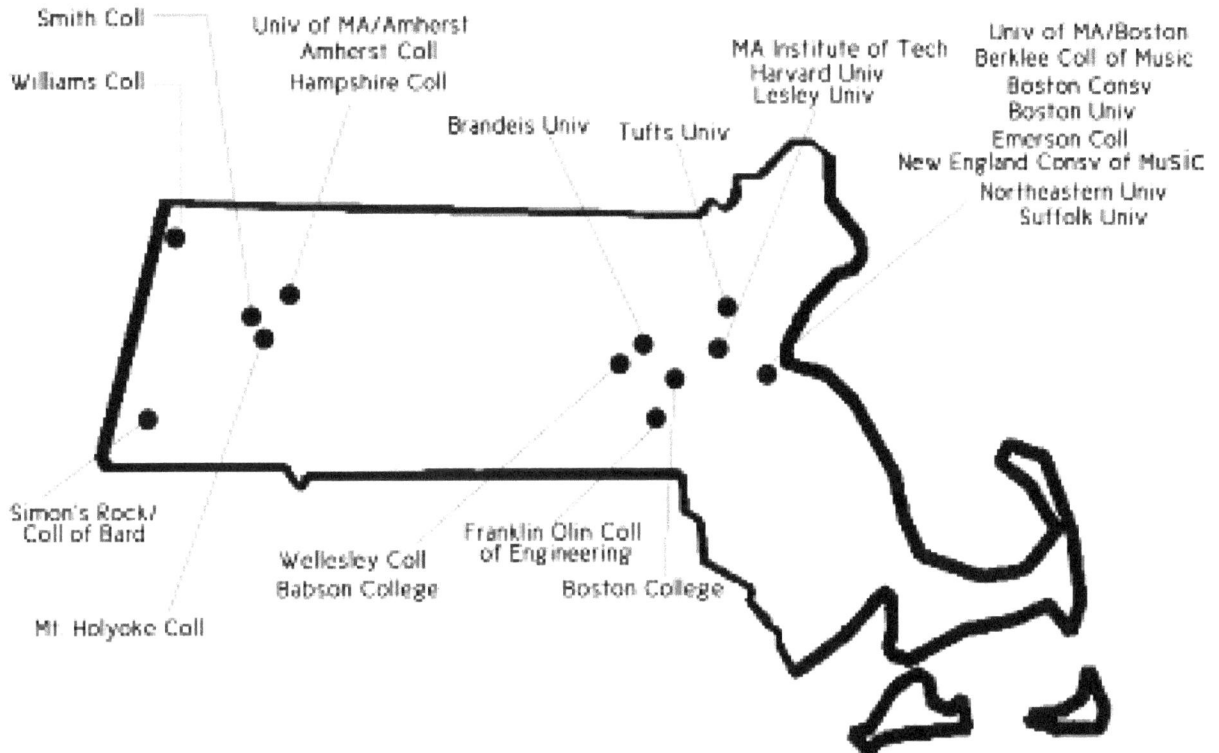

Smith Coll

Williams Coll

Univ of MA/Amherst
Amherst Coll
Hampshire Coll

Brandeis Univ   Tufts Univ

MA Institute of Tech
Harvard Univ
Lesley Univ

Univ of MA/Boston
Berklee Coll of Music
Boston Consv
Boston Univ
Emerson Coll
New England Consv of Music
Northeastern Univ
Suffolk Univ

Simon's Rock/
Coll of Bard

Wellesley Coll
Babson College

Franklin Olin Coll
of Engineering

Boston College

Mt Holyoke Coll

MID-ATLANTIC

Skidmore College

Union College

Albany Medical College
Rensselaer Polytechnic Institute
Siena College

Bard College

Vassar College

Syracuse University

U.S. Military Academy   West Point

University of Rochester

Manhattanville College

Hamilton Coll

Hofstra University

Colgate University

Cornell University
Ithaca College

Barnard College
Columbia University
Cooper Union
Fashion Institute of Technology
Fordham University
Juilliard
Manhattan College
New School University
New York University
Pace Univ   New York
Sarah Lawrence College
Touro College
Yeshiva Univ

Wagner College

Monmouth Univ

Montclair State Univ

Seton Hall Univ

Rutgers Univ   New Brunswick

Drew Univ

Princeton University

University of Delaware

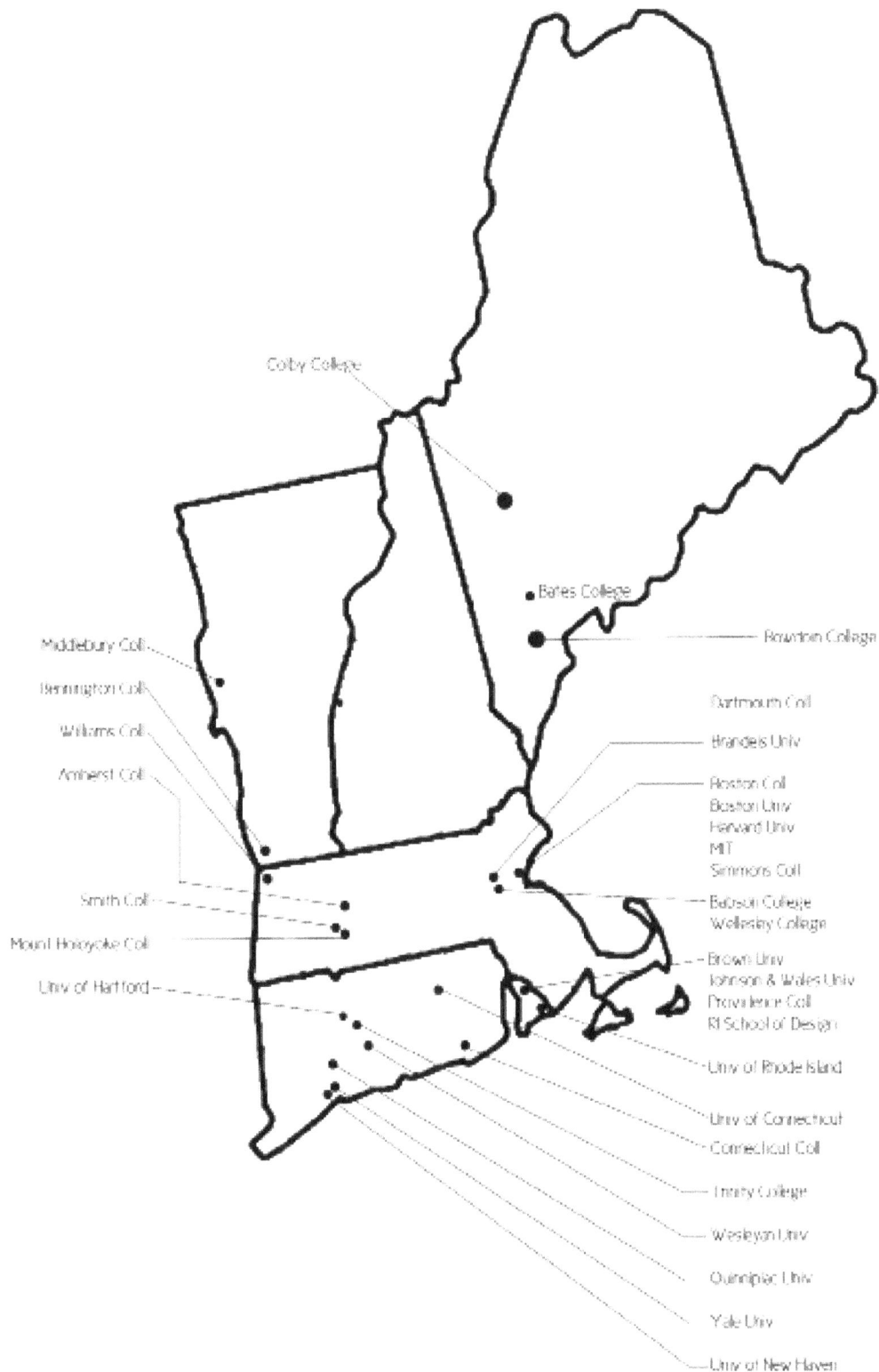

NEW ENGLAND

Colby College

Bates College

Bowdoin College

Middlebury Coll

Bennington Coll

Williams Coll

Amherst Coll

Dartmouth Coll

Brandeis Univ

Boston Coll
Boston Univ
Harvard Univ
MIT
Simmons Coll

Babson College
Wellesley College

Smith Coll

Mount Holyoke Coll

Univ of Hartford

Brown Univ
Johnson & Wales Univ
Providence Coll
RI School of Design

Univ of Rhode Island

Univ of Connecticut

Connecticut Coll

Trinity College

Wesleyan Univ

Quinnipiac Univ

Yale Univ

Univ of New Haven

New Jersey

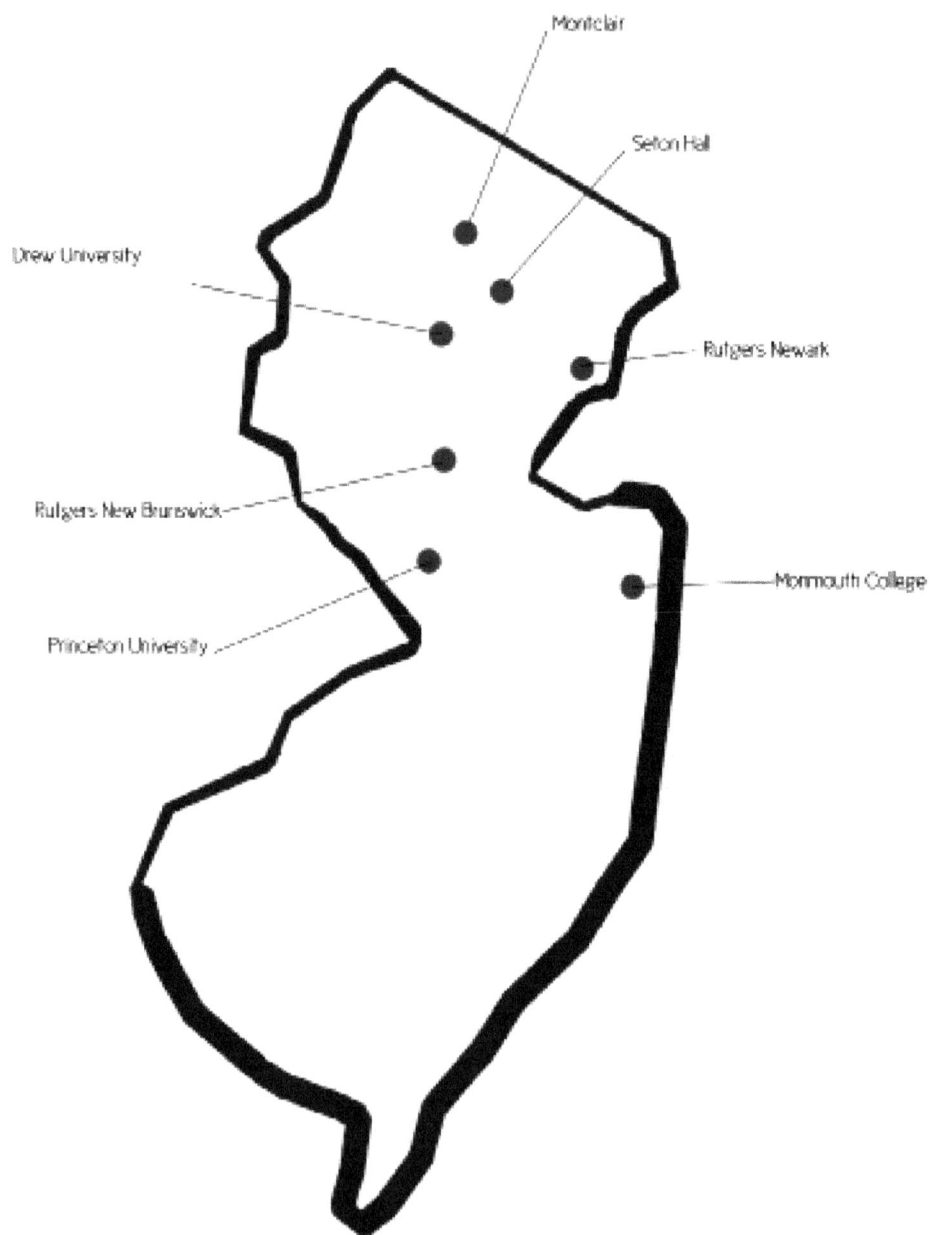

NEW YORK

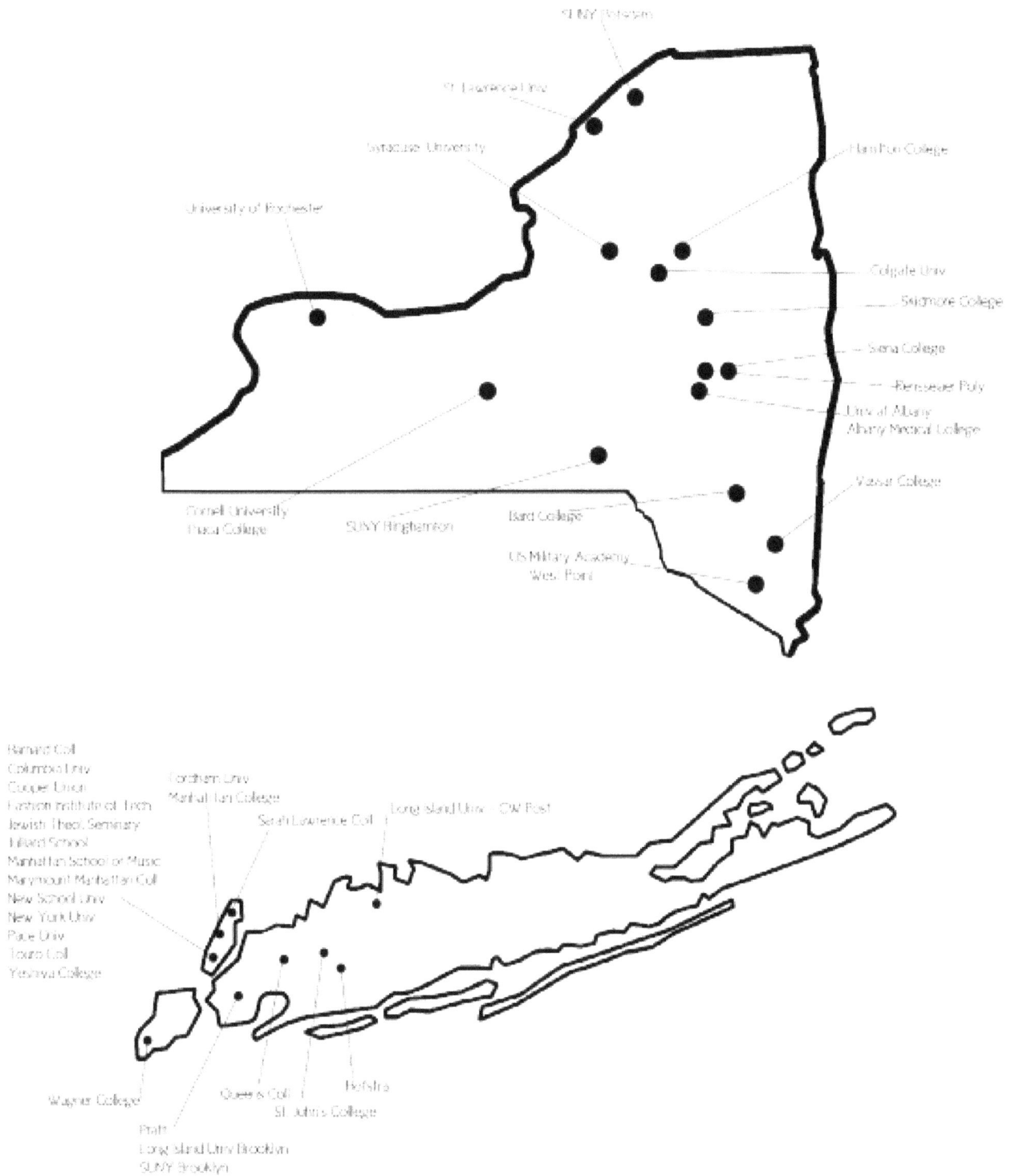

SUNY Potsdam

St. Lawrence Univ

Syracuse University

University of Rochester

Hamilton College

Colgate Univ

Skidmore College

Siena College

Rensselaer Poly

Univ of Albany
Albany Medical College

Cornell University
Ithaca College

SUNY Binghamton

Bard College

Vassar College

US Military Academy
West Point

Barnard Coll
Columbia Univ
Cooper Union
Fashion Institute of Tech
Jewish Theol Seminary
Juliard School
Manhattan School of Music
Marymount Manhattan Coll
New School Univ
New York Univ
Pace Univ
Touro Coll
Yeshiva College

Fordham Univ
Manhattan College

Sarah Lawrence Col

Long Island Univ - CW Post

Wagner College

Queens Coll

St. Johns College

Hofstra

Pratt
Long Island Univ Brooklyn
SUNY Brooklyn

NORTH CAROLINA

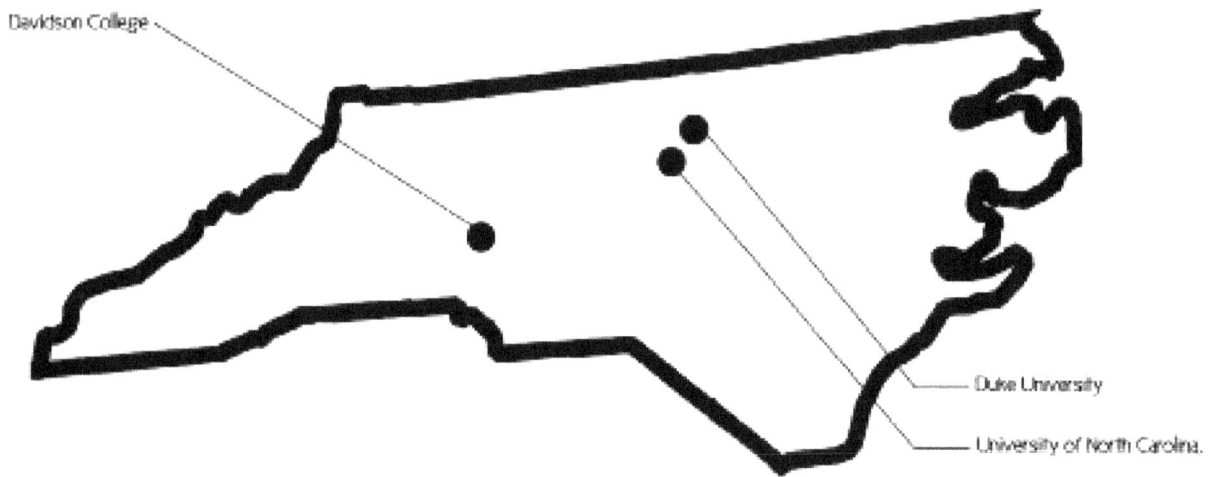

Davidson College

Duke University

University of North Carolina.

PENNSYLVANIA

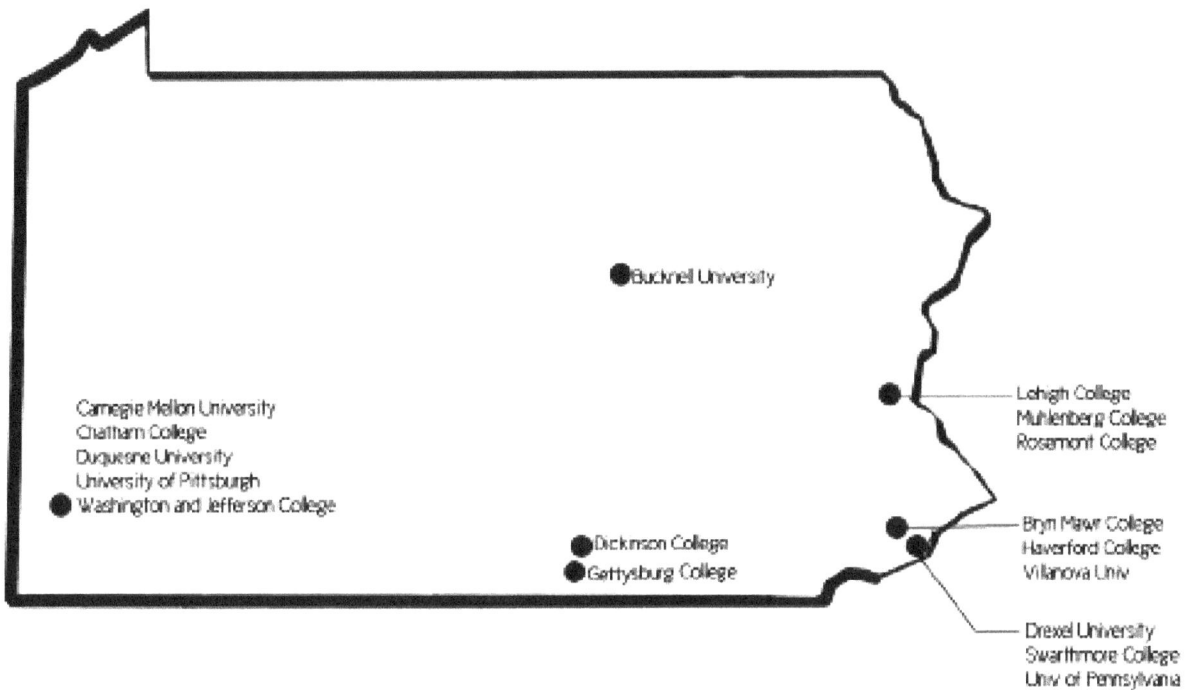

Bucknell University

Carnegie Mellon University
Chatham College
Duquesne University
University of Pittsburgh
Washington and Jefferson College

Dickinson College
Gettysburg College

Lehigh College
Muhlenberg College
Rosemont College

Bryn Mawr College
Haverford College
Villanova Univ

Drexel University
Swarthmore College
Univ of Pennsylvania

SOUTHEAST REGION

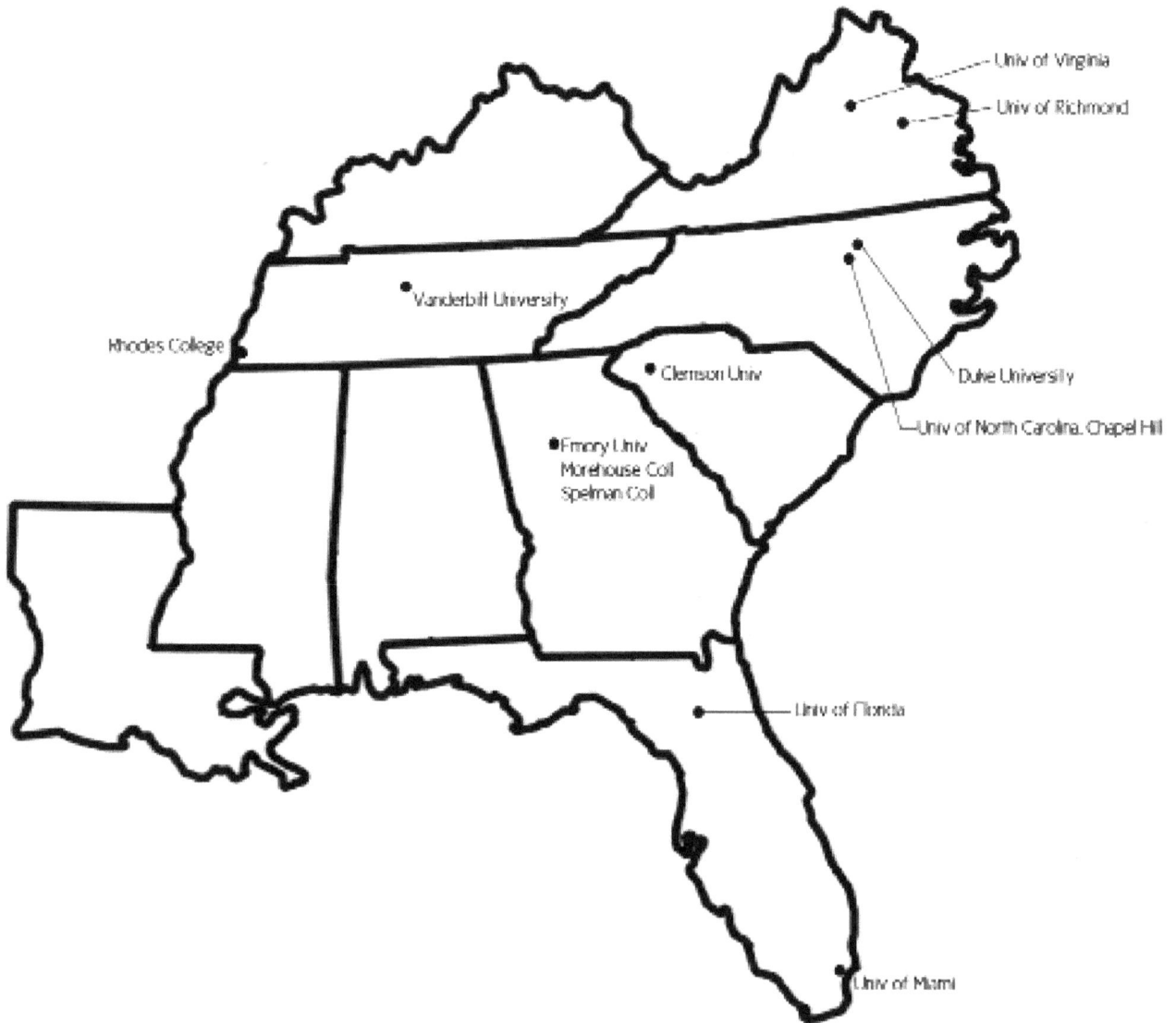

- Univ of Virginia
- Univ of Richmond
- Vanderbilt University
- Rhodes College
- Clemson Univ
- Duke University
- Univ of North Carolina, Chapel Hill
- Emory Univ
- Morehouse Coll
- Spelman Coll
- Univ of Florida
- Univ of Miami

Texas

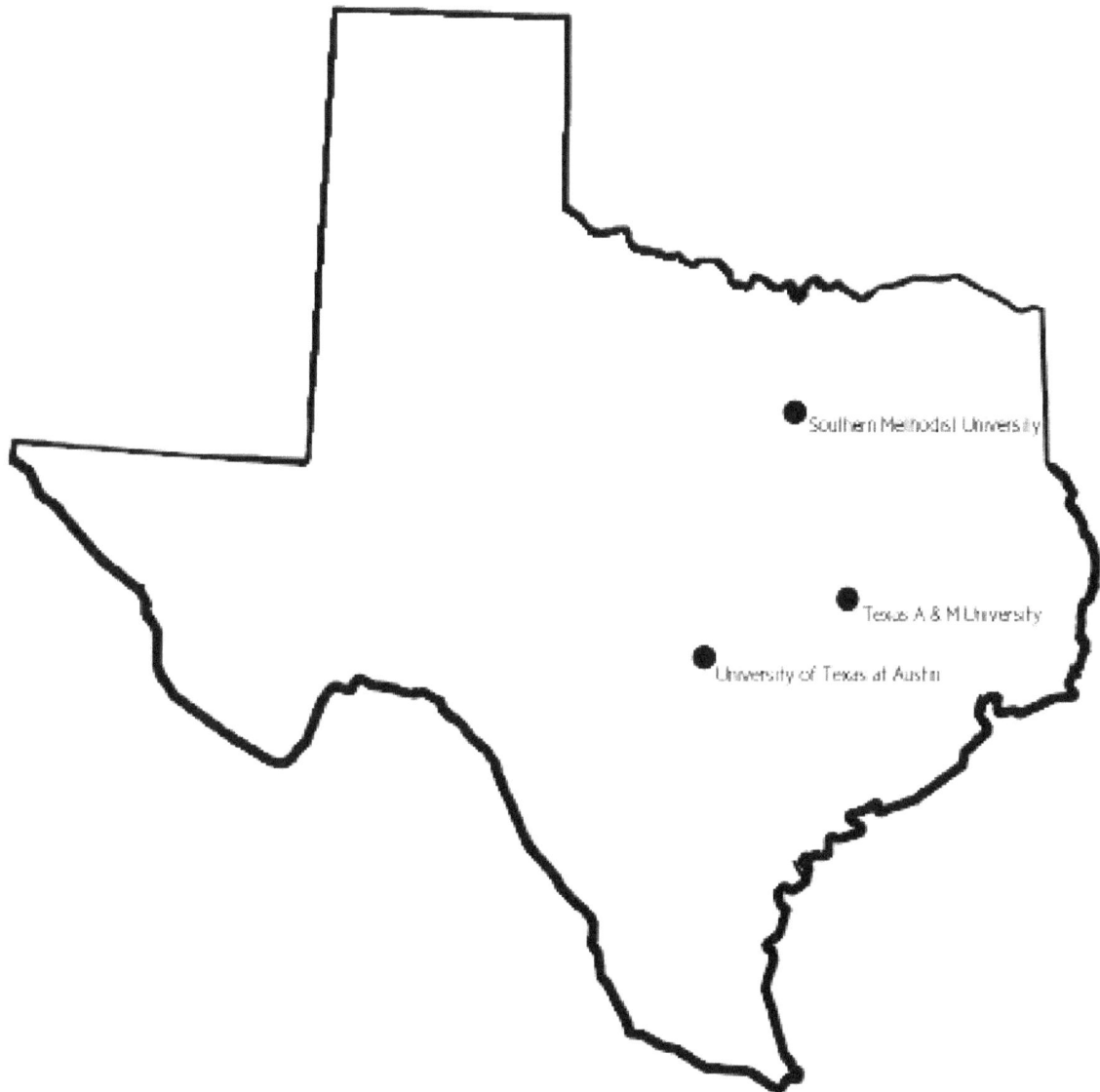

Southern Methodist University

Texas A & M University

University of Texas at Austin

Virginia

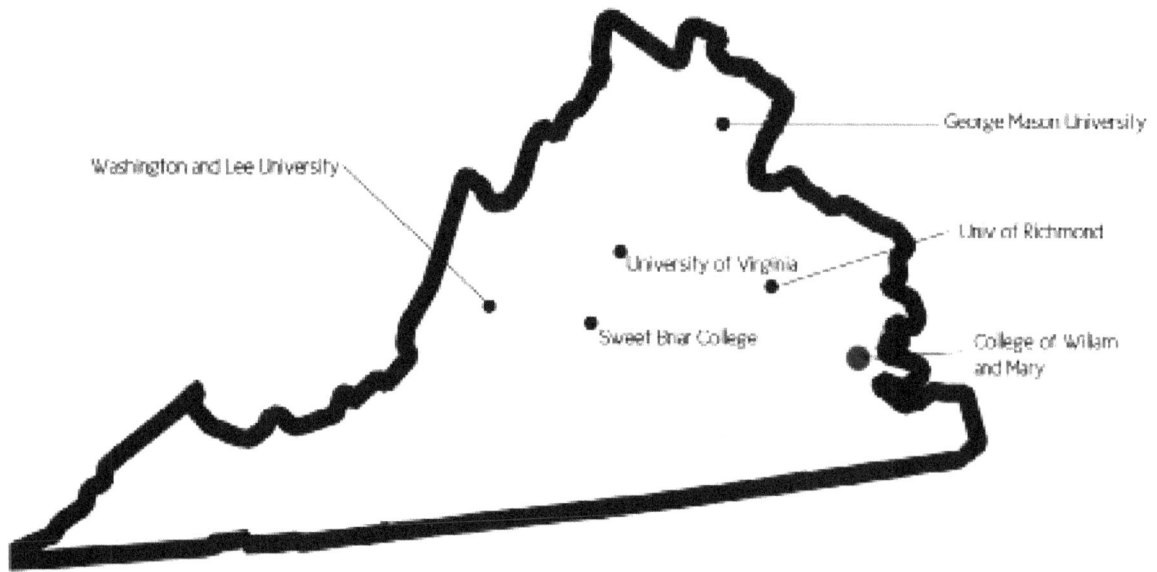

George Mason University

Washington and Lee University

Univ of Richmond

University of Virginia

Sweet Briar College

College of William and Mary

financial
aid

College Costs: Adding it All Up

Student Financial Aid

Determine what amount of financing you will need.

Understand the financial aid process.

Types of Student Financial Aid

1. Scholarships

   You want all of the FREE money you can get. True, most scholarship awards are for athletic and academic merits. But there are other scholarships for talents and affiliations. Use a national database to begin your search.

2. Federal Student Loans

   The most popular form of financial aid. Federal student loans are generally processed through your college. You don't have to repay these loans until after you leave or graduate from school.

3. Federal PLUS Loans

   Federal loans for parents of undergraduate students. Parents can borrow up to the full cost of college attendance minus any financial aid awarded to the student.

4. Private Student Loans

   Sometimes loans, scholarships, grants, and other college aid do not cover the full cost of college, including personal expenses such as a computer. Many students are using private student loans to cover the gap.

5. Home Equity Loans

   Using the security of your home, you can finance college without restrictions.

COLLEGE COSTS: ADDING IT ALL UP

The cost of *attendance* generally includes the following:

- Tuition and fees

- Room and board

- Books and supplies

- Transportation

- Personal expenses

Increasingly, there is some flexibility in what are sometimes called fixed costs, like tuition and fees and room and board. For example, colleges have many dormitory room options and many meal plans. At private institutions, tuition is usually the same for all students, but at public institutions it can depend on a stud state of residence. (Many states have consortia that charge students from neighboring states the same amount as in-state students.)

The invaluable *Counselors and Mentors Handbook on Federal Student Aid*, published by the U.S. Department of Education, explains how a college determines cost. The financial aid administrator at a school usually develops a attendance for different categories of students. Some programs of study might have lab fees or higher charges for books and supplies than other programs. Students living off campus might have slightly higher allowable costs for room and board and transportation expenses than students living on campus. The law specifies that the cost of attendance includes tuition and fees and an allowance for living expenses such as room and board, books and supplies, miscellaneous personal expenses (including a reasonable allowance for renting or purchasing a personal computer), and transportation costs.)

Unfixed costs can be high. Colleges themselves estimate that books and supplies range from $800 to $900 or more a year, and students in fields requiring special equipment (such as architecture and engineering) will spend more. Transportation costs can only be approximate.

Finally, personal expenses. Colleges estimate that students spend between $1,000 and $2,000 a year on personal expenses. The amount may shock some families, but you can help them put the figure into context: Do their children eat snacks, go to the movies, get their hair cut, and buy CDs and clothes now? They will continue to do so in college!

COLLEGES THAT EMPLOY A NEED BLIND POLICY

Institutions that employ a need blind admissions policy do not consider an applicant's financial situation when deciding admission. Generally, an in in students admitted under a need-blind policy and needing financial aid requires the institution to back the policy with an ample endowment or source of funding.

Need-blind admissions systems are rare. Most universities cannot offer it and not all that do offer it to all students; many schools offer need-blind admission to American first-year students but not to internationals or to transfer students.

Amherst College	Georgetown University	University of Chicago
Beloit College	Grinnell College	University of Miami
Boston College	Harvard University	University of Notre Dame
Brandeis University	Haverford College	University of Pennsylvania
Brown University	Knox College	University of Richmond
California Institute of Technology	Massachusetts Institute of Technology	University of Rochester
Claremont McKenna College	Middlebury College	University of Southern California
College of the Holy Cross	Northwestern University	University of Virginia
Columbia University	Phillips Academy	Vassar College
Cornell University	Pomona College	Vanderbilt University
Cooper Union	Princeton University	Wake Forest University
Dartmouth College	Rice University	Wellesley College
Davidson College	Roxbury Latin	Wesleyan University
Duke University	Stanford University	Williams College
Emory University	Swarthmore College	Yale University

COLLEGES THAT CLAIM TO MEET THE FULL FINANCIAL NEED OF STUDENTS

Adrian College
Amherst College
Barnard College
Bates College
Boston College
Bowdoin College
Brown University
Bryn Mawr College
California Institute of Technology
Carleton College
Chapman University
Claremont McKenna College
Colby College
Colgate University
College of Holy Cross
Columbia University
Connecticut College
Cornell University
Dartmouth College
Davidson College
Duke University
Emory University
Georgetown University
Gettysburg College
Grinnell College
Hamilton College
Harvard University
Harvey Mudd College
Haverford College
Lafayette College
Macalester College
Massachusetts Institute of Technology
Middlebury College

Mount Holyoke College
Northwestern University
Oberlin College
Occidental College
Pitzer College
Pomona College
Princeton University
Reed College
Rice University
Salem College
Scripps College
Smith College
St. Olaf College
Stanford University
SUNY College, Environmental Science and Forestry
Swarthmore College
Thomas Aquinas College
Trinity College
Tufts University
University of Chicago
University of North Carolina-Chapel Hill
University of Notre Dame
University of Pennsylvania
University of Richmond
University of Virginia
Vanderbilt University
Vassar College
Wabash College
Washington University in St. Louis
Wellesley College
Wesleyan University
Williams College
Yale University

INSTITUTIONS @ $50,000 TUITION OR MORE PER YEAR

	Tuition, fees, room, and board ($)		
	2010-11	2009-10	1-year increase
Sarah Lawrence College	$57,384	$55,788	2.90%
Landmark College	$56,500	$53,900	4.80%
Columbia University School of General Studies	$54,782	$51,930	5.50%
Wesleyan University	$53,976	$51,432	4.90%
Columbia University	$53,874	$51,544	4.50%
Johns Hopkins University	$53,690	$51,690	3.90%
Georgetown University	$53,591	$52,161	2.70%
New York University	$53,589	$51,993	3.10%
Harvey Mudd College	$53,588	$51,137	4.80%
Barnard College	$53,496	$50,969	5.00%
Bard College	$53,480	$51,180	4.50%
Trinity College (Conn.)	$53,330	$51,400	3.80%
Washington University in St. Louis	$53,315	$51,193	4.10%
Bates College	$53,300	$51,300	3.90%
University of Chicago	$53,244	$51,078	4.20%
Claremont McKenna College	$53,230	$51,035	4.30%
Connecticut College	$53,110	$51,115	3.90%
Fordham Universtiy	$53,093	$50,598	4.90%
Vassar College	$53,090	$51,470	3.10%
Pitzer College	$53,080	$50,770	4.50%
George Washington University	$53,025	$51,775	2.40%
Vanderbilt University	$53,000	$51,228	3.50%
Haverford College	$52,970	$50,975	3.90%
Stevens Institute of Technology	$52,965	$50,750	4.40%
Babson College	$52,916	$50,324	5.20%
Bennington College	$52,900	$50,860	4.00%
Scripps College	$52,900	$50,550	4.60%
Bowdoin College	$52,880	$50,900	3.90%
New School Parsons School of Design	$52,870	$51,270	3.10%
Tufts University	$52,866	$51,088	3.50%
Occidental College	$52,815	$49,702	6.30%

Institutions @ $50,000 Tuition or More Per Year

	Tuition, fees, room, and board ($)		
	2010-11	2009-10	1-year increase
Carnegie Mellon University	$52,690	$51,068	3.20%
Boston College	$52,624	$50,970	3.20%
Bard College at Simon's Rock	$52,610	$50,340	4.50%
Oberlin College	$52,587	$50,484	4.20%
Middlebury College	$52,500	$50,780	3.40%
Northwestern University	$52,463	$50,164	4.60%
Dartmouth College	$52,445	$50,084	4.70%
Eastman School of Music of U. of Rochester	$52,372	$50,326	4.10%
Williams College	$52,340	$49,880	4.90%
Union College (N.Y.)	$52,329	$50,439	3.70%
Cornell University	$52,316	$50,114	4.40%
Bucknell University	$52,280	$50,320	3.90%
Hampshire College	$52,202	$50,450	3.50%
St. John's College (Md.)	$52,176	$50,352	3.60%
St. John's College (N.M.)	$52,176	$49,992	4.40%
Skidmore College	$52,170	$51,196	1.90%
Hobart and William Smith Colleges	$52,168	$50,245	3.80%
Rensselaer Polytechnic Institute	$52,145	$50,310	3.60%
Boston University	$52,124	$50,288	3.70%
Carleton College	$52,110	$50,205	3.80%
Franklin & Marshall College	$52,110	$50,410	3.40%
Colgate University	$52,060	$50,940	2.20%
Mount Holyoke College	$52,036	$50,576	2.90%
Colby College	$51,990	$50,320	3.30%
Boston Conservatory	$51,985	$49,856	4.30%
Dickinson College	$51,975	$50,219	3.50%
Wellesley College	$51,950	$49,848	4.20%
University of Pennsylvania	$51,944	$49,986	3.90%
Franklin W. Olin College of Engineering	$51,925	$50,025	3.80%
University of Rochester	$51,922	$49,890	4.10%
Smith College	$51,898	$50,380	3.00%
Duke University	$51,865	$49,895	3.90%

INSTITUTIONS @ $50,000 TUITION OR MORE PER YEAR

	Tuition, fees, room, and board ($)		
	2010-11	2009-10	1-year increase
Reed College	$51,850	$49,950	3.80%
Bryn Mawr College	$51,780	$50,034	3.50%
Lafayette College	$51,774	$50,289	3.00%
St. Lawrence University	$51,770	$49,925	3.70%
Hamilton College (N.Y.)	$51,760	$49,860	3.80%
Tulane University	$51,708	$50,190	3.00%
Amherst College	$51,520	$49,078	5.00%
Swarthmore College	$51,500	$49,600	3.80%
Brandeis University	$51,488	$49,562	3.90%
Chapman University	$51,481	$49,596	3.80%
Fairfield University	$51,430	$49,410	4.10%
Gettysburg College	$51,390	$48,460	6.00%
Brown University	$51,360	$49,128	4.50%
Eugene Lang College The New School	$51,350	$49,810	3.10%
Berklee College of Music	$51,335	$48,733	5.30%
Pomona College	$51,330	$49,668	3.30%
Wheaton College (Mass.)	$51,264	$49,440	3.70%
Providence College	$51,125	$44,480	14.90%
Wake Forest University	$50,980	$49,032	4.00%
College of the Holy Cross	$50,832	$49,342	3.00%
University of Notre Dame	$50,785	$48,845	4.00%
Harvard College	$50,724	$48,684	4.20%
University of California at Berkeley (out-of-state residents)	$50,649	$47,726	6.10%
Drew University	$50,647	$48,385	4.70%
Washington and Lee University	$50,630	$48,702	4.00%
Stanford University	$50,576	$48,843	3.50%
Villanova University	$50,550	$49,330	2.50%
Pepperdine University	$50,470	$48,750	3.50%
West Coast University	$50,453	n/a	n/a
Massachusetts Institute of Technology	$50,446	$49,142	2.70%
University of Richmond	$50,420	$48,490	4.00%

INSTITUTIONS @ $50,000 TUITION OR MORE PER YEAR

	Tuition, fees, room, and board ($)		
	2010-11	2009-10	1-year increase
Kenyon College	$50,400	$48,240	4.50%
New School Mannes College of Music	$50,360	$48,860	3.10%
Emory University	$50,356	$48,932	2.90%
Loyola Marymount University	$50,334	$48,679	3.40%
Lehigh University	$50,300	$48,830	3.00%
Worcester Polytechnic Institute	$50,240	$48,868	2.80%
American U.	$50,165	$47,903	4.70%

TEN UNIVERSITIES WITH HIGHEST STUDENT DEBT

1. New York University $695 million
2. University of Southern California $631 million
3. Penn State University $590 million
4. Ohio State University $560 million
5. University of Minnesota $495 million
6. Arizona State University $479 million
7. University of Texas $474 million
8. Michigan State University $433 million
9. Indiana University- Purdue $421 million
10. Rutgers University $398 million

Federal & Institutional Methodology

Colleges rely on two basic methods to calculate the expected family contribution.

The Federal Methodology (FM) is a formula established by Congress to determine EFC and federal financial aid eligibility. The formula takes into consideration income, assets, expenses, family size, and other factors to help evaluate a family's financial strength.

The Free Application for Federal Student Aid (FAFSA) is the form used in reporting the information that determines EFC under the Federal Methodology. All students applying for need-based federal aid should complete the FAFSA. (In general, most students applying for financial aid from other sources will also want to file a FAFSA.)

Many colleges and aid-granting programs use a more comprehensive formula, referred to as the Institutional Methodology (IM), to determine student need for nonfederal aid (such as institutional scholarships and grants). Many colleges think that Institutional Methodology provides a better gauge of a family's abilit than FM. IM takes home equity into account and includes a minimum expected contribution from the student. It also permits more generous treatment of medical/ dental expenses, efforts to put money aside for education and emergencies, and other special circumstances.

Because many colleges use IM for the purpose of awarding their own money, the formula can vary from college to college. For example, some colleges offer additional funds to parents who are paying for private school tuition or who live in areas of the country with a higher-than-average cost of living. Most colleges that use an alternative formula to award their funds require families to complete an application form in addition to the FAFSA—frequently the form is the CSS/Financial Aid Profile.

The Federal Methodology EFC serves as an eligibility index used to determine the student's potential qualification for federal and, sometimes, state funds. exception of the Federal Pell Grant, the college determines the amount of federal aid to award a student based on the college's federal funding allocation dollars. The Institutional Methodology EFC helps some colleges determine the student's eligibility for nonfederal institutional funds. (Some colleges use the Methodology EFC to determine eligibility for federal as well as nonfederal funds.)

Expected Family Contribution

Colleges use various approaches to determine a family's estimated contribution to their child's education. The amount of the expected family contribution (EFC) depends on which approach a college uses. Counselors do not have to discuss finances with students or families, but you should understand EFC and how it is determined.

FINANCIAL AID FORMS

FAFSA

Any student applying for federal aid must complete the FAFSA. And, in general, most students applying for aid will want to complete the FAFSA. The federal government mails an excellent booklet—the Counselors and Mentors Handbook on Federal Student Aid—to each school each year. This easy-to-use reference provides information to help counselors advise students about financial aid, with an emphasis on federal student aid programs. If you need a copy, call 1 800 4-FED-AID (1 800 433 -3243) or download it from www.fsa4counselors.ed.gov. The Office of Federal Student Aid has just created "Start Here, Go Further with Federal Student Aid: Money for Education Beyond High School," a video/DVD that may be obtained calling 800 394-7084. The video includes information for counselors as well as for students and parents.

FAFSA has an easily navigated Web site (www.fafsa.ed.gov) where families can register for a PIN (the password is necessary for applying online) and find out everything they need to know about FAFSA. Urge students to complete the FAFSA online (called FAFSA on the Web). There are edit checks that ensure an error-free submission and that will get results much more quickly. The paper FAFSA is available in Spanish as well as English.

CSS/Financial Aid Profile

For purposes of awarding their private funds, some colleges and universities require the CSS Financial Aid PROFILE. This fully web-based financial aid application service is available at www.collegeboard.com. PROFILE provides students with extensive online "eelp sections; customer support is available via e-mail and by phone during normal business hours.

The PROFILE application is customized to the individual needs of each student. Application customization occurs after the student has completed the PROFILE Registration process. Once the registration process is completed, the PROFILE application will only present questions that are relevant to the unique financial and family circumstances of each student.

The PROFILE Registration and Application Guide provides important information about the process and should be reviewed prior to registering for PROFILE. The Guide includes an important section for applicants to review with parents prior to completing the Registration process. The Registration Guide is available in both English and Spanish. Once the PROFILE registration step is complete, students can also review and print the Customized Pre-Application Worksheet, which can help them gather information about the unique PROFILE questions that they will be asked.

The CSS/Financial Aid PROFILE section of the College Board Web site includes a list of the colleges and scholarship programs that require it.

Financial Aid & Early Decision

When applying under an ED program, you fill out a preliminary financial aid form from the college. (Some colleges use the CSS Financial Aid/PROFILE form available on the Internet at www.collegeboard.com.) You will be notified of your financial aid package at the time of your acceptance. The package will be determined by the college based on an assessment of your family's economic needs.

If financial aid is an essential factor for you in selecting a college, you may not wish to apply under an Early Decision program because you will not be able to compare your aid package with financial aid offers from others colleges.

In recent years, college admissions officers and college counselors have seen a growing number of students and parents who, in an attempt to manipulate the system in their favor, are crossing the boundary between helping ensure a desired outcome and taking inappropriate actions.

The admissions process is not a game to be won at any cost. It is a complex process that demands a great deal of integrity on everyone's part, especially the school's. Here are some examples of what we consider crossing the boundary:

- Applying to binding Early Decision programs at more than one college or university. The whole point of a binding ED program is to make a contract: ff you accept me, I will withdraw all my other applications and attend your university. Many colleges now require that the college adviser sign the application along with the student and parents. The school will not send transcripts to more than one ED school or to any other schools once a student has been admitted under a binding ED program.

- Failing to withdraw your applications to other colleges when you have been admitted under a binding ED program. It isn't fair to those colleges or t students who have applied to them for you to continue in the process just to see what happens.

- Attempting to gain release from an ED decision because you have changed your mind. The only acceptable reason for requesting release from your contract with your ED college is the inability to work out appropriate financial aid. You and your parents should discuss the cost factor when you are deciding whether to apply for ED in the first place.

- Having someone else write or heavily edit your essays. When you sign an application, you are indicating it is your work. If it is not, then you may be subject to the school's honor code.

INDEPENDENT STUDENTS

Some of your students may be independent students. If so, their parents' finances are not taken into account by colleges. To be considered independent, a student must:

- be at least 24 years old by December 31 of the award year covered by the FAFSA; or be working on a master's or doctorate program

- be married

- have children who receive more than half their support from the student

- have legal dependents other than children or spouse living with them who receive more than half their support from the student

- be serving on active duty in the U.S. Armed Forces for purposes other than training

- be a veteran of the U.S. armed forces; or

- be otherwise identified as independent by the financial aid administrator

For these students, their ability to contribute to college costs is evaluated on the basis of their own income, assets, and expenses. Special expenses such as child care may be considered by the college.

Sometimes a student under age 24 can be treated as independent when there are unusual circumstances (e.g., he or she is living independently as a result of estrangement from parents). In these cases, the student must provide documentation (usually including letters from clergy or from counseling agencies) to a financial aid administrator who may approve a dependence override. However, such exceptions are made on a limited basis.

Fee Waivers

PROFILE uses the financial aid data provided by the family to determine who is eligible for a fee waiver. PROFILE fee waivers are available to applicants from families with very low incomes and few assets. Generally, students who qualify for the federal reduced-price or free lunch program are also eligible for the PROFILE fee waiver. The fee waiver covers the cost of registration and up to six school or program reports.

Deadlines and Priority Dates

Many colleges have a priority date but no firm deadline for applying for financial aid (many priority dates are in February and March). Urge students to apply by the priority date. This is the date by which the college needs the application in order to award the most attractive aid package. After this date, funds may be limited or depleted, and students may not get as much aid as they need. Getting Financial Aid lists priority dates for each college.